Progressive Business Plan for a Medical Marijuana Dispensary

NON-DISCLOSURE AGREEMENT

_____ (Company)., and _____ (Person Name), agrees:

_____ (Company) Corp. may from time to time disclose to _____ (Person Name) certain confidential information or trade secrets generally regarding Business plan and financials of _____ (Company) corp.

_____ (Person Name) agrees that it shall not disclose the information so conveyed, unless in conformity with this agreement. _____ (Person Name) shall limit disclosure to the officers and employees of _____ (Person Name) with a reasonable "need to know" the information, and shall protect the same from disclosure with reasonable diligence.

As to all information which _____ (Company) Corp. claims is confidential, _____ (Company) Corp. shall reduce the same to writing prior to disclosure and shall conspicuously mark the same as "confidential," "not to be disclosed" or with other clear indication of its status. If the information which _____ (Company) Corp. is disclosing is not in written form, for example, a machine or device, _____ (Company) Corp. shall be required prior to or at the same time that the disclosure is made to provide written notice of the secrecy claimed by _____ (Company) Corp.. _____ (Person Name) agrees upon reasonable notice to return the confidential tangible material provided by it by _____ (Company) Corp. upon reasonable request.

The obligation of non-disclosure shall terminate when if any of the following occurs:
(a) The confidential information becomes known to the public without the fault of _____ (Person Name), or;
(b) The information is disclosed publicly by _____ (Company) Corp., or ;
(c) a period of 12 months passes from the disclosure, or;
(d) the information loses its status as confidential through no fault of _____ (Person Name).

In any event, the obligation of non-disclosure shall not apply to information which was known to _____ (Person Name) prior to the execution of this agreement.

Dated: _____

_____
_____ (Company) Corp.
_____(Person Name)

Business and Marketing Plan Instructions

1. If you purchased this Book via Amazon's Kindle or Print-on-Demand Systems, please send proof-of-purchase to Probusconsult2@Yahoo.com and we will email you the file.

2. Complete the Executive Summary section, as your final step, after you have completed the entire plan.

3. Feel free to edit the plan and make it more relevant to your strategic goals, objectives and business vision.

4. We have provided all of the formulas needed to prepare the financial plan. Just plug in the numbers that are based on your particular situation. Excel spreadsheets for the financials are available on the microsoft.com website and www.simplebizplanning.com/forms.htm http://office.microsoft.com/en-us/templates/

5. Throughout the plan, we have provided prompts or suggestions as to what values to enter into blank spaces, but use your best judgment and then delete the suggested values (?).

6. The plan also includes some separate worksheets for additional assistance in expanding some of the sections, if desired.

7. Additionally, some sections offer multiple choices and the word 'select' appears as a prompt to edit the contents of the plan.

8. Your feedback, referrals and business are always very much appreciated.

Thank you

Nat Chiaffarano, MBA
Progressive Business Consulting, Inc.
Pembroke Pines, FL 33027
ProBusConsult2@yahoo.com

"Progressive Business Plan for a
Medical Marijuana Dispensary"

Medical Marijuana Dispensary
Business Plan
_____ (date)

Business Name: _____

Plan Time Period: 2017 - 2019

Founding Directors:

Name: _____

Name: _____

Contact Information:

Owner: _____

Address: _____

City/State/Zip: _____

Phone: _____

Cell: _____

Fax: _____

Website: _____

Email: _____

Submitted to: _____

Date: _____

Contact Info: _____

Medical Marijuana Dispensary Business Plan: Table of Contents

1.0 Executive Summary

Industry Overview

The year 2017 is shaping up to be a significant year for the cannabis industry. Three states – Illinois, Maryland and New Hampshire – have passed medical marijuana laws since January, creating tens of millions of dollars in opportunities for cannabis businesses. These are clear signs that entrepreneurs are eager to get involved in the industry despite all the challenges and entry barriers. The Gallup organization released a poll in October of 2017, showing that for the first time in 44 years, a wide margin of Americans--58% to 39%-- believe marijuana should be legalized.

Presently, 23 states and Washington D.C. have laws in place legalizing marijuana in some form. As time goes on, it's looking likely that more and more states will be approving programs to legalize marijuana in some capacity. Thus far only Colorado, Washington state, Oregon, Alaska, and Washington D.C. have legalized marijuana for both medical and recreational use.

Resources:

http://www.ncsl.org/research/health/state-medical-marijuana-laws.aspx

Today thanks to lobbying efforts, state legislators realize that MMJ is politically popular, leading to a second wave of legalization and pro-MMJ laws in general. This trend highlights how important it is for cannabis businesses in existing MMJ states to create a favorable perception of the industry by following best practices and operating above-board in every respect.

Although the federal law still prohibits the use of this alternative medicine, certain states allow patients to use this medicinal plant as an alternative medicine for their medical condition but with a recommendation from a doctor. Dispensary Caregivers can easily grow cannabis plants but for medical purposes only.

Resources:

www.buzzfeed.com/dominicholden/6-reasons-why-trump-would-hit-a-wall-if-he-tried-to-crack?utm_term=.dt3OMd8M2#.ykqRQGDQa

Business Overview

_____ (company name) _____ (was/is in the process of being) formed to provide first class Medical Marijuana Dispensary products and services in the _____ area. The company was formed because market research indicates that there is a significant need for quality Medical Marijuana Dispensary products and services within this region. We will be a medical marijuana dispensary serving the _____ (city) and greater _____ areas. We will have over ____ (#) strains and will strive to be the highest recommended clinic in the area according to every major review source.. Our facility's style, security, variety, compassion and knowledgeable professionalism will raise the standard for a medical marijuana dispensary serving the community.

_____ (company name) will be committed to providing high quality medical marijuana to our patients. The healing atmosphere in our dispensary represents what we believe answers the needs of our patients. We will strive to help empower patients with the quality of life they deserve and services beyond just the typical dispensary. The Clinic will pride itself on providing its patients with the highest level of care at its dispensary, which extends beyond simply providing the cleanest, highest quality medical marijuana. Our Clinic's highly-trained staff will be capable of servicing all types of patients, making their experience both pleasurable and comfortable in a clean, safe environment.

Products and Services

_____ (company name) intends to offer the highest quality, organic, pharmaceutical-grade Medical Marijuana products. The intended product line for the first year of operations includes Raw Medical Cannabis Flowers (i.e., dried 'buds'), including at least _____ (fifteen?) strains, concentrated extracts (i.e. bubble hash, tinctures, vaporizer cartridges), pre-rolls (grounded raw medical cannabis flowers prepared in ready-to-consume unbleached rolling papers), medical cannabis-infused olive oil and butter for home use, baked goods and edible products (including cookies, brownies, popcorn/kettle corn), and topical ointments and capsules.

We will have the best laboratory tested marijuana strains, gourmet edibles, smoking devices, vaporizors, clothing and prices in town. We serve all ____ (state) medical marijuana patients with a valid original doctors recommendation and a ____ (state) ID.

We believe that we can become the Medical Marijuana Dispensary service provider of choice in the _____ area for the following reasons:
1.   We will employ competent and well-educated staff and provide them with regularly scheduled training programs.
2.   We will provide the staff with organized and responsive management.
3.   We will offer a one-stop solution to patient personalized health and wellness needs.

In order to succeed, _____ (company name) will have to do the following:
1.   Make superior patient service our number one priority.
2.   Stay abreast of trends in the Medical Marijuana Dispensary industry.
3.   Precisely assess and then exceed the expectations of all patients.
4.   Form long-term, trust-based relationships with patients to secure profitable repeat business and referrals.
5.   Develop process efficiencies to achieve and maintain patient affordability and business profitability.

Critical Risks
Management recognizes there are several internal and external risks inherent in our business concept. Quality and personalization will be key factors in the consumers' decision to utilize our Medical Marijuana Dispensary services on a continual basis. Also, consumers must be willing to accept the various services offered in order for the company to meet its sales projections. A strong marketing strategy and careful screening of employees and contracted service providers will mitigate these risks. Building a loyal and trusting relationship with our patients and referral partners is a key component to the

success of _____ (company name).

Patient Service
We will take every opportunity to help the patient, regardless of what the revenue might be. We will outshine our competition by doing something "extra" and offering added-value. We will treat patients with respect and help them like we would help a friend. We will take a long-term perspective and focus on the patient's possible lifetime value to our business.

Plan Objective
The purpose of this document is to provide a strategic business plan for our company. The plan has been adjusted to reflect the particular strengths and weaknesses of _____ (company name). Actual financial performance will be tracked closely and the business plan will be adjusted when necessary to ensure that full profit potential is realized.

The Company
The business _____ (will be/was) incorporated on _____ (date) in the state of _____, as a _____ (Corporation/LLC), and intends to register for Sub-chapter 'S' status for federal tax purposes. This will effectively shield the owner(s) from personal liability and double taxation.

Business Goals
Our business goal is to continue to develop the _____ (company name) brand name. To do so, we plan to execute on the following:
1. Offer quality Medical Marijuana Dispensary services at a competitive price.
2. Focus on quality controls and ongoing operational excellence.
3. Recruit and train the very best, background checked and licensed employees.
4. Create a branded marketing campaign with a consistent look and message content.

Location
_____ (company name) will be based in the _____ (complex name) on _____ (street address) in _____ (city), ____ (state). The _____ (purchased/leased) space is easily accessible and provides ample parking for ____ (#) patients and staff. The location is attractive due to the area demographics, which reflect our target patient profile. _____ (city name) is also home to a _____ (medical complex/hospital?), which will serve as a good referral base for our services.

Competitive Edge
_____ (company name) will compete well in our market by offering competitive prices, high-quality patient-centric Medical Marijuana Dispensary services and leading edge educational programs. Our Medical Marijuana Dispensary services will require a complimentary consultation, which will aid the staff and the patient in creating a comprehensive treatment plan. Furthermore, we will maintain an excellent reputation for

security, safety, trustworthiness and integrity with the community we serve.

Target Market

Consumers of our services will be those individuals with medical conditions in need of Medical Marijuana Dispensary services. Our patients will be referred by health care professionals. Clients and customers are all patients who have been referred by a physician who has prescribed cannabis as a medical treatment for an existing condition. Our Medical Marijuana Dispensary business has already developed an excellent reputation with many of these medical professionals through the work of our owner, _____ (owner name) who has worked in the _____ industry for the last _____ (#) years. Younger adults between 18 and 29 are much more supportive of legalizing pot (67% to 31%) than folks 65 and older (45% to 53%).

Licensing Requirements

Our company will be licensed by the State of _____ and the city of_____.
We have already initiated the licensure, accreditation and insurance certification processes and expect to easily meet the guidelines for providing Medical Marijuana Dispensary services in _____ region of _____ (state), by acquiring the services of a licensed Medical Director.
Resources:
http://greenrushconsulting.com/open-a-dispensary/
Example:
http://greenrushconsulting.com/open-a-dispensary-in-florida/

Marketing Plan

With the help of an aggressive marketing plan, __ (company name) expects to experience steady growth. _____ (company name) plans to attract its patients through the use of local newspaper advertisements, circulating flyers, a systematic series of direct mailings, press releases, a website, online directories, networking with local professional medical organizations, dedicated commissioned sales reps to call upon medical service providers and Yellow Page ads. We also plan on sponsoring and/or attending community education events and giving presentations to patient support groups and at medical facilities.
Resources:
http://www.who.int/genomics/public/patientsupport/en/
http://www.thisaslife.com/find-support/

The Management Team

_____ (company name) will be lead by _____ (a / two) Medical Marijuana Dispensary industry veteran(s), _____ (owner name) and _____ (co-owner name). _____ (owner name) has a _____ background within the industry, having spent ____ (#) years with _____ (former employer name). During this tenure, ___ (he/she) helped grow the business from $_____ in yearly revenue to over $_____. _____ (co-owner name) has a _____ background, and while employed by _____ was able to increase operating profit by _____ percent.
These acquired skills, work experiences and educational backgrounds will play a big role

in the success of our Medical Marijuana Dispensary. Additionally, our president, _____ (name), has an extensive knowledge of the _____ area and has identified a niche market opportunity to make this venture highly successful, combining his ___ (#) years of work experience in a variety of businesses. _____ (owner name) will manage all aspects of the business and service development to ensure effective patient responsiveness while monitoring day-to-day operations. Qualified and trained staff associates personally trained by _____ (owner name) in patient service skills will provide additional support services. Support staff will be added as seasonal or extended hours mandate.

Past Successful Accomplishments

_____ (company name) is uniquely qualified to succeed due to the following past successes:

1. **Entrepreneurial Track Record**: The owners and management team have helped to launch numerous successful ventures, including a _____.

2. **Key Milestones Achieved**: The founders have invested $___ to-date to staff the company, build the core technology, acquire starting inventory, test market the _____ (product/service), realize sales of $_____ and launch the website.

Start-up Funding

_____ (owner name) will financially back the new business venture with an initial investment of $ _____, and will be the principal owner. Additional funding in the amount of $_____ will be sought from _____, a local commercial bank, with a SBA loan guarantee. This money will be needed to start the company. This loan will provide start-up capital, financing for a selected site lease, vehicle acquisition, inventory strain supply purchases, pay for permits and licensing, staff training and certification, purchase equipment and working capital to cover expenses during the first year of operation.

Financial Projections

We plan to open for business on _____ (date). _____ (company name) is forecasted to gross in excess of $___ in sales in its first year of operation, ending ___ (month/ year). Profit margins are forecasted to be at about ____ percent. Second year operations will produce a net profit of $___. This will be generated from an investment of $___ in initial capital. It is expected that payback of our total invested capital will be realized in less than __ (#) months of operation. It is further forecasted that cash flow becomes positive from operations in year ___ (one/two?). We project that our net profits will increase from $___ to over $ __ over the next three years.

Financial Profile Summary

Key Indicator	2017	2018	2019
Total Revenue			
Expenses			
Gross Margin			
Operating Income			

Net Income   _____

EBITDA   _____

EBITDA = Revenue - Expenses (excluding tax, interest, depreciation and amortization)
       EBITDA is essentially net income with interest, taxes, depreciation, and amortization added back to it, and can be used to analyze and compare profitability between companies and industries because it eliminates the effects of financing and accounting decisions.

Gross Margin (%) = (Revenue - Cost of Goods Sold) / Revenue

Net Income = Total revenue - Cost of sales - Other expenses - Tax

Exit Strategy

If the business is very successful, _____ (owner name) may seek to sell the business to a third party for a significant earnings multiple. Most likely, the Company will hire a qualified business broker to sell the business on behalf of _____ (company name). Based on historical numbers, the business could generate a sales premium of up to __(#) times earnings.

Summary

Through a combination of a proven business model and a strong management team to guide the organization, _____ (company name) will be a long lasting, profitable business. We believe our ability to create future product and service opportunities and growth will only be limited by our imagination and our ability to attract talented people who understand the concept of branding.

1.1.0   Tactical Objectives   (select 3)

The following tactical objectives will specify quantifiable results and involve activities that can be easily tracked. They will also be realistic, tied to specific marketing strategies and serve as a good benchmark to evaluate our marketing plan success. (Select Choices)

1. To create a company whose primary goal is to exceed patient expectations.
2. To develop a cash flow that is capable of paying all salaries, as well as grow the business, by the end of the _____ (first?) year.
3. To be an active networking participant and productive member of the community by _____ (date).
4. Create over ___ (60?) % of revenues from repeat patients by _____ (date).
5. Achieve an overall patient satisfaction rate of ____ (98?) % by _____ (date).
6. Get a business website designed, built and operational by _____ (date), which will include an online shopping cart.
7. Achieve total sales revenues of $_____ in _____ (year).
8. Begin franchise efforts by the end of Fiscal _____ (year).
9. Realize gross margins higher than _____ (80?) percent by _____ (date).

10. Achieve net income more than ___ (15?) percent of net sales by the ____ (#) year.
11. Increase overall sales by _____ (20?) percent from prior year through superior service and word-of-mouth referrals.
12. Reduce the cost of new patient acquisition by ___ % to $ ___ by _____ (date).
13. Turn in profits from the _____ (#) month of operations.
14. Expand mobile operations to include all of the _____ (city) area, including _____, _____ and _____.
15. Provide employees with continuing training, benefits and incentives to reduce the employee turnover rate to _____% by _____ (date).
16. To pursue a growth rate of ____ (20?) % per year for the first ____ (#) years.
17. Establish mutual referral relationships with ___ (#) businesses and practices that have similar patient profiles in order to cross-promote offerings.
18. Allocate at least $ ____ or _____ % of sales in the first year, whichever is greater, to our marketing campaign.
19. To pursue a growth rate of ____ (25?) % per year for the first ____ (#) years.
20. Enable the owner to draw a salary of $ _____ by the end of year ____ (one?).
21. To reach cash break-even by the end of year ____ (one?).
22. Increase market share to ___ percent over the next ___ (#) months.
23. Become one of the top ___ (#) players in the emerging _____ category in __ (#) months.
24. Increase Operating Profit by ___ percent versus the previous year.
25. Achieve market share leadership in the ____ category by ____ (date).
26. Reduce the cost of new patient acquisition by ___ % to $ ___ by _____ (date).

Note: Research indicates that more established operations can enjoy 40-50% profit margins, while newer shops may only see 20%.

Source: www.forbes.com/sites/debraborchardt/2015/06/04/marijuana-businesses-find-it-hard-to-measure-success/2/#e49dd35280ce

1.1.1   Strategic Objectives

We will seek to work toward the accomplishment of the following strategic objectives:
1. Improve the overall quality and menu of Medical Marijuana Dispensary services.
2. Promote patient education by providing greater access to service benefit info.
3. Improve patient convenience, affordability and accessibility.
4. Make the dispensary experience better and more user friendly.
5. Improve access for seniors and minorities.
6. Strengthen personal relationships with patients.
7. Improve the coordination of referrals across professions.
8. Give consumers more control over and options to realize a healthier lifestyle.
9. Foster a spirit of innovation.

1.2.0   Mission Statement

Our Mission Statement is a written statement that spells out our organization's overall goal, provides a sense of direction and acts as a guide to decision making for all levels of management. In developing the following mission statement we will encourage input from employees, volunteers, and other stakeholders, and publicize it broadly in our website and other marketing materials.

It is the Mission of _____ (company name) to offer quality and affordable Medical Marijuana Dispensary products and services to our patients in the _____ area. Our mission is to provide safe alternatives to the more dangerous and addictive prescription medications currently available. Our mission is to realize 100% patient satisfaction, and generate long-term profits through professional referrals and repeat business. Our mission is to provide friendly, compassionate and professional patient service to our patients on an individual basis. Our goal is to provide safe and affordable access to a variety of cannabis medicines.

Our goal is to set ourselves apart from the competition by making patient satisfaction our number one priority and to provide patient service that is responsive, informed and respectful. Our mission is to improve dispensary service accessibility for all community residents and promote cultural diversity. To be the innovative leader of Medical Marijuana Dispensary services in _____ (city). Our goal is to provide a personal touch through our broad range of services, unparalleled convenience and exceptional patient service.

1.2.1   Our Goals

1.   To assist every patient who visits our facilities in a secure environment that projects professionalism and knowledge, and providing safe access to medicine.

2.   To provide patients an alternative to illegal means of obtaining high quality cannabis medicine within State of _____ Law.

3.   To protect the citizens of _____ (state) by following all requirements of the _____ (state) Medical Marijuana Act and Department of Health Services rules, with an emphasis on maintaining the integrity and safety of all patients and non-patients.

4.   To not have an adverse effect on neighborhoods and businesses surrounding our facilities, and provide a positive influence on the community.

5.   To maintain the high standards patients expect from traditional medical facilities.

1.2.2 Mantra

We will create a mantra for our organization that is three or four words long. Its purpose will be to help employees truly understand why the organization exists. Our mantra will serve as a framework through which to make decisions about product and business direction. It will boil the key drivers of our company down to a sentence that defines our most important areas of focus and resemble a statement of purpose or significance.
Our Mantra is _____

1.2.3 Core Values Statement

The following Core Values will help to define our organization, guide our behavior, underpin operational activity and shape the strategies we will pursue in the face of various challenges and opportunities:
> Being legal, respectful and ethical.
> Building enduring partnerships and relationships with individuals, families and
> > corporations.
> Seeking innovation in our Medical Marijuana Dispensary industry.
> Practicing accountability to our colleagues and stakeholders.
> Pursuing continuous learning as individuals and as a business entity.

1.3 Vision Statement

The following Vision Statement will communicate both the purpose and values of our organization. For employees, it will give direction about how they are expected to behave and inspires them to give their best. Shared with patients, it will shape patients' understanding of why they should work with our organization.

_____ (company name) will strive to become one of the most respected and favored Medical Marijuana Dispensary service providers in the _____ area. To increase the number, variety and effectiveness of the treatments that are available. It is our desire to become a landmark business in _____ (city), _____ (state), and become known not only for the quality of our Medical Marijuana Dispensary products and services and eco-friendly practices, but also for our community and charity involvement.

_____ (company name) is dedicated to operating with a constant enthusiasm for learning about the Medical Marijuana Dispensary services business, being receptive to implementing new ideas, and maintaining a willingness to adapt to changing market needs and wants. To be an active and vocal member of the community, and to provide continual reinvestment through participation in community activities and financial contributions. Our success in fulfilling our vision will be measured by patient wellness, health and satisfaction, team member happiness, and local and larger community involvement.

In five years,_____ (company name) will be an area leader in the Medical Marijuana Dispensary industry, and plans will be developed and implemented to pursue national business through the franchising of our business model concept.

In summary, our vision is to accomplish the following:

1. To better understand and facilitate the needs of our patients, making sure they have the most enjoyable, result-oriented and comfortable experiences with medical marijuana.
2. To respect and honor the laws about medical marijuana set forth by the state of _____ under _____ (law title).
3. To create and maintain an atmosphere in our dispensary based on professionalism, compassion, safety, security, and privacy.
4. To provide the widest variety of the highest tested grade of medical marijuana for our patients.
5. To set and maintain the highest standard for customer service in the medical marijuana industry.
6. To help keep our local community safe, clean, and peaceful.
7. To help eliminate the negative stigmas attached to medical marijuana dispensaries and patients in need through industry-leading research, service and through charitable outreach.
8. To support local charities, local culture and the local economy.
9. To create a positive example in both the medical marijuana industry and for the other communities working to revise medical marijuana laws.

1.4 Keys to Success

In broad terms, the success factors relate to providing what our patients want, and doing what is necessary to be better than our competitors. The following critical success factors are areas in which our organization must excel in order to operate successfully and achieve our objectives:

1. Carefully check and follow local business licensing and employee certification requirements for a Medical Marijuana Dispensary business.
2. Introduce special packages targeted at diverse patient groups.
3. Introduce discounts and incentives to attract first-time patients.
4. Apply environmentally sustainable practices, such as recycling, utilizing sustainable packaging, offering organic products and becoming LEED certified.
5. Increase partnerships with suppliers who practice earth-friendly principles.
6. Ensure friendly patient service to make the patient feel comfortable.
7. Assemble a pool of well-trained staff to draw upon when needed.
8. Form personal relationships with patients to create repeat and loyal business partners.

9. Hire the very best horticulturist.
10. Customize each patient's experience to his or her preferences using a needs analysis worksheet.
11. Give the kind of service that brings people back for regular treatments.
12. Encourage patients to recommend friends, and other health professionals to recommend their patients.
13. Utilize the latest in techniques with the best products from around the world.
14. Target niche markets such as golfers at country clubs, weight trainers at fitness centers, and travelers at hotels.
15. Use an incentive, such as a discount or free extra service, to encourage patients to sign-up for an automatic repeat patient program, so that you can better schedule your time, on a monthly basis.
16. Build an ideal patient profile to more efficiently locate other patients with similar needs and wants.
17. Service our patient needs with personalized attention and expert knowledge.
18. Launch a website to showcase our services and patient testimonials, provide helpful information and facilitate online registrations.
19. Local community involvement and business partnerships.
20. Conduct a targeted and cost-effective marketing campaign that seeks to differentiate our dispensary products and educational services from traditional offerings.
21. Institute a program of profit sharing among all employees to reduce employee turnover and improve productivity.
22. Control costs and manage budgets at all times in accordance with company goals.
23. Institute management processes and controls to insure the consistent replication of operations.
24. Institute an employee training to insure the best techniques are consistently practiced.
25. Network aggressively within the community, as word of mouth will be our most powerful advertising asset.
26. Maintain a highly regarded reputation for excellence in dispensary services, education and community involvement.
27. Adhere to our strategic business plan for growth and expansion, and reinvesting in the business and its employees.
28. Competitive pricing in conjunction with a differentiated service business model.
29. Stay abreast of new Medical Marijuana Dispensary service concepts.
30. Build our brand awareness, which will drive patients to increase their usage of our services and make referrals.
31. Maintain a reputable and untarnished reputation in the community.
32. Business planning with the flexibility to make changes based on gaining new insightful perspectives as we proceed.
33. Build trust by circulating and adhering to our Code of Ethics and Service Guarantees.
34. Achieve vehicle fuel savings with regular vehicle maintenance, keeping tires properly inflated, reducing vehicle trunk weight and using the recommended grade of motor oil.

35. Ask employees and subcontractors to sign 'non-compete agreements' (if legal in your state)
36. Develop several different Medical Marijuana Dispensary packages.
37. Maintain the highest levels of hygiene and use equipment that is either disposable or sterilized.
38. Arrange for a reasonable degree of involvement by an experienced physician.
39. Advertise our relatively new Medical Marijuana Dispensary services to attract the initial group of patients and build a long-term stream of referrals.
40. Thoroughly investigate the efficacy of the technology or service promised by the manufacturer before promoting it to the public.
41. Install security cameras in the parking lot to discourage loitering and dealing.
42. Do not initially spend an excessive amount of capital on leasehold improvements.
43. Develop a tracking system to capture lead acquisition costs and patient acquisition costs to wisely allocate marketing dollars.

44. Provide an easily accessible location for patients.

45. Provide an environment conducive to giving professional service.

46. Offer patients a range of services in one setting, and extended business hours.

47. Promote the reputation of the owner and other employees as providing superior, knowledgeable personal service.

48. All members of management must be cognizant of the specific laws and regulations for the region in which they operate.

49. Must continue to produce and release educational materials explaining how the active ingredients of marijuana enter the body and work to prevent nausea, seizures, spasms and pain.

50. Must monitor state and federal legislation, through state boards, for bill proposals that will affect the Medical Marijuana Dispensary business.

51. Must be prepared for unusual business challenges such as raising capital, finding investors, and setting up merchant accounts with banking institutions.

52. Be prepared to spend major dollars to meet the security and operational requirements of city building code inspectors.

53. Keep shelves stocked with only high quality product, because Medical Marijuana users are usually looking for high quality herb and consistent delivery of the same weed.

54. Must keep aware of state approved, qualifying conditions, such as:
- Cancer   -Glaucoma

- Human Immunodeficiency Virus (HIV)   - AIDS
- Hepatitis C   - Amyotrophic Lateral Sclerosis
- Crohn's disease   - Agitation of Alzheimer's disease

A chronic or debilitating disease or medical condition or the treatment for a chronic or debilitating disease or medical condition that causes:
- Cachexia or wasting syndrome
- Severe and chronic pain
- Severe nausea
- Seizures, including those characteristic of epilepsy
- Severe or persistent muscle spasms, including multiple sclerosis

55. Medical Marijuana Dispensaries that also have approval to sell recreational cannabis should segment the market, and create two distinct brands to avoid negatively impacting their existing brand equity and positioning.
Source:
https://smallbiztrends.com/2017/01/marijuana-marketing.html

56. Seek to establish good relationships with city officials by doing the following:
A.   Consistently practice regular communication, honesty and transparency.
B.   Publish your mission statement and code of ethics.
C.   Strive to give back to the community, such as by generating funding for substance abuse education and a substance abuse coordinator.
D.   Start a charitable initiative that donates proceeds from a designated product, such as infused chocolates, to a local organization, such as a domestic violence shelter.

57. Conduct surveys with customers to determine which infused edibles may be of interest to them.

58. Set up a Goolge.com/alerts with following types of keywords; medical marijuana dispensary _____ (your state) to keep up-to-date with new laws and regulations.
Example:
www.miaminewtimes.com/news/how-to-get-rich-in-the-medical-marijuana-
        business-or-go-broke-trying-6395479

59. Use Social media to build a regular clientele as well as to offer sales promotions, including special deals, loyalty rewards, and referral incentives.

60. Create a blog on the business website to educate existing and potential customers about the benefits of our products.

2.0 Company Summary

_____ (company name) will give patients a clinical assessment before prescribing a strain of marijuana.. During their visit we will present professional and credible information and various marijuana strains and extraction options tailored to the patient's individual needs. It will be our responsibility to only to sell to patients, who have doctor approvals to use the drug and who have registered with the state. We will also sign-up for the first phase of the vetting process, which includes a criminal background check and a financial review. This will be followed by a more detailed review of our proposed locations and operations. As an applicant, we must also prove that we have local support for the dispensary, as regulators have also established a limit on the number of dispensaries in each county.

____ (company name) is a start-up ____ (Corporation/Limited Liability Company) consisting of __ (#) principle officers with combined industry experience of __ (#) years. We will form a corporation because it offers the best protection overall. We will research whether it should be a general C-Corp or a Not-for-Profit entity under State Law. We cannot be a Federal 501 (c)(3) corporation because marijuana, medical or not, is not recognized by Federal Law.

The owner of the Dispensary will be investing $_____ of his/her own money as startup capital into the business, and will be seeking a loan of $_____ to cover additional start-up and short-term operating costs, and future growth objectives. We will also investigate and satisfy what the state requires for start-up capital reserves.

We understand that we must first receive local zoning approval for the dispensary as a necessary first step in the process of obtaining permission under recently approved state legislation, and that only patients registered with the state and who have prescriptions from qualifying physicians may use our medical marijuana dispensary. In other words, only registered patients and their caregivers will be the only people who can enter our dispensary. In addition, security measures will include a perimeter alarm, motion detector, video cameras in all areas that may contain marijuana, a panic alarm, a silent holdup alarm, an automatic voice dialer, the ability to remain open during a power outage and a back-up alarm system approved by the state. The medical marijuana will be kept in locked safes or vaults when the dispensary is closed and complete records of the receipt and sale of marijuana will be maintained.

_____ (company name) will be located in a ___ (purchased/rented) ___ (suite/complex) in the _____ on _____ (address) in _____ (city), _____ (state). The facilities _____ (will be/were designed) to meet strict design standards, under the supervision of the _____ County's licensing board.

The company plans to use its existing contacts and patient base to generate short-term sales. Its long-term profitability will rely on focusing on referrals, networking within community organizations and a comprehensive marketing program that includes public relations activities and a structured referral program.

Sales are expected to reach $_____ within the first year and to grow at a conservative rate of _____ (20?) percent during the next two to five years.

Facilities Renovations

The necessary renovations are itemized as follows:	Estimate
Partition of space into secure areas and offices.	_____
Build inventory storage areas.	_____
Painting and other general cosmetic repairs	_____
Install equipment and communication lines	_____
Build Reception and Product Display Areas	_____
Other _____	_____
Total:	_____

Operations

_____ (company name) will open for business on _____ (date) and will maintain the following business hours:

Monday through Thursday:	_____	(9 to 6 ?)
Friday:	_____	(9 to 8 ?)
Saturday:	_____	(8 to 5 ?)
Sunday:	_____	(?)

The company will invest in patient relationship management software (CRM) to track sales and collect patient information, including names, email addresses, key reminder dates and preferences. This information will be used with email, e-newsletter and direct mail campaigns to build personalized fulfillment programs, establish patient loyalty and drive revenue growth.

2.0.1   Traction (optional)

We will include this section because investors expect to see some traction, both before and after a funding event and investors tend to judge past results as a good indicator of future projections. It will also show that we can manage our operations and develop a business model capable of funding inventory purchases. Traction will be the best form of market research and present evidence of patient acceptance.

Period	_____
Product/Service Focus	_____
Our Sales to Date:	_____
Our Number of Users to Date:	_____
Number of Repeat Users	_____
Number of Pending Orders:	_____
Value of Pending Orders:	_____
Reorder Cycle:	_____

Key Reference Sites   _____
Mailing List Subscriptions   _____
Competitions/Awards Won   _____
Notable Product Reviews   _____
Actual Percent Gross Profit Margin   _____
Industry Average: GPM   _____
Actual B/(W) Industry Average   _____

Note: Percent Gross Profit Margin equals the sales receipts less the cost of goods sold
        divided by sales receipts multiplied by 100.

2.1   Company Ownership

_____ (company name) is a _____ (Sole-proprietorship /Corporation/Limited
Liability Corporation (LLC)/Not-for-Profit Corporation) and is registered to the principal
owner, _____ (owner name). The company was formed in _____ (month)
of ____ (year).

An _____ (PLLC/LLC/Corporation) establishment limits personal liability in which
all business matters will be separate from the individual's personal assets. As an ___
(LLC) the members will only be held liable for the amount they each invest into the
business and not for the other members' debts or obligations. The business will be
registered as a Subchapter S Corporation to avoid double taxation, with ownership
allocated as follows: _____ (owner name) ____ % and ___ (owner name) ____ %.

We will seek a special license for the Department of _____ (Public Health). Their
role is to do the following:
1.   Permit and regulate medical cannabis dispensaries in accordance with state and
        local laws.
2.   Inspect each permitted medical cannabis dispensary twice annually.
3.   Respond to complaints.

The owner is a _____ (year) graduate of _____ (institution name), in
_____ (city, ____ (state), with a _____ degree. He/she has ____ years of
executive experience in the _____ (?) industry as a _____, performing the
following roles: _____.

His/her major accomplishments include: _____.

Ownership Breakdown:

Shareholder Name	Responsibilities	Number and Class of Shares	Percent Ownership

The remainder of the issued and outstanding common shares are retained by the Company for ___ (future distribution / allocation under the Company's employee stock option plan).

Shareholder Loans

The Company currently has outstanding shareholder loans in the aggregate sum of $_____. The following table sets out the details of the shareholder loans.

Shareholder Name	Loan Amount	Loan Date	Balance Outstanding

Directors

The Company's Board of Directors, which is made up of highly qualified business and industry professionals, will be a valuable asset to the Company and be instrumental to its development. The following persons will make up the Board of Directors of the Company:

Name of Person	Educational Background	Past Industry Experience	Other Companies Served

2.2   Company Licensing & Liability Protection

Because federal law doesn't allow medical marijuana businesses, but the state law allows it already, we will seek the services of a trusted lawyer with a specialty knowledge of this aspect of the law to develop an understanding of the legalities of the proper usage of marijuana.
Resource: http://www.canorml.org/laws/find-a-marijuana-lawyer-in-California

Since our Medical Marijuana Dispensary incorporates procedures and services that most States consider the "practice of medicine", a qualified physician will be involved with our business. The Professional Liability Coverage we obtain will cover the physician in his/her role.

The following documents/information will be submitted as part of our Medical Marijuana Dispensary Permit application:
1.   Completed permit application
2.   Background investigation form for applicant and all primary care givers
3.   Complete set of fingerprints for applicant and all primary care givers
4.   Indemnification Agreement and Affidavit of Acknowledgement
5.   Documentation addressing compliance with dispensary regulations
6.   Property Owner Affidavit (if applicable)

7. $_____ Non-refundable application fee payable to the City of _____
8. $____ fingerprint processing fee payable to the ___ (state) Bureau of Investigation

The business will consider the need to acquire the following types of insurances. This will require extensive comparison shopping, through several insurance brokers, listed with our state's insurance department:
1.   Workman's Compensation,
2.   Business Owner's Policy: Property & General Liability Insurance
3.   Health insurance.
4.   Commercial Auto Insurance
5.   Professional Liability/ Medical Malpractice Insurance
6.   State Unemployment Insurance
7.   Surety Bonds
8.   Business Interruption Insurance / Loss of Income
9.   Cyber Liability
10. Cargo Insurance

We will explore the following specialty coverages:

- Buildings/Equipment/Crops
- Transit/Delivery Coverage
- Theft/Fire/Vandalism
- Wind/Hail/Falling Objects
- Other Standard Perils
- Finished Stock/Marijuana

Workman's compensation covers employees in case of harm attributed to the workplace. The property and liability insurance protects the building from theft, fire, natural disasters, and being sued by a third party. Employee health insurance will be provided for the full time employees. We will make certain to procure adequate malpractice insurance for our Medical Marijuana Dispensary business. This will be our Medical Marijuana Dispensary's basic legal protection. We will also make sure that the medical personnel have individual malpractice insurance plans of their own.

Liability Insurance includes protection in the face of day-to-day accidents, unforeseen results of normal business activities, and allegations of abuse or molestation, food poisoning, or exposure to infectious disease.
Property Insurance - Property Insurance should take care of the repairs less whatever deductible you have chosen.
Loss of Income Insurance will replace our income during the time the business is shut-down. Generally this coverage is written for a fixed amount of monthly income for a fixed number of months.

To help save on insurance cost and claims, management will do the following:
1.   Stress employee safety in our employee handbook.
2.   Screen employees with interview questionnaires and will institute pre-employment drug tests and comprehensive background checks.

3. Videotape our equipment and inventory for insurance purposes.
4. Create an operations manual that shares safe techniques.
5. Limit the responsibilities that we choose to accept in our contracts.
6. Consider the financial impact of assuming the exposure ourselves.
7. Establish loss prevention programs to reduce the hazards that cause losses.
8. Consider taking higher deductibles on anything but that which involves liability insurance because of third-party involvement.
9. Stop offering services that require expensive insurance coverage or require signed releases from patients using those services.
10. Improve employee training and initiate training sessions for safety.
11. Require Certificate of Insurance from all subcontractors.
12. Make staff responsible for a portion of any damages they cause.
13 We will investigate the setting-up of a partial self-insurance plan.
14. Convince underwriters that our past low claims are the result of our ongoing safety programs and there is reason to expect our claims will be lower than industry averages in the future.
15. At each renewal, we will develop a service agreement with our broker and get their commitment to our goals, such as a specific reduction in the number of incidents.
16. We will assemble a risk control team, with people from both sides of our business, and broker representatives will serve on the committee as well.
17. When an employee is involved in an accident, we will insist on getting to the root cause of the incident and do everything possible to prevent similar incidents from re-occurring.
18. At renewal, we will consult with our brokers to develop a cost-saving strategy and decide whether to bid out our coverage for competitive quotes or stick with our current carrier.
19. We will set-up a captive insurance program, as a risk management technique, where our business will form its own insurance company subsidiary to finance its retained losses in a formal structure.
20. Review named assets (autos and equipment), drivers and/or key employees identified on policies to make sure these assets and people are still with our company.
21. As a portion of our business changes, that is, closes, operations change, or outsourcing occurs, we will eliminate unnecessary coverage.
22. We will make sure our workforce is correctly classified by our workers' compensation insurer and liability insurer because our premiums are based on the type of workers used.
23. We will become active in Trade Organizations or Professional Associations, because as a benefit of membership, our business may receive substantial insurance discounts.
24. We will adopt health specific changes to our work place, such as adopting a no smoking policy at our company and allow yoga or weight loss classes to be held in our break room.
25. We will consider a partial reimbursement of health club membership as a benefit.
26. We will find out what employee training will reduce rates and get our employees

involved in these programs.

The required business insurance package will be provided by _____ (insurance carrier name) . The business will open with a ____ (#) million dollar liability insurance policy, with an annual premium cost of $ _____..

All required licenses to own and operate a Medical Marijuana Dispensary business will be obtained through the local city and county government offices. Many state governments have asked local governments to regulate medical marijuana facilities by location and the hours and manner of operation. Each state has its own guidelines for the staff qualifications, proper physical environment, proper health and safety practices. Some State Laws require dispensaries to be 500 feet from a school or gathering place of children. We will first check with the Department of Health Services as a starting point. In most states the company was secure a letter of support or non-opposition from the County to be sent to the State's Department of Public Health, as dispensaries also require approval from the state.

Note: Many states are requiring background checks for all of the investors and operators of the business, with disqualification for certain previous felony charges. Some states also specify a required minimum number of years as a resident for all persons involved. Also make note that several states, such as Massachusetts and Illinois, are severely limiting the maximum number of dispensaries, which greatly reduces the chance of getting a license.

The Medical Marijuana Dispensary business will need to acquire the following special licenses, accreditations, certifications and permits:
1.   A sales tax license is required through the State Department of Revenue.
2.   A County and/or City Occupational License.
3.   Business License from State Licensing Agency
4.   Permits from the Fire Department and State Health Department.
5.   Building Code Inspections by the County Building Department.
6.   Cardiopulmonary Resuscitation Certificate (CPR)
7.   Sign Permit.

A medical marijuana dispensary is generally run out of a storefront. Businesses operating out of a physical location typically require a Certificate of Occupancy (CO). A CO confirms that all building codes, zoning laws and government regulations have been met.

Our _____ (nonprofit?) was awarded a provisional license by the Department of Public Health after a stringent application process. Our dispensary plans to open by ____ (date), but still needs a special permit from the Zoning Board of Appeals, which is scheduled to consider the matter when it meets on _____ (date). If the company receives that approval, it will still need to pass a state inspection right before opening its doors in order to receive a full license.

County governments are beginning to detail the steps each applicant will need to take to become fully licensed. They include the "verification phase," a process in which the controlling department would verify letters of support submitted on behalf of applicants, and the group's meetings with municipalities. Also reviewed would be dispensary sites and operational plans, including the group's management members and the board of directors.

Resource:
Status of State Medical Marijuana Laws

      http://medicalmarijuana.procon.org/view.resource.php?resourceID=000881

License Application Process
It is expected that the states' Department of Public Health will contract independent experts in this subject matter, such as _____ (ICF International) and in background investigations _____ (Creative Services, Inc?) to support their selection committee in the license decision making process. The expert review will score the applications in areas including ties to the community, public health focus, security procedures and strength of business plan. The expert review will determine the score for each applicant, based on a scale of 0 to ____ possible points. Scores of qualifying applicants will all be ____ (#) or higher. Other factors in making final recommendations will include geographic diversity, local support, and a strong focus on the ability to meet patient needs, while ensuring public safety. The Management Team, Board of Directors, and investors of dispensaries will also be subject to extensive civil and criminal background checks.

Example: In Massachusetts a medical-marijuana dispensary operator must first file an "Application of Intent" to seek a dispensary license with the State Department of Public Health and the State Executive Office of Health and Human Services.

Licensing Consulting Support
Medbox, Inc.   **www.medbox.com**
A leading dispensary infrastructure and licensing specialist, patented technology provider, and partner to the cannabis industry. Helps businesses with the application process to qualify to be awarded a medical marijuana dispensary authorization from state governments. Headquartered in Los Angeles, CA, Medbox, through its wholly owned subsidiary, Medicine Dispensing Systems, offers its patented systems, software and consulting services to pharmacies, alternative medicine dispensaries and local governments in the U.S. In addition, through its wholly owned subsidiary, Vaporfection International, Inc. (www.vaporfection.com), the company offers an industry award winning medical line of vaporizer products. Medbox, through its newly established subsidiaries, is also developing ancillary services tailored to the alternative medicine industry, including real estate acquisitions and subsequent lease programs to alternative medicine dispensaries and cultivation centers, and alternative medicine dispensary and cultivation management services.
Source: http://www.digitaljournal.com/pr/2463025

Green Rush Consulting, LLC   **www.greenrushconsulting.com**

A cannabis consulting firm that has over 20 years of experience operating in the industry, and provides education, training, market analyses, and expertise to medical marijuana cultivators and dispensary operators across the nation. We specialize in developing winning applications for medical marijuana businesses seeking licenses. Green Rush Consulting has helped entrepreneurial groups win cultivation and dispensary licenses in Arizona, California Connecticut, Nevada, New Jersey, Oregon, Washington D.C., and Illinois.
Source: http://news.sys-con.com/node/3438791

Some states require all dispensaries to be non-profits, while others can be registered as C-Corporations. In most states, you are legally required to obtain a business license, and a dba certificate. A business license is usually a flat tax assessment and a percentage of your gross income. A dba stands for Doing Business As, and it is the registration of your trade name if you have one. You will be required to register your trade name within 30 days of starting your business. Instead of registering a dba, you can simply form an LLC or Corporation and it will have the same effect, namely register your business name.

Resources:
Workers Compensation Regulations
            http://www.dol.gov/owcp/dfec/regs/compliance/wc.htm#IL
New Hire Registration and Reporting
            www.homeworksolutions.com/new-hire-reporting-information/
State Tax Obligations
            www.sba.gov/content/learn-about-your-state-and-local-tax-obligations
Resource:
www/sba.gov/content/what-state-licenses-and-permits-does-your-business-need

Note: Check with your local County Clerk and state offices or Chamber of Commerce to make sure you follow all legal protocols for setting up and running your business.
Note: To find out about your local business licensing office, visit SBA.gov. This government website compiles information on business licenses and permits at the state level.

Resource:
http://www.profitableventure.com/starting-a-medical-marijuana-dispensary/

Note: Cannabis Career Institute (https://cannabiscareerinstitute.com/) creates Medical Marijuana Industry Business Standards and offer educational seminars around the country.

Resources:
Statewide MMD Insurance   www.mmdinsurance.com/
Cannassure Insurance Services   www.cannassure.com/products/dispensaries/
Insurance Information Institute   www.iii.org/individuals/business/
National License Directory   www.sba.gov/licenses-and-permits
National Association of Surety Bond Producers   www.nasbp.org

Hands on Trade Insurance   www.handsontrade.com
Medical Marijuana Dispensary Insurance
     http://medicaldispensaryinsurance.com/
Find Law   http://smallbusiness.findlaw.com/starting-business/starting-business-
     licenses-permits/starting-business-licenses-permits-guide.html
Business Licenses   www.iabusnet.org/business-licenses
Legal Zoom   www.legalzoom.com
Business Filings   www.bizfilings.com

Novus Acquisition & Development Corp. ("Novus")   www.novusqc.com/
Provides health insurance and related insurance solutions to the medical marijuana industry in states where legal programs exist. The Company also plans to offer physicians' education programs, pharmaceutical R&D, compliance, and business development services within the industry.

2.3   Start-up To-Do Checklist

1. Describe your business concept and model, with special emphasis on planned multiple revenue streams and services to be offered.
2. Create Business Plan and Opening Menu of Products and Services.
3. Determine our start up costs of Medical Marijuana Dispensary business, and operating capital and   capital budget needs.
4. Seek and evaluate alternative financing options, including SBA guaranteed loan, equipment leasing, social networking loan (www.prosper.com) and/or a family loan (www.virginmoney.com).
5. Do a name search: Check with County Clerk Office or Department of Revenue and Secretary of State to see if the proposed name of business is available.
6. Decide on a legal structure for business.
   Common legal structure options include Sole Proprietorship, Partnership, Corporation or Limited Liability Corporation (LLC).
7. Make sure you contact your State Department of Revenue, Secretary of State, and the Internal Revenue Service to secure EIN Number and file appropriate paperwork. Also consider filing for Sub-Chapter S status with the Federal government to avoid the double taxation of business profits.
8. Protect name and logo with trademarks, if plan is to go national.
9. Find a suitable location with proper zoning.
10. Research necessary permits and requirements your local government imposes on your type of business. (Refer to: www.business.org)
11. Call for initial inspections to determine what must be done to satisfy Fire Marshall, and Building Inspector requirements.
12. Adjust our budget based on build-out requirements.
13. Negotiate lease or property purchase contract.
14. Obtain a building permit.
15. Obtain Federal Employee Identification Number (FEIN).

16. Obtain State Sales Tax ID/Exempt Certificate.
17. Open a Business Checking Account.
18. Obtain Merchant Credit Card /PayPal Account.
19. Obtain City and County Business Licenses
20. Create a prioritized list for equipment, furniture and décor items.
21. Comparison shop and arrange for appropriate insurance coverage with product liability insurance, public liability insurance, commercial property insurance and worker's compensation insurance.
22. Locate and purchase all necessary equipment and furniture prior to final inspections.
23. Get contractor quotes for required alterations.
24 Manage the alterations process.
25. Obtain information and price quotes from possible supply distributors.
26. Set a tentative opening date.
27. Install 'Coming Soon' sign in front of building and begin word-of-mouth advertising campaign.
28. Document the preparation, project and payment process flows.
29. Create your accounting, purchasing, payroll, marketing, loss prevention, employee screening and other management systems.
30. Start the employee interview process based on established job descriptions and interview criteria.
31. Contact and interview the following service providers: uniform service, security service, trash service, utilities, telephone, credit card processing, bookkeeping, cleaning services, etc.
32. Schedule final inspections for premises.
33. Correct inspection problems and schedule another inspection.
34. Set a Grand Opening date after a month of regular operations to get the bugs out of the processes.
35. Make arrangements for website design.
36. Train staff.
37. Schedule a couple of practice lessons for friends and interested prospects.
38. Be accessible for direct patient feedback.
39. Distribute comment cards and surveys to solicit more constructive feedback.
40. Remain ready and willing to change our business concept and offerings to suit the needs of our actual patient base.

2.3.1 EMPLOYER RESPONSIBILITIES CHECKLIST

1. Apply for your SS-4 Federal Employer Identification Number (EIN) from the Internal Revenue Service. An EIN can be obtained via telephone, mail or online.
2. Register with the State's Department of Labor (DOL) as a new employer. State Employer Registration for Unemployment Insurance, Withholding, and Wage Reporting should be completed and sent to the address that appears on the form. This registration is required of all employers for the purpose of determining whether the applicants are subject to state unemployment insurance taxes.

3. Obtain Workers Compensation and Disability Insurance from an insurer. The insurance company will provide the required certificates that should be displayed.
4. Order Federal Tax Deposit Coupons – Form 8109 – if you didn't order these when you received your EIN. To order, call the IRS at 1-800-829-1040; you will need to give your EIN. You may want to order some blanks sent for immediate use until the pre-printed ones are complete. Also ask for the current Federal Withholding Tax Tables (Circular A) – this will explain how to withhold and remit payroll taxes, and file reports.
5. Order State Withholding Tax Payment Coupons. Also ask for the current Withholding Tax Tables.
6. Have new employees complete an I-9 Employment Eligibility Verification form. You should have all employees complete this form prior to beginning work. Do not send it to Immigration and Naturalization Service – just keep it with other employee records in your files.
7. Have employees complete aW-4 Employees Withholding Allowance Certificate.

2.4.0   Company Location

Because there are certain places in the _____ area that don't allow this type of business, we will seek advice from our lawyer and the local Municipal or County Clerk's Office about any zoning restrictions for a medical marijuana dispensary. We will make certain that we are going to put up a dispensary in a place where dispensaries are allowed to avoid problems later on. In most states, dispensaries must be located outside the residential areas, schools, churches and parks. It must typically be located in the commercial district of a particular county. We will also check with the city of _____ regarding controlling ordinances to determine if this city will allow a dispensary to be put up.

_____ (company name) will be located in the _____ (commercial complex name) in _____ (city), ___ (state). It is situated on a _____ (turnpike/street/avenue) just minutes from _____ (benchmark location), in the commercial district of _____. It borders a large parking lot which is shared by all the businesses therein.

If we decide to rent a building for the dispensary, we will make certain to tell the landlord our plans in advance. A suitable location will typically be one that is away from schools, churches and parks.

The location has the following advantages: (Select Choices)
It is easy to locate and accessible to a number of major roadways.
Plentiful parking.
Proximity to _____ and _____ growth areas.
Proximity to businesses in same affinity class with same ideal patient profiles.
Reasonable rent.
Storefront Visibility

Shares a facility with the _____ community organization.
Shortage of Medical Marijuana Dispensary service providers in area.
Similar types of businesses have had a good track record in this area.
Limited number of direct competitors.
Proximity to the _____ light industrial park with a sizeable workforce.

Note: Some cities are adopting zoning laws that allow dispensaries where new physician's offices are located, with requirements keeping them 200 feet from schools.

2.4.1   Company Facilities

_____ (company name) signed a _____ (#) year lease for _____ (#) square foot of space. The cost is very reasonable at $____/sq. foot. We also have the option of expanding into an additional _____ sq. ft. of space and subletting the space. A leasehold improvement allowance of $___ /sq. ft. would be given. Consolidated area maintenance fees would be $___/month initially. _____ (company name) has obtained a _____ (three) month option on this space effective _____ (date), the submission date of this business plan, and has deposited refundable first and last lease payments, plus a $ _____ security deposit with the leasing agent.

The facilities will feature the following:
1.   Computer lab equipped with state-of-the-art hardware and software.
2.   Secure Marijuana Strains Inventory Storage
3.   Product Shipping/Receiving Area
4.   Marijuana Juice bar
5.   Assessment/Treatment Rooms.
6.   Reception/Waiting Area
7.   Admin/Sales Offices
8.   Classroom/Conference Room.
9.   Retail Boutique
10.   _____

2.4.2   Medical Marijuana Dispensary Design

Our dispensary will feature a pharmacy, waiting room, patient meeting rooms and office space, as well as areas dedicated to security. The building will deploy a "man trap" where clients are buzzed into an area where their credentials will be checked before they are let into the locked dispensary area.

There will a bud room where patients get to examine and choose their buds. About ____ (#) jars will contain a bud or two each of various strains. Patients will be able to peruse them, discuss their effects with the bud tender stationed in the area, and even read lab reports on the THC and CBD cannabinoid levels in each sample. THC is known for its pain reduction, and appetite inducing properties. CBD is known for anxiety, nausea and convulsion reduction,

We will document the existing or proposed security and lighting systems for our medical marijuana dispensary. This will include a diagram on 8.5 by 11 inch paper of the facility with all security devices and lighting identified. Security devices will include: motion detectors, alarms, video cameras, solid core doors, electric door openers, safes, exterior lighting, etc. We will also include a written description of existing ventilation system and whether smoking or vaporization of cannabis will be permitted on premise. We will specifically include a description of the carbon filtration system for odor control.

The exterior branding of our dispensary will allow patients to easily locate, and spend safely their money, at our store. Creating curb appeal and clearly marking our location with professional signage and branding, while still being discrete and safe will ensure that patients feel secure and comfortable when visiting our facility.
 Note: Attach floor plan to Appendix Section.

As the customer experience becomes more important, we will offer more services to clients, and also aim to serve as wellness centers for the community at-large. This will require spaces that are designed to serve multiple purposes, including: education areas, private consultation rooms, classroom space for activities like yoga, dining options, and interactive sales floors.

The design of our dispensary will be shaped more in the images of lifestyle retailers like Apple and Whole Foods, and wellness retailers like lululemon. Another example of this philosophy will be in our product presentation. As concentrates and edibles become more popular, we will be moving away from convenience-store-style displays and more toward displays found in confectionaries and even jewelry stores, with products on well-lit tables that lend themselves to more intimate patient consultations and more tactile customer experiences.

We will also search for ways to integrate security measures into the design of our space so that safety and security are still paramount without putting customers and community members on edge with barred windows, barbed-wire fences, and air-lock entryways.

Examples:
https://www.curbed.com/2015/3/30/9976266/medical-marijuana-dispensaries

Note: Research indicates that an interior design resembling a head shop may be better fitting for recreational users whereas medical patients may prefer a pharmacy type of layout that endorses simplicity and privacy.

Resources:
http://thrdesignstudio.com/building-your-dispensary-brand-through-interior-design/
http://4frontpublishing.org/designing-dispensaries-for-success/

Sand Studios   www.sandstudios.com/
A multidisciplinary design firm with a poetic approach to design.

The High Road Design Studio   http://thrdesignstudio.com/
A cannabis retail design and consulting firm aiming to educate industry business owners
on the correlation between design and professionalism, branding and customer loyalty.

2.5.0   Start-up Summary

The start-up costs for the Medical Marijuana Dispensary business will be financed
through a combination of an owner investment of $ _____ and a short-term bank loan
of $ _____. The total start-up costs for this company are approximately $
_____ and can be broken down in the following major categories:

1.	Computer hardware & software	$ _____
2.	Legal, Accounting and Consulting Fees	$ _____
3.	Office Furniture, Display Cases, Work Tables and Fixtures	$ _____
4.	Inventory: Marijuana Strains	$ _____
5.	Working Capital	$ _____
	For day-to-day operations, including payroll, etc.	
6.	Location Build-out	$ _____
7.	Marketing/Advertising Expenses	$ _____
	Includes sales brochures, direct mail, opening expenses.	
8.	Utility and Rent Deposits	$ _____
9.	Insurance	$ _____
10.	Business Licensing and Employee Registration Fees	$ _____
11.	Vehicle	$ _____
12.	Contingency Fund	$ _____
13.	Build Cultivation Facility (optional)	$ _____
14.	Security Systems	$ _____
15.	Other (Includes training, legal expenses, software, etc.)	$ _____
Totals:		$ _____

Resource:
http://www.profitableventure.com/starting-a-medical-marijuana-dispensary/

Note: Considering legal and consulting fees, an entrepreneur can expect to pay between
$30,000 to $100,000 just to make an application. Then, if granted a license, the build-out
will run between $100,000 to $300,000. And if our state allows a cultivation location,
that will run anywhere between $200,000 to $400,000.

The state will require $ _____ in initial cash reserves and additional $ _____ in
assets. The start-up costs are to be financed by the equity contributions of the owner in
the amount of $ _____ , as well as by a _____ (#) year commercial loan in the

amount of $ _____ . The funds will be repaid through earnings.
These start-up expenses and funding requirements are summarized in the tables below.

2.5.1   Inventory

Inventory:	Supplier	Qty	Unit Cost	Total
Marijuana Strains				
Marijuana infused edibles				
Logo-imprinted Packaging				
Aromatherapy Oils				
Display Bottles/Glass Jars				
Hash Containers				
Glass Tincture Vials				
Rolling papers	8			
Water pipes				
Vaporizers				
Edibles Plastic Containers				
Glass Extract Containers				
Pre-roll Tubes				
Storage/Display Sets				
Butane				
Rx Labels				
Uniforms				
Disposables				
Testing Supplies				
Candles				
Cleaning Supplies				
Office Supplies				
Computer Supplies				
Marketing Materials				
Strain Inventory				
Edibles Inventory				
Supplies Inventory				
Business Forms				
Patient Sign-in Sheets				
Employee Time Cards				
Invoices				
Misc. Supplies				
Totals:				

Resource:
www.thenorthwestleaf.com/pages/articles/post/guide-to-24-medical-marijuana-strains

2.5.2   Supply Sourcing

We will search for and contact several wholesale suppliers for our Medical Marijuana Dispensary. We will first contact the National Association of Wholesaler-Distributors, (www.naw.org) and ask our contact person if they can supply a list of _____ wholesalers. We will also visit the Tradepub.com website, and order some free trade publications on retailing. We will read through the classified ads for potential _____ wholesalers. We will consider the wholesalers that offer the best mix of lowest unit cost of marijuana products, the fastest re-order turnaround service, and the best open credit terms. We will meet up with suppliers and inquire if we can avail discounted prices if we buy in bulk.

Initially, ____ (company name) will purchase all of its equipment from _____and supplies from _____, the _____ (second/third?) largest supplier in _____ (state), because of the discount given for bulk purchases. However, we will also maintain back-up relationships with two smaller suppliers, namely _____ and _____.
These two suppliers have competitive prices on certain products.

Resources:
Business Directory   http://entrepotneurmagazine.com/marijuana-business-directory/
Mile High Ice Cream   www.milehighicecream.com
Dispensary Depot   www.dispensarydepot.com

Packaging Supplies:
CoolJarz   www.cooljarz.com
Cannaline   www.cannaline.com/420/
Kush Bottles   www.kushbottle.com

Other:
Alternaturals, Inc.   www.alternaturals.com/
Manufactures and sells alternative healthcare products including an all-natural sleep aids, as well as Hemp and Cannabis related products and many natural substitutes for popular prescription drugs. The company also plans to operate as a distribution company to centralize the fragmented alternative health product, and medical marijuana industries. Alternaturals recently announced its highly anticipated medical marijuana product, five hour high, which has been developed with the leading manufacturer of marijuana drinks and elixirs in the US. The product will be available in dispensaries starting in Colorado around June 30th and plans are in motion to expand to several other "legal" states shortly thereafter to place the product out onto dispensary shelves.
Resource: http://investorshub.advfn.com/Alternaturals-Inc-ANAS-7966/

Easton Pharmaceuticals   www.eastonpharmaceuticalsinc.com
A specialty pharmaceutical company involved in various pharmaceutical sectors that owns, designs, develops, and markets topically-delivered drugs and therapeutic / cosmetic healthcare products, focused on cancer and other health issues related towards male and female sexual dysfunction, wound healing, pain, motion sickness, scar and

stretch marks, cellulite, varicose veins and other conditions. The company is also endeavoring to enter other potentially lucrative industries such as medical marijuana.

Neutra Corp.   **www.neutracorp.com**
A healthy lifestyle company that specializes in the development and marketing of natural wellness solutions, including cannabis-related products.

TDM Financial
Provides marketing, outreach and management services. TDM Financial also owns and operates the CannabisFN website, a leading financial network serving the medical marijuana (MMJ) and cannabis industries.

Dixie Elixirs
This Denver-based Dixie Elixirs produces a wide variety of infused cannabis sodas. Note: Dixie Elixirs & Edibles took its THC-infused drinks off the market because new packaging regulations for recreational marijuana edibles went into effect in Colorado and the screw top aluminum bottles were no longer compliant. The new rules require that drinkable cannabis products come in childproof, resealable packaging. Dixie also had to come with a way to measure out a single dose, like the tiny plastic cup on a bottle of cough syrup.
Source: www.fastcompany.com/3045240/how-to-brand-market-and-sell-weed-without-
            breaking-the-law

The Sweet Grass Kitchen   **www.sweetgrasskitchen.com/**
A Denver-based artisanal bakery producing and distributing high quality cannabis-infused edibles for recreational and medicinal purposes.

Bhang Chocolates   **www.gotbhang.com**
The industrial standard in medicated cannabis edible chocolate bars.

Cheeba Chews   **www.cheebachews.com/**   .
Cannabis infused edibles.

OM Edibles   **http://www.omedibles.org/**

B-Edibles   **http://www.b-edibles.com/**
An infused edibles manufacturer that creates infused sugar products and is particularly well-known for offering medicated cotton candy.
Source:
www.ganjapreneur.com/vanessa-corrales-infusing-edibles-brand-with-personality/

Input Products	Description	Source	Back-up	Cost

2.5.3   Supplier Assessments

We will use the following form to compare and evaluate suppliers, because they will play a major role in our procurement strategies and significantly contribute to our profitability.

	Supplier #1	Supplier #2	Compare
Supplier Name			
Address			
Website			
Contacts			
Annual Sales			
Distribution Channels			
Memberships/Certifications			
Quality System			
Positioning			
Pricing Strategy			
Payment Terms			
Discounts			
Delivery Lead-time			
Return Policy			
Rebate Program			
Technical Support			
Core Competencies			
Primary Product			
Primary Service			
New Products/Services			
Innovative Applications/Uses			
Competitive Advantage			
Capital Intensity			
State of Technology			
Capacity Utilization			
Price Volatility			
Vertical Integration			
References			
Overall Rating			

2.5.4   Equipment Leasing

Equipment Leasing will be the smarter solution allowing our business to upgrade our equipment needs at the end of the term rather than being overly invested in outdated equipment through traditional bank financing and equipment purchase. We also intend to explore the following benefits of leasing some of the required equipment:

1.   Frees Up Capital for other uses.   2.   Tax Benefits
3.   Improves Balance Sheet   4.   Easy to add-on or trade-up

5.	Improves Cash Flow	6.	Preserves Credit Lines
7.	Protects against obsolescence	8.	Application Process Simpler

Our leasing strategy will also be shaped by the following factors:
1.   Estimated useful life of the equipment.
2.   How long our business plans to use the equipment.
3.   What our business intends to do with the equipment at the end of the lease.
4.   The tax situation of our business.
5.   The cash flow of our business.
6.   Our company's specific needs for future growth.

List Any Leases:

Leasing Company	Equipment Description	Monthly Payment	Lease Period	Final Disposition

Resource:

LeaseQ   www.leaseq.com
An online market place that connects businesses, equipment dealers, and leasing companies to make selling and financing equipment fast and easy. The LeaseQ Platform is a free, cloud based SaaS solution with a suite of on-demand software and data solutions for the equipment leasing industry. Utilizes the Internet to provide business process optimization (BPO) and information services that streamline the purchase and financing of business equipment across a broad array of vertical industry segments.

Innovative Lease Services   http://www.ilslease.com/equipment-leasing/
This company was founded in 1986 and is headquartered in Carlsbad, California. It is accredited by the Better Business Bureau, a long standing member of the National Equipment Finance Association and the National Association of Equipment Leasing Brokers and is the official equipment financing partner of Biocom.

2.5.5   Funding Source Matrix

Funds Source	Amount	Interest Rate	Repayment Terms	Use

2.5.6   Distribution or Licensing Agreements   (if any)

Note: These are some of the key factors that investors will use to determine if we have a competitive advantage that is not easily copied.

Licensor	License Rights	License Term	Fee or Royalty

2.5.7   Trademarks, Patents and Copyrights (if any)

Our trademark will be virtually our branding for life. Our choice of a name for our business is very important. Not only will we brand our business and services forever, but what may be worthless today will become our most valuable asset in the years to come. A trademark search by our Lawyer will be a must, because to be told down the road that we must give up our name because we did not bother to conduct a trademark search would be a devastating blow to our business. It is also essential that the name that we choose suit the expanding product or service offerings that we plan to introduce.

Note: These are some of the key factors that investors will use to determine if we have a competitive advantage that is not easily copied.

Resources:

Patents/Trademarks   www.uspto.gov
Copyright   www.copyright.gov

2.5.8   Innovation Strategy   (optional)

_____ (company name) will create an innovation strategy that is aligned with not only our firm's core mission and values, but also with our future technology, supplier, and growth strategies. The objective of our innovation strategy will be to create a sustainable competitive advantage . Our education and training systems will be designed to equip our staff with the foundations to learn and develop the broad range of skills needed for innovation in all of its forms, and with the flexibility to upgrade skills and adapt to changing market conditions. To foster an innovative workplace, we will ensure that employment policies facilitate efficient organizational change and encourage the expression of creativity, engage in mutually beneficial strategic alliances and allocate adequate funds for research and development. Our radical innovation strategies include _____ to achieve first mover status. Our incremental innovation strategies will include modifying the following _____ (products/services/processes) to give our patients added value for their money.

Resource:

https://hbr.org/2015/04/the-5-requirements-of-a-truly-innovative-company

2.5.9   Summary of Sources and Use of Funds

Sources:

Owner's Equity Investment $ _____
Requested Bank Loans $ _____
Total: $ _____

Uses:

Capital Equipment	$ _____
Beginning Inventory	$ _____
Start-up Costs	$ _____
Working Capital	$ _____
Total:	$ _____

2.5.9.1   Funding To Date   (optional)

To date, _____'s (company name) founders have invested $_____ in _____
(company name), with which we have accomplished the following:

1.   _____ (Designed/Built) the company's website
2.   Developed content, in the form of ___ (#) articles, for the website.
3.   Hired and trained our core staff of __(#) full-time people and ___ (#) part-time people.
4.   Generated brand awareness by driving ___ (#) visitors to our website in a ___(#) month period.
5.   Successfully _____ (Developed/Test Marketed) ___ (#) new _____ (products/services), which compete on the basis of _____.
6.   _____ (Purchased/Developed) and installed the software needed to _____ (manage _____ operations?)
7.   Purchased $ _____ worth of _____ (supplies)
8.   Purchased $ _____ worth of _____ dispensary equipment.

2.6   Start-up Requirements

Start-up Expenses:		Estimates
Legal	_____	400
Accountant	_____	300
Accounting Software Package	_____	300
Annual Licenses & Permit fees	_____	5000
Employee Registration Fees	_____	
Market Research Survey	_____	300
Office Supplies	_____	300
Sales Brochures	_____	300
Direct Mailing	_____	500
Other Marketing Materials	_____	2000
Logo Design		500
Advertising (2 months)	_____	2000
Consultants	_____	1000
Insurance	_____	1200

Rent (2 months security)	_____		3000
Rent Deposit	_____		1500
Utility Deposit			600
DSL Installation/Activation	_____		100
Telephone System Installation			200
Telephone Deposit	_____		200
Expensed Equipment	_____		1000
Website Design/Hosting	_____		2000
Computer/Printer	_____		
Used Office Equipment/Furniture	_____		2000
Organization Memberships	_____		300
Vehicle Customization	_____		5000
Cleaning Supplies	_____		200
Security System	_____		
Office Renovation	_____		500
Training Materials	_____		
Vehicle Signs	_____		
Other	_____		
Total Start-up Expenses	_____	**(A)**	

Start-up Assets:

Cash Balance Required	_____	(T)	5000
Start-up Equipment	_____	See schedule	
Start-up Inventory	_____	See schedule	
Other Current Assets	_____		
Long-term Assets	_____		
Total Assets	_____	**(B)**	
Total Requirements	_____	(A+B)	

Start-up Funding

Start-up Expenses to Fund	_____	(A)
Start-ups Assets to Fund	_____	(B)
Total Funding Required:	_____	**(A+B)**

Assets

Non-cash Assets from Start-up	_____	
Cash Requirements from Start-up	_____	(T)
Additional Cash Raised	_____	(S)
Cash Balance on Starting Date	_____	(T+S=U)
Total Assets:	_____	**(B)**

Liabilities and Capital

Short-term Liabilities:

Current Borrowing	_____
Unpaid Expenses	_____
Accounts Payable	_____

Interest-free Short-term Loans   _____

Other Short-term Loans   _____

Total Short-term Liabilities   _____ **(Z)**

Long-term Liabilities:

Commercial Bank Loan   _____

Other Long-term Liabilities   _____

Total Long-term Liabilities   _____ **(Y)**

Total Liabilities   _____ **(Z+Y = C)**

Capital

Planned Investment

Owner   _____

Family   _____

Other   _____

Additional Investment Requirement   _____

Total Planned Investment   _____ **(F)**

Loss at Start-up (Start-up Expenses) (-)_____ **(A)**

Total Capital (=)_____ **(F+A=D)**

Total Capital and Liabilities   _____ **(C+D)**

Total Funding   _____ (C+F)

2.6.1   Capital Equipment List   (select)

Equipment Type	Model No.	New/ Used	Lifespan	Quantity	Unit Cost	Total Cost
Computer System						
Fax Machine						
Digital Camera						
Copy Machine						
Answering Machine						
Weight Scales						
Cordless Vacuum						
Mobile Storage						
Company Vehicle						
Office Furniture						
Surge Protector						
Accounting Software						
Appointment Scheduling Software						
Microsoft Office Software						
Personal Organizer						
CD Collection						
CD Music Player						
Rolling Suitcase Carrier						

Air Filtration System _____

Security System _____

Video surveillance system _____

Cell Phones _____

Internet Broadband Connection _____

GPS System _____

Telephone headsets _____

Greenhouse _____

Daborizer Wax Vaporizer _____

HID Grow Lights _____

Fertigation Systems _____

Automatic Timer _____

De-humidifier System _____

Filtration System _____

Micron Vacuum _____

Refrigerator _____

Microwave _____

Paper Shredder _____

Postal Meter _____

Calculator _____

Other _____

Total Capital Equipment _____

Notes: Equipment costs are dependent upon buying new or used equipment or leasing. All items that are assets to be used for more than one year will be considered a long-term asset and will be depreciated using the straight-line method.

Specialized Equipment

MagicalButter   A patent-pending Botanical Extractor(TM)

The MagicalButter.com recipe section guides visitors through easy-to-grasp directions for a variety of dishes. l, Magical Butter sells a kitchen appliance that helps pot enthusiasts make THC-infused butter and oil. Last year, the Seattle-based company sold an average of 4,500 units per month.

Source:

www.marketwatch.com/story/medical-marijuana-gets-a-magical-touch-2017-10-23

Water Technologies International, Inc. and its wholly owned subsidiaries, GR8 Water, Inc. (Great Water) and Aqua Pure International, Inc. (Specializing in Filtration Systems) are engaged in the manufacture and distribution of technologically advanced Atmospheric Water Generators (AWG). These unique devices utilize a patent pending air purification input system to produce clean, great-tasting, safe water from the humidity in the air. GR8 Water makes freestanding water factory units for the home or office and large, industrial-sized water units using a modular design that can produce up to thousands of gallons of water each day from ambient air. GR8 Water strives to make safe drinking water available to everyone on the planet, making the world a better place in which to live while nurturing the environment. Their custom units will be able to generate water as well as clean, dehumidify, cool and heat the air in the marijuana grow areas.

The most common types of lights used indoor with marijuana is **High Intensity Discharge (HID) lights** such as **High Pressure Sodium (HPS)** and **Metal Halide (MH) lights**.
Source: www.growweedeasy.com/growing-marijuana-what-type-of-lights#intro

Fertigation Systems
Fertigation is the application of fertilizers, soil amendments, or other water-soluble products through an irrigation system. Effective automated fertigation systems for cannabis are available from the following companies;

Dosatron	http://www.dosatronusa.com/
Envirotech	http://envirotechgreenhouse.com/
Gryphon Automation	http://www.gryphonautomation.com/

Greenhouses
http://www.hightimes.com/read/greenhouse-grow-basics

2.7.0   SBA Loan Key Requirements

In order to be considered for an SBA loan, we must meet the basic requirements:
1. Must have been turned down for a loan by a bank or other lender to qualify for most SBA Business Loan Programs. 2. Required to submit a guaranty, both personal and business, to qualify for the loans. 3. Must operate for profit; be engaged in, or propose to do business in, the United States or its possessions; 4. Have reasonable owner equity to invest; 5. Use alternative financial resources first including personal assets.

All businesses must meet eligibility criteria to be considered for financing under the SBA's 7(a) Loan Program, including: size; type of business; operating in the U.S. or its possessions; use of available of funds from other sources; use of proceeds; and repayment. The repayment term of an SBA loan is between five and 25 years, depending on the lift of the assets being financed and the cash needs of the business.
Working capital loans (accounts receivable and inventory) should be repaid in five to 10 years. The SBA also has short-term loan guarantee programs with shorter repayment terms.

A Business Owner Cannot Use an SBA Loan:

To purchase real estate where the participant has issued a forward commitment to the developer or where the real estate will be held primarily for investment purposes. To finance floor plan needs. To make payments to owners or to pay delinquent withholding taxes. To pay existing debt, unless it can be shown that the refinancing will benefit the small business and that the need to refinance is not indicative of poor management.

SBA Loan Programs:

Low Doc: www.sba.gov/financing/lendinvest/lowdoc.html

SBA Express www.sba,gov/financing/lendinvest/sbaexpress.html

Basic 7(a) Loan Guarantee Program

> For businesses unable to obtain loans through standard loan programs. Funds can be used for general business purposes, including working capital, leasehold improvements and debt refinancing.
> www.sba.gov/financing/sbaloan/7a.html

Certified Development Company 504 Loan Program

> Used for fixed asset financing such as purchase of real estate or machinery.
> www. Sba.gov/gopher/Local-Information/Certified-Development-Companies/

MicroLoan 7(m) Loan Program

> Provides short-term loans up to $35,000.00 for working capital or purchase of fixtures.
> www.sba.gov/financing/sbaloan/microloans.html

2.7.1   Other Financing Options

1. Grants:

   Health care grants, along with education grants, represent the largest percentage of grant giving in the United States. The federal government, state, county and city governments, as well as private and corporate foundations all award health care grants. The largest percentage of health care grants are awarded to non-profit organizations, health care agencies, colleges and universities, local government agencies, tribal institutions, and schools. For profit organizations are generally not eligible for health care grants unless they are conducting research or creating jobs.

   A.   Contact your state licensing office.

   B.   Child Care Resource and Referral Agency

   C.   Children's and Family Service Office

   D.   Foundation Grants to Individuals: www.fdncenter.org

   E.   US Grants   www.grants.gov

   F.   Foundation Center   www.foundationcemter.org

   G.   The Grantsmanship Center   www.tgci.com

   H.   Contact Local Chamber of Commerce

   G.   The Catalog of Federal Domestic Assistance is a major provider of business grant money.

   H.   The Federal Register is a good source to keep current with the continually changing federal grants offered.

   I.   FedBizOpps is a resource, as all federal agencies must use FedBizOpps to notify the public about contract opportunities worth over $25,000.

   J.   Fundsnet Services   http://www.fundsnetservices.com/

   K.   SBA Women Business Center
   www.sba.gov/content/womens-business-center-grant-opportunities

Local Business Grants

Check with local businesses for grant opportunities and eligibility requirements. For example, Bank of America sponsors community grants for businesses that endeavor to improve the community, protect the environment or preserve the neighborhood.
Resource:
www.bankofamerica.com/foundation/index.cfm?template=fd_localgrants

Green Technology Grants

If you install green technology in the business as a way to reduce waste and make the business more energy efficient, you may be eligible for grant funding. Check your state's Economic Development Commission. This grant program was developed as part of the American Recovery and Reinvestment Act.
Resource: www.recovery.gov/Opportunities/Pages/Opportunities.aspx

2.	Friends and Family Lending	www.virginmoney.com
3.	National Business Incubator Association	www.nbia.org/
4.	Women's Business Associations	www.nawbo.org/
5.	Social Networking Loans	www.prosper.com
7.	Peer-to-Peer Programs	www.lendingclub.com
8.	Extended Credit Terms from Suppliers	30/60/90 days.
9.	Community Bank w/ Established Relationship	
10.	Leasing Companies	www.businessfinance.com
11.	Prepayments from patients	
12.	Seller Financing: When purchasing an existing Medical Marijuana Dispensary.	
13.	Business Funding Directory	www.businessfinance.com
14.	FinanceNet	www.financenet.gov
15.	SBA Financing	www.sbaonline.sba.gov
16.	Private Investor	

17.	Use retirement funds to open a business without taxes or penalty. First, establish a C-corporation for the new business. Next, the C-corporation establishes a new retirement plan. Then, the owner's current retirement funds are rolled over into the C-corporation's new plan. And last, the new retirement plan invests in stock of the C-corporation. Warning: Check with your accountant or financial planner.
Resource: http://www.benetrends.com/

18.	Business Plan Competition Prizes
www.nytimes.com/interactive/2009/11/11/business/smallbusiness/Competitions-table.html?ref=smallbusiness

19.	Unsecured Business Cash Advance based on future credit card transactions.

20.	Kick Starter	www.kickstarter.com

21.	Capital Source	www.capitalsource.com
www.msl.com/index.cfm?event=page.sba504
Participates in the SBA's 504 loan program. This program is for the purchase of fixed assets such as commercial real estate and machinery and equipment of a capital nature, which are defined as assets that have a minimum useful life of ten

years. Proceeds cannot be used for working capital.

22. Commercial Loan Applications   www.c-loans.com/onlineapp/
23. Sharing assets and resources with other non-competing businesses.
24. Angel Investors   www.angelcapitaleducation.org
25. The Receivables Exchange   http://receivablesxchange.com/
26. Bootstrap Methods: Personal Savings/Credit Card/Second Mortgages
27. Community-based Crowd-funding   www.profounder.com
                                       www.peerbackers.com

      A funding option designed to link small businesses and entrepreneurs with pools of prospective investors. Crowdfunding lenders are often repaid with goods or services.

28. On Deck Capital   www.ondeckcapital.com/

      Created the Short Term Business Loan (up to $100,000.00) for small businesses to get quick access to capital that fits their cash flow, with convenient daily payments.

29. Royalty Lending   www.launch-capital.com/

      With royalty lending, financing is granted in return for future revenue or company performance, and payback can prove exceedingly expensive if a company flourishes.

30. Stock :Loans   Southern Lending Solutions, Atlanta. GA.
                                         Custom Commercial Finance, Bartlesville, OK

      A stock loan is based on the quality of stocks, Treasuries and other kinds of investments in a businessperson's personal portfolio. Possession of the company's stock is transferred to the lender's custodial bank during the loan period.

31. Lender Compatibility Searcher   www.BoeFly.com
32. Micro-Loans   www.accionusa.org/
33. Strategic Investors

      Strategic investing is more for a large company that identifies promising technologies, and for whatever reason, that company may not want to build up the research and development department in-house to produce that product, so they buy a percentage of the company with the existing technology.

34. Bartering
35. Small Business Investment Companies   www.sba.gov/INV
36. Cash-Value Life Insurance
37. Employee Stock Option Plans   www.nceo.org
38. Venture Capitalists   www.nvca.org
39. Initial Public Offering (IPO)
40. Meet investors through online sites, including LinkedIn (group discussions), Facebook (BranchOut sorts Facebook connections by profession), and CapLinked (enables search for investment-related professionals by industry and role).
41. SBA Community Advantage Approved Lenders
            www.sba.gov/content/community-advantage-approved-lenders
42. Small Business Lending Specialists
     https://www.wellsfargo.com/biz/loans_lines/compare_lines
     http://www.bankofamerica.com/small_business/business_financing/
     https://online.citibank.com/US/JRS/pands/detail.do?ID=CitiBizOverview

https://www.chase.com/ccp/index.jsp?pg_name=ccpmapp/smallbusiness/home/page/bb_business_bBanking_programs

43. United States Economic Development Administration   www.eda.gov/
44. Small Business Loans   http://www.iabusnet.org/small-business-loans
45. Tax Increment Financing (TIF)

    A public financing method that is used for subsidizing redevelopment, infrastructure, and other community-improvement projects. TIF is a method to use future gains in taxes to subsidize current improvements, which are projected to create the conditions for said gains. The completion of a public project often results in an increase in the value of surrounding real estate, which generates additional tax revenue. Tax Increment Financing dedicates tax increments within a certain defined district to finance the debt that is issued to pay for the project. TIF is often designed to channel funding toward improvements in distressed, underdeveloped, or underutilized parts of a jurisdiction where development might otherwise not occur.

46. Gust   https://gust.com/entrepreneurs

    Provides the global platform for the sourcing and management of early-stage investments. Gust enables skilled entrepreneurs to collaborate with the smartest investors by virtually supporting all aspects of the investment relationship, from initial pitch to successful exit.

47. Emerald Ocean Capital   http://emeraldocean.com/

    The company intends to position itself as the leader in the legal cannabis sectors through both acquisitions and continued pioneering with first-to-market legal cannabis verticals.

48. Biz2Credit   www.biz2credit.com
49. Funding Circle   www.fundingcircle.com

    A peer-to-peer lending service which allows savers to lend money directly to small and medium sized businesses

50. Lending Club   www.lendingclub.com

51. Equity-based Crowdfunding www.Indiegogo.com
                               www.StartEngine.com
                               www.SeedInvest.com
54. National Funding   www.nationalfunding.com

    Their customers can to get working capital, merchant cash advances, credit card processing, and, equipment leasing.

55. Quick Bridge Funding   www.quickbridgefunding.com

    Offers a flexible and timely financing program to help assist small and medium sized businesses achieve their goals.

56. Go Fund Me   www.gofundme.com

Resources: www.sba.gov/category/navigation-structure/starting-managing-business/starting-business/local-resources
http://usgovinfo.about.com/od/moneymatters/a/Finding-Business-Loans-Grants-Incentives-And-Financing.htm

The Ghost Group   http://ghostgroup.com/
Their cannabis-related portfolio currently includes WeedMaps and Cannabinoid Science
Systems – a company that is designing a number of cannabis products
including terpene extracts, chewing gum, and topicals, while working to secure patents
for their processes. The Ghost Group also launched the Emerald Ocean Fund, with which
they intend to raise $10-$25 million this year to acquire and invest in cannabis-related
businesses. Resource: http://www.medicaljane.com/directory/company/ghost-group/

Privateer Holdings   www.privateerholdings.com/
Located in Seattle. Founded in 2011, Privateer claims to be the first private equity firm
that only invests in cannabis-related companies. Because cannabis cultivation and
distribution is federally illegal, their true focus is on ancillary businesses – companies
that don't "touch the leaf." This company uses strategic investments in the cannabis
industry to acquire and create mainstream brands, professionalizing the cannabis business
landscape through the power of private enterprise.

The Arc View Group   http://arcviewgroup.com/
The ArcView Group is ushering in the next generation of cannabis-related businesses
with The ArcView Investor Network, ArcView Market
Research, CanopyBoulder, Cannasure Insurance Services, and other ground-breaking
ventures.
Source: www.medicaljane.com/2013/10/02/medical-marijuana-legal-cannabis-earns-
           investors-interest/

GUD Capital   www.gudcapital.com
A nationally recognized leader in the financing industry for providing the best business
lending solutions available to small and mid-sized businesses. We leverage our network
of 4,000 competing commercial lenders to provide your business the largest selection of
commercial financing options.

The Canna Law Group   www.cannalawblog.com/
A team of business attorneys focusing on the corporate, compliance, intellectual property,
and consumer product issues impacting the cannabis industry. They represent medical
and recreational businesses in multiple states, and continue to offer their clients the
proactive approach and strategic edge that this unique industry demands.

Articles:
www.cannalawblog.com/marijuana-fundraising-top-5-tips-on-approaching-investors/
https://gudcapital.com/cannabis-business-loans-dispensary-financing-and-marijuana-
           industry-investment/
www.medicaljane.com/2013/12/08/ten-tips-for-raising-start-up-funding-in-the-cannabis-
           industry/
https://mjbizdaily.com/5-tips-for-a-successful-cannabusiness-investment-pitch/

3.0 Products and Services

In this section, we will not only list all of our planned products and services, but also describe how our proposed products and services will be differentiated from those of our competitors and solve a real problem or fill an unmet need in the marketplace.

We will offer prepackaged Cannabis, from the most popular size — one gram — on up to the ____ (2.5?) -ounce limit set by the ____ (state) Medical Marihuana Act. We will offer 8tinctures and oils made with THC extracts, and edibles will range from the traditional brownies and cookies to pizza and lollipops. We will also introduce topical marijuana products, infused waters and a cannabis lozenge. The plants used to make the products will be free of contamination and sent to a third party testing laboratory to test for potency and contaminants.

We will also provide marijuana infused products including edibles, soaps, lotions, tinctures and salves. Medicinal marijuana can also be made into sodas, bars, elixirs, and lozenges. Concentrates are also potent marijuana substances that can be used with vaporizers or similar devices. We will also pursue sales of smoking and non-smoking paraphernalia.

Paraphernalia includes devices, contrivances, instruments and paraphernalia for inhaling or otherwise consuming marijuana, including, but not limited to, rolling papers and related tools, water pipes, and vaporizers.
l
We also intend to purchase equipment and product in bulk quantities, at substantial discounts. We also plan to investigate the private labeling of our products.

3.1.0   Service Overview

_____ (company name) patients will be able to contact our service desk manager by telephone 24/7 or via our website for consultation information and appointment reservations.

3.1.1   Service Descriptions   (select)

In creating our service descriptions, we will provide answers to the following types of questions:
1.   What does the service do or help the patient to accomplish?
2.   Why will people decide to buy it?
3.   What makes it unique or a superior value?
4.   How expensive or difficult is it to make or copy by a competitor?
5.   How much will the service be sold for?

The Patient Servicing Process

1. Doctors who recommend medical marijuana will write a letter explaining the patient's diagnosis and the doctor's choice of cannabis as treatment.

2. Patients keep this letter close at hand and/or apply to the state for an ID card, issued only to medical marijuana patients, which can serve in place of the recommendation letter.

3. A doctor's recommendation will remain valid as long as the doctor continues to treat the patient and believes the patient should use the drug to treat a condition.

4. The dispensary will maintain a list of doctors who are willing to recommend medical marijuana.

5. Marijuana-laced edibles are a popular alternative to smoking medical marijuana.

6. Once a patient has a valid recommendation letter or ID card, he or she simply presents it at a dispensary. A patient may also have to join the dispensary as a member.

7. He or she can then purchase different types of herbal marijuana and numerous marijuana-based products and prepared foods (chocolate, smoothies, cakes, cookies and butter).

8. Since there's no standard dosage for marijuana, patients are left to regulate their own intake of medication.

9. Many patients smoke it, but it has some side effects, besides producing intoxication. Smoke, of course, isn't good for the lungs. However, the effect is nearly immediate, and some studies indicate that marijuana smoke is less toxic than that from cigarettes.

10. Alternatives to smoking include marijuana-laced foods or using a vaporizer. A vaporizer is a device that burns marijuana at a lower temperature than when it's smoked. The vaporizer releases the THC from the plant but produces fewer harmful byproducts.
    Resource: Volcano, a popular model of vaporizer, sells for around $500.

11. Vending machines now vend marijuana in some locations, with strictly controlled access. These machines require a fingerprint scan and the insertion of an ID card provided by the dispensary. They are monitored by security guards and patients and offer convenient access to the medicine.

Our dispensary will basically be a private club. A new kitchen will serve meals (medicated and non-medicated) to members, prepared by different chefs who will work on a rotating schedule.

There will be a community room with a small stage to accommodate about ___ (#)

people. We will schedule bands, poetry readings and the like in community room. There will also be classes on how to build a grow room, cultivation and cooking with marijuana. When there is no entertainment people will be able to watch cable TV on the flat-screen wall mounted television.

We will offer home delivery services on orders above $ _____ (50.00) and facilitate the meeting of support groups on our premises. Note: The state law governing the dispensaries allows them to deliver medicine as long as the service is approved by the health department.

We will help our patients to obtain physician approvals and referrals.
Resource: http://www.canorml.org/prop/MDRecForm.jpg

3.1.2 The Health Benefits of Marijuana

The health benefits of marijuana are as follows: alleviates pain, and certain, disabilities illnesses and diseases. In _____ (state), a broad range of illnesses, disabilities, and diseases were approved to use medical marijuana as a treatment for therapy, and medication. _____ (state) has approved medical marijuana to effectively treat symptoms associated with cancer, muscle spasms associated with Multiple Schlerosis, chronic pain, symptoms associated with HIV and AIDS, Anorexia, migraine, headache, Glacucoma, persistent epileptic seizures, nausea, Cachexia, and other re-occurring medical conditions.

In addition to the above list marijuana can be a treatment for arthritis, Chrohn's Disease,PMS, Bipolar Disorder, Tourette Syndrome tics, ADD, ADHD, Insomnia, Parkinsons, Alzheimers, and stress reduction.

3.2 Alternative Revenue Streams

1. Classified Ads in our Newsletter
2. Errand Running/ Concierge
3. Exercise and Yoga Classes
4. Product sales and rentals.
5. Website Banner Ads
6. Content Area Sponsorship
7. Seminars and Workshops
8. ATM Machines

We will make an automated teller machine (ATM) available at our dispensary to help our customers to make cash payments.
ATM Resource: Sky Processing   www.skyprocessing.net/

We also plan to consider subletting our space to complementary businesses. This could include a Chiropractor, a Naturopath, an expert in Chinese medicine or even an Endocrinologist or Nutritionist.

3.3 Production of Products and Services

We will use the following methods to locate the best suppliers for our business:
- **Attend trade shows and conferences to spot upcoming trends, realize networking opportunities and compare prices.**

World Medical Cannabis Conference and Expo
www.compassionatecertificationcenters.com/2017-world-medical-cannabis-conference-expo/

Marijuana Cannabis Conferences
https://inhalemd.com/blog/3-biggest-2017-marijuana-business-conferences/

- **Subscribe to appropriate trade magazines, journals, newsletters and blogs.**

Cannabis Times Magazine   www.cannabistimesmagazine.com

Green Rush Daily   https://www.greenrushdaily.com/
A cannabis-oriented publication offering up-to-date and breaking content on cannabis politics, news, business, technology, and culture.

MMJ Business Daily
          http://mmjbusinessdaily.com/medical-marijuana-news-by-us-state/
A business news source for the US medical marijuana and cannabis industry.

Entrepotneur Magazine   http://entrepotneurmagazine.com
Culture Magazine
High Times Magazine   www.hightimes.com
Cannabis Health News   www.cannabishealthnews.com/

Stop the Drug War   http://stopthedrugwar.org/chronicle/2017/oct/02/med_marijuana_update
The Hot Box Magazine   http://thehotboxmagazine.com/
The Weed Blog   www.theweedblog.com

- **Join our trade association to make valuable contacts, get listed in any online directories, and secure training and marketing materials.**

Medical Marijuana Association   www.medicinalmarijuanaassociation.com/
Their mission is to promote and support the use of medicinal marijuana by providing patients with information about its many benefits. Our purpose is to help you discover if medicinal marijuana is right for you and to teach you how to have an effective conversation with your doctor. They also provide access to reputable producers and health professionals, and provide ongoing monitoring and dosing.

American Medical Marijuana Association   http://americanmarijuana.org/
A group of volunteers working together to implement, preserve and protect the rights of medicinal cannabis patients through political activism. Their platform is based on the idea of not bargaining away people's rights. They believe that each person will have

different needs, which are best determined by the patient and physician. .

National Cannabis Industry Association   http://thecannabisindustry.org/
NCIA is the only trade association in the U.S. that works to advance the interests of cannabis-related businesses on the national level.

The American Alliance for Medical Cannabis   www.letfreedomgrow.com/
AAMC is dedicated to bringing patients, caregivers and volunteers the facts they need to make informed decisions about whether Cannabis is the right medicine for them, the laws surrounding Medicinal Marijuana in your area, political activism and even handy recipes and guides to growing your own nontoxic medicine.

Cannabis Business Alliance   http://cannabisalliance.org/
Advocates for sensible and collaborative public policy that protects employees, patients, and clients of the medical and retail marijuana industry.

Infused Products Council
2A subgroup of CBA focused specifically on issues that impact edibles and infused companies. Developed an educational flyer to promote responsible use of edibles and prevent over consumption.

Canadian Association of Medical Cannabis Dispensaries   www.camcd-acdcm.ca/
A not-for-profit corporation, has been established with the mandate to promote a regulated community-based approach to medical cannabis access and to support medical cannabis dispensaries to provide the highest quality of patient care.

Schools
Northeastern Institute of Cannabis
        Focuses on training medical marijuana dispensary workers.

Oaksterdam University in California
        The best-known cannabis institute.

New England Grass Roots Institute
        Offers a range of classes, such as the history and science of cannabis as well
        as patient caregiving and cooking with cannabis.

Cannabis University of Florida
The university puts on seminars each month in big Florida cities like Orlando, Daytona Beach and Jacksonville. The seminars, which cost around $300 and go from 9 a.m. to 5 p.m., offer attendees the chance to speak to doctors, lawyers, CPAs and other marijuana experts about the ins and outs of the business.

3.4 Competitive Comparison

According to _____ County Records, the city of _____, _____ (state) has only ____(#) licensed Medical Marijuana Dispensary facilities. We expect to filling the growing local market need for convenient Medical Marijuana Dispensary services.

According to US Census 2000 data, the city of _____ has _____ (#) single family homes. There are only ___ (#) other Medical Marijuana Dispensary facilities in the neighborhood. _____ (company name) will differentiate itself from its local competitors by offering an alternative to these traditional service provider approaches at a competitive price based on the expanded value of our convenient Medical Marijuana Dispensary services.

Our market strategy is based on providing an activity based learning environment. We will offer the services of professional bud tenders with the credentials to improve a person's lifestyle.

By forming strategic referral alliances with local physicians, we plan to become the market leader in Medical Marijuana Dispensary services.

3.5 Sales Literature

____ (company name) has developed sales literature that illustrates a professional organization with vision. ____ (company name) plans to constantly refine its marketing mix through a number of different literature packets. These include the following:
- direct mail with introduction letter and product price sheet.
- product information brochures
- press releases
- new product/service information literature
- email marketing campaigns
- website content
- corporate brochures

A copy of our informational brochure is attached in the appendix of this document. This brochure will be available to provide referral sources, leave at seminars, and use for direct mail purposes.

3.6 Fulfillment

The key fulfillment and delivery of services will be provided by our director/owner, and certified staff workers. The real core value is the industry expertise of the founder, and staff education, training, experience and certifications.

CannLabs   **www.cannlabs.com**
The nation's premier provider of scientific methods and intellectual property for cannabis test labs. Offers clients accurate, reliable and scientifically validated results that are easily accessible from our proprietary cloud-based technology platform. The results can be

published in real-time via our web-based customer portal and can be published on our Product Locator map. This tool allows consumers to locate products that have been tested and certified by a licensed cannabis laboratory.

3.7 Technology

__ (company name) will employ and maintain the latest technology to enhance its programs, job scheduling, office management system, payment processing and record keeping.

We will also use a Cash Register POS system to manage our Medical Marijuana Dispensary. Each item that gets sold will be deducted from our inventory list. Additionally, tracking items in our dispensary will easily be managed with handheld inventory devices that integrate with Cash Register system. Our point of sale system will include a small form factor computer, cash drawer, receipt printer and laser bar code scanner or tabletop scanner. An optional pole display will be easily added, which will inform our patients how much they are paying so they are likely to have the cash out quickly. A laser bar code scanner will aggressively scan bar codes that might be on bags or around bottles and quickly add the item to the invoice. All of these devices help to reduce the time it takes to process a patient.

Our software systems will support the following Medical Marijuana Dispensary functions:

1.	Custom branded public pages	2.	Import existing patients & inventory
3.	Integrates with POS hardware	4.	Custom labels and barcodes
5.	Leafly integration	6.	Twitter integration
7.	iPhone, iPad & Andriod friendly	8.	Real-time inventory tracking
9.	Manage multiple locations	10.	Accept inventory on consignment
11.	Generate invoice for vendor purchase	12.	Place online orders with vendors
13.	Download and generate sales reports	14.	Manage employees and track hours
15.	Allow patient to check in themselves	16.	Online ordering for patients
17.	Low inventory alerts	18.	Email and text message patients
19.	Manage patient data and documents	20.	Notifications for medical expirations
21.	Patient visit tracking & reward program		

The opening of our new dispensary will allow our business to implement our Dispensary Management System (DMS), which we have spent a great deal of time and effort planning. This includes a full suite of cannabis management software that provides seed to sale inventory control, point of sale and financial reporting. Our systems will meet or exceed current ____ (state) rules and regulations. We will also implement a state of the art audio/video security system and 24 hour monitoring.

Resources:
MMJ Menu Software   https://mmjmenu.com/
Cafe Cartel   http://cafecartel.com/retail-pos-systems/medical-marijuana-dispensary-pos.html

THC Biz   www.thcbiz.com/directory/dispensary-resources/management-software.html

Marketing Resources

Hemp American Media Group   http://hempamerican.com/sites/
Operates high-traffic marijuana-related website businesses which provide services and products to an audience that reaches into the millions annually.

Medical Cannabis Payment Solutions, Inc.   www.refg.co

Their mission is to provide end-to-end management, across multiple management systems, for medicinal marijuana operations. Many medicinal marijuana companies have experienced such rapid growth that they are finding it difficult to manage all aspects of their operation. In order to become a successful and compliant medicinal marijuana operation, effective management must depend on many different systems. REFG solves the fragmentation problem by identifying tools that are important to dispensaries, and customizing those tools specifically catered to the industry. They strive to create awareness within the medicinal marijuana industry and to develop an environmentally friendly, economically sustainable business while increasing shareholder value.

MediSwipe, Inc.   www.mediswipe.com/

Provides both online and wireless merchant payment solutions. The company offers a range of secure transaction processing solutions using Internet point-of-sale (POS), e-commerce, social networks and mobile terminals through its alliance partner network. The Company's electronic payment processing .

MJ Freeway   www.mjfreeway.com/

The firm provides software to businesses for tracking every gram of marijuana from cultivation facility to retail sale. It also helps companies maintain compliance with state regulations.

Mobile Phone Credit Card Reader   https://squareup.com/

Square, Inc. is a financial services, merchant services aggregator and mobile payments company based in San Francisco, California. The company markets several software and hardware products and services, including Square Register and Square Order. Square Register allows individuals and merchants in the United States, Canada, and Japan to accept offline debit and credit cards on their iOS or Android smartphone or tablet computer. The app supports manually entering the card details or swiping the card through the Square Reader, a small plastic device which plugs into the audio jack of a supported smartphone or tablet and reads the magnetic stripe. On the iPad version of the Square Register app, the interface resembles a traditional cash register.

Google Wallet   https://www.google.com/wallet/

A mobile payment system developed by Google that allows its users to store debit cards, credit cards, loyalty cards, and gift cards among other things, as well as redeeming sales promotions on their mobile phone. Google Wallet can be used NFC to make secure payments fast and convenient by simply tapping the phone on any PayPass-enabled terminal at checkout.

Apple Pay   http://www.apple.com/apple-pay/
A mobile payment and digital wallet service by Apple Inc. that lets users make payments using the iPhone 6, iPhone 6 Plus, Apple Watch-compatible devices (iPhone 5and later models), iPad Air 2, and iPad Mini 3. Apple Pay does not require Apple-specific contactless payment terminals and will work with Visa's PayWave, MasterCard's PayPass, and American Express's ExpressPay terminals. The service has begun initially only for use in the US, with international roll-out planned for the future. Resource:
www.wired.com/2017/01/shadow-apple-pay-google-wallet-expands-online-reach/

WePay   https://www.wepay.com/
An online payment service provider in the United States. WePay's payment API focuses exclusively on platform businesses such as crowdfunding sites, marketplaces andsmall business software. Through this API, WePay allows these platforms to access its payments capabilities and process credit cards for the platform's users.

Chirpify
Connects a user's PayPal account with their Twitter account in order to enable payments through tweeting.

Article: www.prnewswire.com/news-releases/tips-to-leverage-mobile-payments-in-your-marketing-strategy-300155855.html

3.8   Future Products and Services

___ (company name) will continually expand our offering of services based on Medical Marijuana Dispensary industry trends and changing patient needs. We will not only solicit feedback via surveys and comments cards from patients on what they need in the future, but will also work to develop strong relationships with all of our patients and vendors.

We also plan to open _____ (#) additional locations in the _____ area starting in ____ (year). Franchise start-ups will be offered in _____(city) after ___ (#) years of successful operation. We plan to expand our line of products as a source of holiday gift items.

We plan to expand our offering of services into the following areas:
1.   Weight Management Counseling
2.   Stress Reduction Programs
3.   Rental, Sales and Service of Portable Equipment.
4.   Consignment arrangements with suppliers.
5.   24/7 Emergency Delivery Services
6.   Mobile Medical Marijuana Dispensary Services
7.   Online registration and order placement
8.   Monthly publication of newsletter with info about new medicines and services.

We will give patients the option to verify online via the dispensary's website, and, once verified, to place orders for delivery service. The stated purpose for this service is that many patients prefer the privacy of having their medicine delivered to them rather than visiting a dispensary. There are also a lot of patients with serious medical conditions for whom it can be difficult to do a lot of driving around. Many of them cannot afford the luxury of a caretaker to pick up and deliver their medicine for them.

We will publish profiles with several online medical marijuana social networking communities such as Leafly and Weedmaps to keep our patients informed of the current selection of medicines and services.

Scheduled Tours
We also plan to offer marijuana tours to cash in on tourists expected to be attracted to our local resorts.

Subscription Programs
A purchase that is made repeatedly by way of a signed order. The subscription add-on module is designed for businesses that have to invoice their customers for their goods or services in specific intervals. Involves someone paying a fee to receive a product, service, or the like in regular intervals.

Examples:

Marvina   **https://marvina.com/**
Similar in style to other subscription models, the cannabis arrives monthly on the customer's doorstep. Based in San Francisco, Marvina was conceived when its founder Dane Pieri recognized that once the medical sale of the pain-alleviating drug was legalized in the state of California that customers would be overwhelmed with choice. The monthly medical marijuana delivery service aims to create a culture of "cannabis connoisseurs" by offering high quality strains. Every month this company works to create a new strain assortment. They feature popular classics, but also try to mix in rare or new strains that the customer may have never tried before. Marvina is not a dispensary and does not sell marijuana. Marvina is a service that connects qualified patients with local dispensaries.

Resources:

Order Groove   **www.ordergroove.com/**

Marijuana Food Truck
Example: The Samich
A marijuana food truck that serves THC-infused sandwiches. From grilled cheese to pulled pork and peanut butter and jelly. Created by MagicalButter Studio, The Samich will set up a permanent spot in Seattle, Washington. Each meal is created with the help of MB2, a device that inserts botanical extracts into butter, cooking oil and alcohol. The modified 40-foot Freightliner C2 school bus is known as the SAMICH Truck, according to the company. That stands for Savory Accessible Marijuana Infused Culinary Happiness. It serves dishes like pulled pork sandwiches, cheese sandwiches and tomato soup.
Resources: https://magicalbutter.com/

Source:
www.forbes.com/sites/karstenstrauss/2014/05/08/marijuana-food-truck-makes-its-denver-debut/

Online Ordering
To register for online ordering, customers will have to visit our physical location and speak with a budtender about setting up their online account. This is not a delivery service and customers will not have to pay until they pick up their order.

Examples:
http://www.thecliniccolorado.com/online-ordering/
https://shop.essencevegas.com/menu/dispensary/essence-henderson

Resources:
http://www.trybaker.com/products/shop
https://ecommerce.shopify.com/c/payments-shipping-fulfilment/t/payment-gateways-for-
      medical-marijuana-195824
https://ecommerce.shopify.com/c/bab-general/t/how-to-create-a-six-figure-cannabis-
      business-w-out-selling-weed-434004

Delivery Service
We will deliver purchases that are over $_____ in a designated service area.
Resource:
http://theweedbusiness.com/what-is-a-medical-marijuana-delivery-service/
Examples:
http://www.thegreencross.org/

Stress Management
We will establish programs and sell products that help our patients to reduce their stress levels by finding natural everyday stress and anxiety relief. These products will be made from organic herbs such as Kava Kava Root.
Resource:
One Hour Break   https://www.1hourbreak.com/

Health and Wellness Center
We will transition our dispensary into a health and wellness center, and offer weekly health enhancing programs, such as Yoga, Pilates, therapeutic massages or acupuncture.
We will also offer the following types of alternative or natural approaches to health and wellness:

Acupuncture
Acupuncture stimulates the body's chi, or life energy, accelerating movement from disharmony towards health.

Yoga Classes
An avenue toward healthy living by improving flexibility, strength and posture while calming the mind and relaxing the spirit.

Cannabis-infused Massage Therapies
Within the category of massage topicals, there are a growing number of cannabidiol (CBD) containing salves, creams, oils and patches touted as relaxing and pain-relieving. Massage therapists must obtain information about the legal use of these topicals directly from their state.
Source:
Care By Design Guild   https://www.cbd.org/
Manufacturers CBD sprays, oil, vape pens and other products

Example:
http://dragonflywellness.org/what-we-do/

Resources:
www.massagemag.com/marijuana-massage-5-questions-answered-32929/
https://www.leafly.com/news/health/cannabis-oil-topical-massage

Range of New Business Opportunities in the Cannabis Industry
      https://smallbiztrends.com/2016/10/marijuana-business-opportunities.html
      https://www.entrepreneur.com/slideshow/282008
      www.dailyworth.com/posts/3564-how-to-make-money-from-the-growing-
          marijuana-industry

4.0 Market Analysis Summary

Our Market Analysis will serve to accomplish the following goals:
1.   Define the characteristics, and needs and wants of the target market.
2.   Serve as a basis for developing sales, marketing and promotional strategies.
3.   Influence the e-commerce website design.

This industry is in the growth phase of its lifecycle, with strong growth over recent years expected to continue over the immediate future. The aging population, increasing consumer awareness and advancements in horticulture and technology will continue to stimulate growth going forward. With more patients opting for treatments in the comfort of their own home, the need for Mobile Medical Marijuana Dispensary services by seniors is likely to keep increasing.

The consumer base for _____ (company name) will be patients referred by the following:

1.	Physicians	2.	Discharge planners
3.	Health care facilities	4.	Nutritionists
5	Oncologists	6.	Optometrists
7.	Physical Therapists	8.	Chiropractors
9.	Other Medical Professionals		

Additionally, a recent research study identified Medical Marijuana Dispensary services, as a significant market opportunity in _____ (city).
.

The next step will be to identify market opportunities and arrange introductions to referral agents and medical service providers in the _____ (city).

4.1 Secondary Market Research

We will research demographic information for the following reasons:
1.   To determine which segments of the population, such as Hispanics and the elderly, have been growing and may now be underserved.
2.   To determine if there is a sufficient population base in the designated service area to realize the company's business objectives.
3.   To consider what products and services to add in the future, given the changing demographic profile and needs of our service area.

We will pay special attention to the following general demographic trends:
1.   Population growth has reached a plateau and market share will most likely be increased through innovation and excellent patient service.
2.   Because incomes are not growing and unemployment is high, process efficiencies and sourcing advantages must be developed to keep prices competitive.
3.   The rise of non-traditional households, such as single working mothers, means

4. As the population shifts toward more young to middle aged adults, ages 30 to 44, and the elderly, aged 65 and older, there will be a greater need for child-rearing and geriatric personal care products and services.

5. Because of the aging population, increasing pollution levels and high unemployment, new alternative medicine remedies will need to be developed.

We will collect the demographic statistics for the following zip code(s):

_____

We will use the following sources: www.census.gov, www.zipskinny.com, www.city-data.com, www.demographicsnow.com, www.freedemographics.com, www.ffiec.gov/geocode, www.esri.com/data/esri_data/tapestry and www.claritas.com/claritas/demographics.jsp. This information will be used to decide upon which targeted programs to offer and to make business growth projections. **Resource:** www.sbdcnet.org/index.php/demographics.html

Snapshots of consumer data by zip code are also available online:
http://factfinder.census.gov/home/saff/main.html?_lang=en
http://www.esri.com/data/esri_data/tapestry.html
http://www.claritas.com/MyBestSegments/Default.jsp?ID=20

1.	**Total Population**	_____
2.	**Number of Households**	_____
3.	**Population by Race:**	White ____% Black ___% Asian Pacific Islander ___% Other ____%
4.	**Population by Gender**	Male ____% Female ____%
5.	**Income Figures:**	Median Household Income $_____ Household Income Under $50K ____% Household Income $50K-$100K ____% Household Income Over $100K ____%
6.	**Housing Figures**	Average Home Value - $_____ Average Rent $_____
7.	**Homeownership**:	Homeowners % _____ Renters % _____
8.	**Education Achievement**	High School Diploma % _____ College Degree % _____ Graduate Degree % _____
9.	**Stability/Newcomers**	Longer than 5 years % _____
10.	**Marital Status**	___% Married ___% Divorced ___% Single ___% Never Married ___% Widowed ___% Separated
11.	**Occupations**	___%Service ___% Sales ___% Management ___% Construction ___% Production ___% Unemployed ___% Below Poverty Level
12.	**Age Distribution**	___%Under 5 years ___%5-9 yrs ___%10-12 yrs ___% 13-17 yrs ___%18-years ___% 20-29 ___% 30-39 ___% 40-49 ___% 50-59

		___% 60-69 ___% 70-79 ___% 80+ years

13. **Prior Growth Rate** _____ % from _____ (year)

14. **Projected Population Growth Rate** _____ %

15. **Employment Trend** _____

Secondary Market Research Conclusions:

This area will be demographically favorable for our business for the following reasons:

_____

_____

_____

Resources:

www.allbusiness.com/marketing/segmentation-targeting/848-1.html

http://www.sbdcnet.org/industry-links/demographics-links

http://factfinder2.census.gov/faces/nav/jsf/pages/index.xhtml

4.1.1   Primary Market Research

We plan to develop a survey for primary research purposes and mail it to a list of local home, senior and parenting magazine subscribers, purchased from the publishers by zip code. We will also post a copy of the survey on our website and encourage visitors to take the survey. We will use the following survey questions to develop an Ideal Patient Profile of our potential patient base, so that we can better target our marketing communications. To improve the response rate, we will include an attention-grabbing _____ (discount coupon/ dollar?) as a thank you for taking the time to return the questionnaire.

1. What is your zip-code? _____
2. Are you single, divorced, separated, widowed or married? _____
3. Are you male or female? _____
4. What is your age? _____
5. What is your approximate household income? _____
6. What is your educational level? _____
7. What is your profession? _____
8. Are you a dual income household?
9. Do you have children? If Yes, what are their ages? _____
10. What are your favorite magazines? _____
11. What is your favorite local newspaper? _____
12. What is your favorite radio station? _____
13. What are your favorite television programs? _____
14. What organizations are you a member of? _____
15. Does our community have adequate Medical Marijuana Dispensary services?
16. Is your family currently a patient of a dispensary?   Yes / No

17. What are the ages of your children?
18. Are you satisfied with your current service arrangements?   Yes / No
19. Would you patronize a new Medical Marijuana Dispensary?   Yes / No
20. What are the strengths of your current pain management provider?
21. What are their weaknesses or shortcomings?
22. What would it take for us to earn your Medical Marijuana Dispensary business?
23. What is the best way for us to market our products and services?
24. What is your general need for Medical Marijuana Dispensary services?
   Circle Months: J F M A M J J A S O N D
   Circle Days: S M T W T F S
   Indicate Hours: _____
26. Would you be willing to pay a higher fee for personalized Medical Marijuana Dispensary services?
28. Do you live in _____ community?
29. Do you work or study in _____ community?
31. What type of Medical Marijuana Dispensary services would you prefer?
32. Describe your experience with other dispensary service providers.
33. Please rank (1 to 18) the importance of the following factors when choosing a dispensary service provider:

   ___ Right education focus   ___ Hours of service
   ___ Convenient location   ___ Staff education and experience
   ___ Staff turnover   ___ Member Benefits.
   ___ Patient Service   ___ Strain Selection
   ___ Scheduling Convenience   ___ Value Proposition
   ___ Price   ___ Referral
   ___ Other _____

34. What information would you like to see in Medical Marijuana Dispensary newsletter?
35. Which online social groups have you joined? Choose the ones you access.

   ___ Facebook   ___ MySpace
   ___ Twitter   ___ LinkedIn
   ___ Ryze   ___ Ning

36. What types of new medical marijuana related services would most interest you?
37. What are your suggestions for realizing a better Medical Marijuana Dispensary experience?
38. Are you on a mailing list? Yes/No   If No, can we add you?   Yes / No
39. Can you supply the name and contact info of person who might be interested in Medical Marijuana Dispensary services?

Please note any comments or concerns about Medical Marijuana Dispensary services. We very much appreciate your participation in this survey. If you provide your name, address and email address, we will sign you up for our e-newsletter, inform you of our survey results, advise you of any new medical marijuana service facilities opening in your community, and enter you into our monthly drawing for a free _____.

Name   Address   Email   Phone

4.1.2 Market Research Conclusions

The above compiled market research leads us to make the following conclusions:

1. About _____ % of the public would make use of a Medical Marijuana Dispensary in the _____ area.
2. The ideal demographic profile of the Medical Marijuana Dispensary patient is

   _____
3. The ideal lifestyle profile of the Medical Marijuana Dispensary patient is

   _____
4. _____

4.1.3 Voice of the Patient

To develop a better understanding of the changing needs and wants of our Medical Marijuana Dispensary patients, we will institute the following ongoing listening practices:

1. Focus Groups
   Small groups of patients (6 to 8) will be invited to meet with a facilitator to answer open-ended questions about priority of needs and wants, and our company, its products or other given issues.
2. Individual Interviews
   We will conduct face-to-face personal interviews to understand patient thought processes, selection criteria and entertainment preferences.
3. Patient Panels
   A small number of patients will be invited to answer open-ended questions on a regular basis.
4. Patient Tours
   We will invite patients to visit our facilities to discuss how our processes can better serve them.
5. Visit patients
   We will observe patients as they actually use our products to uncover the pains and problems they are experiencing during usage.
6. Trade Show Meetings
   Our trade show booth will be used to hear the concerns of our patients.
7. Toll-free Numbers
   We will attach our phone number to all products and sales literature to encourage the patient to call with problems or positive feedback.
8. Patient Surveys
   We will use surveys to obtain opinions on closed-ended questions, testimonials, constructive feedback, and improvement suggestions.
9. Mystery Shoppers
   We will use mystery shoppers to report on how our employees treat our

patients.

10. Salesperson Debriefing
   We will ask our salespeople to report on their patient experiences to obtain insights into what the patient faces, what they want and why they failed to make a sale.

11. Patient Contact Logs
   We will ask our sales personnel to record interesting patient revelations.

12. Patient Serviceperson's Hotline
   We will use this dedicated phone line for service people to report problems.

13. Discussions with competitors.

14. Installation of suggestion boxes to encourage constructive feedback.

4.2 Market Segmentation

Market segmentation is a technique that recognizes that the potential universe of users may be divided into definable sub-groups with different characteristics. Segmentation enables organizations to target messages to the needs and concerns of these subgroups. We will segment the market based on the needs and wants of select patient groups. We will develop a composite patient profile and a value proposition for each of these segments. The purpose for segmenting the market is to allow our marketing/sales program to focus on the subset of prospects that are "most likely" to purchase our Medical Marijuana Dispensary products and services. If done properly this will help to insure the highest return for our marketing/sales expenditures.

Our target market is primarily the ___ (city) residents and employees. This is a young market with a great deal of potential. It consists of the following groups:

1. **Business Women**
   This group makes up the majority of our target market. There are a significant number of young women (22-35 yrs old) that live and/or work in ____ (city). We will be advertising by placing fliers at local grocers, bars, restaurants, etc. with ads that stress the benefits of the alternative treatment options available at our Medical Marijuana Dispensary. Location will be our primary advantage. This group most likely has been to one of our competitors. We will key in on the fact that we are right around the corner. We will also have delivery services available for the busy business woman.

2. **College Students**
   This group makes up a ___ % of our target market. Price will be our advantage to this market. These individuals are always seeking news remedies with fewer harmful side effects. We will offer value-driven pricing. We will be advertising to this group by placing ads at local grocers, apartment complexes, college bulletin boards, and direct mailers. We will also have coupons to encourage this group to seek referrals from their physicians and try our medical marijuana dispensary.

3. **Young Business Men**
   This group we hope to reach because they represent a significant percentage of the population of ___ (city). We hope to accomplish this by overcoming the beliefs that medical marijuana is just for potheads. We will be placing brochures and ads at physician offices and local health clubs that emphasize the importance of an alternative approach to anxiety and stress relief.

4. **Personal Injury Sufferers**
   This includes those individuals who have suffered a personal injury and require personalized restorative services. These patients will be referred by medical practitioners, attorneys and insurance companies looking for a less expensive course of treatment.

5. **Seniors**
   We will educate this group to be receptive to new ways to manage pain with fewer harmful side effects.

_____ (company name) will focus on meeting the local community need for Medical Marijuana Dispensary services within a ____ mile radius of _____ (neighborhood).

The population in _____ region of _____ (state) is aging, and more people are opting for the convenience of having products delivered to their homes.

Consumer Profile of Recreational and Medical Cannabis Users

Recreational users are typically characterized as having:
1. A strong interest in the psychoactive effects of cannabis.
2. A high willingness to experiment with cannabis in a variety of forms.
3. An inclination towards new product adoption.
4. Sensitivity to product pricing.
5. Greater reception for more than one method of administration.

Medical cannabis patients are often:
1. Loyal to a particular product or category of products.
2. Purpose-driven to treat their condition and improve overall quality of life.
3. More personally connected to the dispensary agents/staff, whose product guidance they come to rely upon
4. Concerned with quality, product consistency and predictable effects.
5. Three times as likely as recreational users to use cannabis on a daily or almost daily basis.
6. Higher consumers of non-psychoactive products.
Source:
https://smallbiztrends.com/2017/01/marijuana-marketing.html

Composite Ideal Patient Profile:

By assembling this composite patient profile we will know what patient needs and wants our company needs to focus on and how best to reach our target market. We will use the information gathered from our patient research surveys to assemble the following composite patient profile:

Ideal Patient Profile

Who are they?
- age _____
- gender _____
- occupation _____
  location: zip codes _____
- income level _____
  marital status _____
  ethnic group _____
  education level _____
  family life cycle _____
  number of household members _____
  household income _____
  homeowner or renter _____
  association memberships _____
  leisure activities _____
  hobbies/interests _____
  core beliefs _____
Where are they located (zip codes)? _____
Most popular product/service purchased? _____
Lifestyle Preferences? Trendsetter/Trend follower/Other _____
How often do they buy? _____
What are most important purchase factors? Price/Brand Name/Quality/Financing/Sales Convenience/Packaging/Other_____

What is their key buying motivator? _____
How do they buy it? Cash/Credit/Terms/Other_____
Where do they buy it from (locations)? _____
What problem do they want to solve? _____
What are the key frustrations/pains that these patients have when buying? _____
What search methods do they use? _____
What is preferred problem solution? _____

Table: Market Analysis

Potential Patients	Growth	Number of Potential Patients		
		2017	2018	2019
Business Women	10%			
Young Business Men	10%			
College Students	10%			
Injury Rehabilitation	10%			

Seniors	10%	_____
Other	10%	_____
Totals:	10%	_____

4.3   Target Market Segment Strategy

Our target marketing strategy will involve identifying a group of patients to which to direct our Medical Marijuana Dispensary products and services. Our strategy will be the result of intently listening to and understanding patient needs, representing patients' needs to those responsible for product production and service delivery, and giving them what they want. In developing our targeted patient messages we will strive to understand things like: where they work, worship, party and play, where they shop and go to school, how they spend their leisure time, what magazines they read and organizations they belong to, and where they volunteer their time. We will use research, surveys and observation to uncover this wealth of information to get our product details and brand name in front of our patients when they are most receptive to receiving our messaging. As a legal cannabis dispensary, we will be permitted to sell pharmaceutical-grade cannabis and paraphernalia to qualified ___ (city) residents registered with the Department of Health's Medical Marijuana Program.

Referral marketing, direct-mail campaigns and community activities will be the primary types of marketing strategies employed. Enhancing our reputation for trust with families and in the community will be crucial in establishing our brand image and obtaining the planned market share growth that we have forecasted. To this end, we will draft and publish our Code of Ethics and any service guarantees that we decide to offer.

We will seek to build meaningful relationships with physicians as to educate them on our program's specifics in an effort to boost their comfort level when recommending cannabis to patients.

We will target medical professionals who treat the following types of conditions:

1.	Premenstrual Syndrome	2.	Crohn's Disease
3.	Glaucoma	4.	HIV/AIDS
5.	Cancer	6.	Multiple Sclerosis
7.	Cachexia	8.	Anxiety Disorder
9.	Chronic Pain	10.	Nausea
11.	Arthritis	12.	Epilepsy
13.	Muscle spasms	14.	Hepatitis
15.	Migraines		

Resource: **www.marijuanadoctors.com/blog/marijuana-medical-conditions**

Target Community Support Groups
We will identify and engage organizations and community support groups that are established and working with qualified individuals and physicians to boost awareness and drive them to connect with our dispensary.

Target Hospices

We will seek to engage individuals battling terminal disease.

Target Assisted Living Facilities and Senior Centers

Present free seminars to establish expertise and build interest in the need for our services and products. Present content as article reprints with sales flyers or direct mail pieces. Possible Seminar Topics Include:

1. Wellness and Complementary Alternative Medicine
2. How to Evaluate Medical Marijuana Therapies and Products
3. New Pain Management and Stress Reduction Techniques

Target Retired People and Seniors

This group may have pain management, mobility, insomnia, and anxiety problems, and the desire to save money with home care services. They can be reached through community and daycare centers. For this group, edibles are a great alternative to pain medications because they don't hurt your liver.

Target Baby Boomers

They want to feel younger and live longer. According to the National Center for Health Statistics, half of middle-aged adults between 55 and 64 have high blood pressure and two in five are obese. The dramatic growth in the numbers of obese seniors in the U.S. requires Medical Marijuana Dispensary providers to provide more personal care services for these patients.

Target Working Women

We will market our Medical Marijuana Dispensary services as a form of stress relief for working women. We will form marketing alliance partnerships with the following types of businesses:

1.	Day Care Centers	2.	Clothing Boutiques
3.	Fitness Centers	4.	Beauty Salons
5.	Catering Companies	6.	Event Planners

Target Older Women

Women have higher average expenditures for Medical Marijuana Dispensary and long-term care than men, because they make up a higher proportion of the older population, need more help with both personal care needs and routine needs, and are less likely to have a spouse available to help them. It will be important for us to identify creative approaches to connecting with the social and community causes that are important to women and reinforce the role of a total wellness and lifestyle solution, rather than a product-centric or service-centric brand approach.

Target Millennials

Millennials, which comprise of 10 million people, are the biggest spenders, and the ones that the entrepreneurs are fighting over for a market share. They account for 21 to 25 percent of consumer discretionary purchases, and that is going to increase has they acquire more earning power. Presently, millennial buyers are struggling with higher prices, tighter mortgage-lending procedures, and a still-unsteady job market. Millennials are reaching out to social networks and observing behaviors of their friends to look for new, novel, authentic experiences. Millennials don't look exclusively to their friends for information. They also process information from lots of sources, because they do want an accurate, authoritative portrayal of an experience they are hoping to enjoy. As marketers, we will provide useful information to potential clients via social networking sites. In fact, JWT data from March 2015 suggests that millennial travelers are more likely to grab their smartphones to access their social networks, Yelp reviews or foursquare users to garner real-time suggestions and find local information while on the go. We will provide these types of "concierge-like" services to reach millennials. And to gain the initial trust of these customers, we will join conversations, participate in forums and comment on blogs, already in progress, rather than interrupt them in order to start and control conversations of our own. We will also practice nostalgia marketing to connect with millenials and use content that reminds them how they have changed from their common, shared experiences in the 90s.

Resource:

www.thestorestarters.com/3-ways-tailor-new-stores-media-plan-speak-millennials/

Target Local Ethnic Groups

Increasingly excellent marketing techniques reveal that diverse ethnic groups have a strong loyalty to those that can best cater to their specific needs. Different ethnic groups will be drawn to physicians and aesthetic services professionals that recognize their specialized needs. Ongoing demographic trends suggest that, in the coming decades, early childhood programs will be serving a population of children which is increasingly diverse in economic resources, racial and ethnic background, and family structure. Our plan is to reach out to consumers of various ethnic backgrounds, especially Hispanics, who comprise nearly 13 percent of the country's total population. In addition to embarking on an aggressive media campaign of advertising with ethnic newspapers and radio stations, we will set up programs to actively recruit bilingual employees and make our store more accessible via signage printed in various languages based on the store's community. We will accurately translate our marketing materials into other languages. We will enlist the support of our bilingual employees to assist in reaching the ethnic people in our surrounding area through a referral program. We will join the nearest _____ (predominate ethnic group) Chamber of Commerce and partner with _____ (Hispanic/Chinese/Other?) Advocacy Agencies. We will also develop programs that reflect cultural influences and brand preferences.

Helpful Resources:

U.S. census Bureau Statistics   www.census.gov
U.S. Dept. of Labor/Bureau of Labor Statistics   www.bls.gov/data/home.htm
National Hispanic Medical Association

4.3.1   Market Needs

ProCon.org, an online resource for research on polemic issues, estimates there are more than 2,400,000 registered medical marijuana patients in the U.S.

According to Forbes, "The U.S. medical marijuana market, worth some $1.7 billion in 2011, is expected to blossom into a $9 billion industry by 2019." See Change Strategy, LLC, in their extensive report, The State of the Medical Marijuana Markets 2011, informed there were 24.8 million potential patients eligible for medical marijuana under existing state laws. In a survey released last week, the Tulchin Research organization, polling for the ACLU, found that nearly two-thirds of California voters (65%) now support a proposal to legalize, regulate and tax marijuana sales to adults.

Approved conditions for which medical marijuana is allowed as a treatment vary by state, but nearly all medical marijuana states include HIV/AIDS, cancer, chronic pain, epilepsy and other seizures, glaucoma, severe nausea, and multiple sclerosis. A number of states define "approved conditions" much more broadly, as including a variety of chronic conditions that "interfere with basic functions of life" and "other chronic or persistent medical symptoms."

The Medical Marijuana Growing industry has benefited from increased acceptance and legitimacy of medical marijuana products. Revenue is expected to grow 22.8% in 2017 alone, largely due to favorable regulatory environment, a steadily aging population and an increase in per capita disposable income. Adults aged 50 and older are a major industry market because they tend to require more healthcare services and treatment than the rest of the population. The number of adults in this age group has been steadily expanding and is expected to total about 104.8 million in 2017. Consequently, medical marijuana demand from this demographic has risen during the past five years.

To open a dispensary, we will need to sign up a physician, who will sit on our dispensary or cooperative's board of directors. They will not usually be on-site, but are there to make sure patients are being treated according to a protocol. It also provides assurance to the community, that it's not merely a drug-dealing business.

4.4 Buying Patterns

A Buying Pattern is the typical manner in which /buyers consumers purchase goods or services or firms place their purchase orders in terms of amount, frequency, timing, etc. In determining buying patterns, we will need to understand the following:
   - Why consumers make the purchases that they make?
   - What factors influence consumer purchases?
   - The changing factors in our society.

Typically, a patient will go to a doctor who prescribes medical marijuana and have a physical and/or a medical history taken. The doctor will then ask the patient whether they think medical marijuana would be a benefit to their current health regimen and then they can agree and say you can try it. The average dispensary is not very comprehensive in its assessment of patients, so it is important to first see a doctor, who is likely to do a more thorough evaluation.

Consequently, medical marijuana dispensary business owners need to be ambassadors for sharing the many ways that cannabis can be used to promote health. Most people don't know about vaporization, tinctures (an alcohol-based solution taken under the tongue), balms, and oils that don't get them high but still relieve medical symptoms.

The following the key factors considered by both consumers and referring professionals when purchasing Medical Marijuana Dispensary services:
1.   Trusted Reputation   2.   Reliability
3.   Quality of Service.   4.   Health Benefit Knowledge

_____ (company name) will gear its offerings, marketing, and pricing policies to establish a loyal patient base. Our affordable pricing, innovative Medical Marijuana Dispensary service offerings, educational programs, and personalized services will be welcomed in _____ (city) and contribute to our success.

4.5   Market Growth

We will assess the following general factors that affect market growth:

Current Assessment

1. Interest Rates
2. Government Regulations
3. Perceived Environment Impact
4. Consumer Confidence Level
5. Population Growth Rate
6. Unemployment Rate
7. Political Stability
8. Currency Exchange Rate
9. Innovation Rate
10. Home Sales
11. Trend Linkage
12. Overall Economic Health

Medical marijuana is rapidly becoming a mainstream industry because of the growing popularity of alternative consumption methods that don't scream "stoner," such as vaporizing pens, dabs and infused products, such as brownies, ice creams and beverages. All of these focus on derivatives of cannabis concentrates, the essential oil of the plant. Some dispensaries are seeing sizable month-over-month revenue growth in concentrates, and some report that these products account for as much as 50% of their sales.

U.S. legal cannabis sales jumped 34 percent to $6.9 billion in 2016, according to ArcView Market Research. The research firm forecasts legal sales growth of 26 percent annually for the next five years, bringing the market to $21.6 billion by 2021.

The _____ area is expected to grow _____ % annually. The _____ zip code area is expected to grow ____% annually. These estimates are based on the most recent US Census Data and the _____ County Chamber of Commerce figures.

The general industry analysis shows that ____ (city) is expected to experience substantial population, housing and commercial business growth. This suggests that as more families continue to move into the _____ area, there will be an increasing demand for quality Medical Marijuana Dispensary services, and this makes it a prime location for a Medical Marijuana Dispensary business.

4.6 Service Business Analysis

It is expected that investment in and the business development of medical marijuana dispensaries will continue to be dampened until the federal government definitively changes its position on the legality of medical marijuana.

_____ (company name) will be a Medical Marijuana Dispensary serving the _____ area. Medical Marijuana Dispensary services are typically utilized by individuals and families, with service referrals coming most often from physicians, oncologists, horticulturists, optometrists, pharmacists, etc..

There are currently ____ (#) other Medical Marijuana Dispensary businesses serving the same area, but we are unique in that we plan to offer community-based services as well as Medical Marijuana Dispensary services and other wraparound therapy and treatment services. There will be an eventual need to diversify and broaden the spectrum of services offered.

4.7 Barriers to Entry   (select)

_____ (company name) will benefit from the following combination of barriers to entry, which cumulatively present a moderate degree of entry difficulty or obstacles in the path of other Medical Marijuana Dispensary businesses wanting to enter our market.

1.	Industry Experience.	2.	Community Networking
3.	Referral Program Set-up	4.	People Skills
5.	Marketing Skills	6.	Licensing and Certification
7.	Operations Management	8.	Cash Flow Management
9.	Website Design	10.	Licensed Medical Director
11.	Adherence to industry standards	12.	Cost of capital equipment
13.	Limited labor pool	14.	Regulatory hurdles
15.	Uniqueness of services and amenities.		

Specialized Skills

1. Knowledge of the medicinal properties of cannabis.
2. Negotiation skills for contracting the best prices from growers.
3. Interpersonal skills for communicating with patients about their needs and experiences with products.
4. Managerial skills for training and supervising staff.
5. Accounting skills and a knowledge of State versus Federal allowable expense deductions.
6. Advertising and promotional skills for competing successfully within the industry.
7. Capital sourcing skills.

4.7.1 Porter's Five Forces Analysis

We will use Porter's five forces analysis as a framework for the industry analysis and business strategy development. It will be used to derive the five forces which determine the competitive intensity and therefore attractiveness of our market. Attractiveness in this context refers to the overall industry profitability.

Competitors	The degree of rivalry is moderate in this segment, but less when compared to the overall dispensary category. Major competitors include: _____
Substitutes	Substitutes are moderate for this industry. These include other medical marijuana dispensaries, home growers, drug dealers, etc.
Buyer Power	Buyer power is moderate in this business. Buyers are sensitive to quality and pricing as the segment attempts to capitalize on the pricing and quality advantage.
Supplier Power	Supplier power is moderate in this industry. Supplies can be obtained from a number of cultivation sources. A high level of operational efficiency for managing supplies can be achieved.
Threat of New Entrants	Relatively moderate in this segment. The business model can be copied. Must be supervised by a licensed physician.

Conclusions: _____ (company name) is in a competitive field and has to move fast to retain its competitive advantage. The key success factors are to develop operational efficiencies, an innovative menu of packaged services, cost-effective marketing campaigns and patient service excellence.

4.8 Competitive Analysis

Competitor analysis in marketing and strategic management is an assessment of the strengths and weaknesses of current and potential competitors. This analysis will provide both an offensive and defensive strategic context through which to identify our business opportunities and threats. We will carry out continual competitive analysis to ensure our market is not being eroded by developments in other firms. This analysis needs to be matched with the target segment needs to ensure that our products and services continue to provide better value than the competitors. The competitive analysis needs to be able to show very clearly why our products and services are preferred in some market segments to other offerings and to be able to offer reasonable proof of that assertion.

Competitor	What We Can Do and They Can't	What They Can Do and We Can't

Competitive analysis conducted by the company owners has shown that there are _____ (# or no other?) companies currently offering the same combination of Medical Marijuana Dispensary services in the _____ (city) area. However, the existing competitors offer only a limited range of dispensary programs. In fact, of these _____ (#) competitors only _____ (#) offered a range of Medical Marijuana Dispensary services and packaged options comparable with what _____ (company name) plans to offer to its patients.

We will conduct good market intelligence for the following reasons:
1. To forecast competitors' strategies.
2. To predict competitor likely reactions to our own strategies.
3. To consider how competitors' behavior can be influenced in our own favor.

Overall competition in the area is _____ (weak/moderate/strong).

Self-assessment
Competitive Rating Assessment: **1 = Weak ....5 = Strong**

	Our Company	Prime Competitor	Compare
Our Location			
Our Facilities			
Our Product Quality			
Our Services and Amenities			
Our Management Skills			
Our Training Programs			
Our Research & Development			
Our Company Culture			
Our Business Model			
Overall Rating			

Rationale: _____

The following establishments are considered direct competitors in _____ (city):

Competitor	Address	Market Share	Primary Focus	Secondary Prod/Svcs	Strengths	Weaknesses

Indirect Competitors include the following:

Alternative Competitive Matrix

Competitor Name: <u>Us</u> _____ _____ _____

Location: _____

Distance _____

Website _____

Comparison Items:

Sales Revenue _____

Focus _____

Programs _____

Registration Fee _____

Profitability _____

Market Share _____

Brand Reputation _____

Medical Director _____

Services Selection _____

Technology/Equipment _____

Training Programs _____

Funding Source _____

Capitalization _____

Target Market _____

Operating Hours _____

Pricing Strategy _____

Yrs in Business _____

Law Compliance _____

Reputation _____

Reliability _____

No. of Strains _____

Delivery Service _____

Quality _____

Marketing Strategy _____

Alliances _____

Sales Brochure/Catalog _____

Website _____

Sales Revenues _____

No. of Staff _____

Competitive Advantage _____

Threats _____

Comments _____

_____

Competitor Profile Matrix

Critical Success Factors	Our Score	Competitor 1 Rating	Score	Competitor 2 Rating	Score	Competitor 3 Rating	Score
Advertising							
Product Quality							
Service Quality							
Price Competition							
Management							
Financial Position							
Patient Loyalty							
Brand Identity							
Market Share							
Total							

We will use the following sources of information to conduct our competition analysis:

1. Competitor company websites.
2. Mystery shopper visits.
3. Annual Reports (www.annual reports.com)
4. Thomas Net (www.thomasnet.com)
5. Trade Journals and Associations
6. Local Chamber of Commerce
7. Sales representative interviews
8. Research & Development may come across new patents.
9. Market research surveys can give feedback on the patient's perspective
10. Monitoring services will track a company or industry you select for news.
    Resources: www.portfolionews.com www.Office.com
11. Hoover's www.hoovers.com
12. www.zapdata.com (Dun and Bradstreet) You can buy one-off lists here.
13. www.infousa.com (The largest, and they resell to many other vendors)
14. www.onesource.com (By subscription, they pull information from many sources)
15. www.capitaliq.com (Standard and Poors).
16. Obtain industry specific information from First Research (www.firstresearch.com) or IBISWorld, although both are by subscription only, although you may be able to buy just one report.
17. Get industry financial ratios and industry norms from RMA (www.rmahq.com) or by using ProfitCents.com software.
18. Company newsletters
19. Industry and Market Research Consultants
20. Local Suppliers and Distributors
21. Patient interviews regarding competitors.
22. Analyze competitors' ads for their target audience, market position, product features, benefits, prices, etc.
23. Attend speeches or presentations made by representatives of your competitors.
24. View competitor's trade show display from a potential patient's point of view. 25.

Search computer databases (available at many public libraries).
26. Review competitor Yellow Book Ads.
27. www.bls.gov/cex/ (site provides information on consumer expenditures nationally, regionally, and by selected metropolitan areas).
28. www.sizeup.com
29. Business Statistics and Financial Ratios   www.bizstats.com

4.9 Market Revenue Projection

For each of our chosen target markets, we will estimate our market share in number of patients, and based on consumer behavior, how often do they buy per year? What is the average dollar amount of each purchase? We will then multiply these three numbers to project sales volume for each target market.

Target Market	Number of Patients		No. of Purchases per Year		Average Dollar Amount per Purchase		Total Sales Volume
	A	x	B	x	C	=	D

Using the target market number identified in this section, and the local demographics, we have made the following assessments regarding market opportunity and revenue potential in our area:

Location: _____

Potential Revenue Opportunity =

a	_____	Number of Households
b	% _____	Projected Percentage of Household Targeted (0.5?%)
a x b= c	_____	Number of likely households
d	$ _____	Average annual amount spent on personal services
e	% _____	Projected Percent of Personal Services Share (10?%)
d x e =f	$ _____	Amount of Personal Services Share
c x f =g	$ _____	Projected Dollar Amount of Sales Obtained

Note: Must perform calculations for each location and add to arrive at cumulative amount.

Or…
Note: Some metrics that are being used are counting the average customers per day and the average spend per customer.

	No. of Patients per Day	(x)	Avg Spend per Patient	(=)	Daily Income
Products	_____		_____		_____

Weed Sales	_____	_____	_____
Edibles	_____	_____	_____
Accessories	_____	_____	_____
Services	_____	_____	_____
Seminars	_____	_____	_____
Other:	_____	_____	_____
Total:			_____

Times:	Open Days per month		_____ (22?)
Equals:	Monthly Revenue		_____
Annualized:		(x)	12
Annual Revenue Potential:			_____

Note: Marijuana Business Daily (MBD) has published its 2015 fact book and it has begun to calculate sales per square foot, which is a metric used in traditional retail. MBD determined that an average sales per square foot for a recreational marijuana store is $1,773 and $1,143 for a medical marijuana dispensary.

Source: www.forbes.com/sites/debraborchardt/2015/06/04/marijuana-businesses-find-it-hard-to-measure-success/#7e6639f24e56

Recap:

Month	Jan Feb Mar Apr May Jun Jul Aug Sep Oct Nov Dec Total
Products/Services	
	_____
	_____
	_____
Gross Sales:	_____
(-) Returns	_____
Net Sales	_____

Revenue Assumptions:

1.   The sources of information for our revenue projection are:

_____

2.   If the total market demand for our product/service = 100%, our projected sales volume represents ____% of this total market.

3.   The following factors might lower our revenue projections:

_____

5.0   Industry Analysis

SIC Code: 512227

In the mid-90's, many activists began to rally around the drug's purported medicinal benefits. The Medical Marijuana Project was founded in 1995 to "increase public support for non-punitive, non-coercive marijuana policies" and to gain influence in Congress. A number of studies, both public and private, were funded to test the veracity of marijuana's medicinal worth. One such study in 1999 found that "The active ingredients in marijuana appear to be useful for treating pain, nausea and the severe weight loss associated with AIDS," according to the *The New York Times*.

Slowly, states began to adopt legislation to make it easier for medical marijuana to be disseminated. Over the past 15 years, led by California, 15 states plus the District of Columbia have adopted laws permitting some form of marijuana consumption or distribution for medical use. These laws have been adopted by public referendums as well as legislation. Medical marijuana is legal in Arizona, Alaska, California, Colorado, Connecticut, Washington, D.C., Delaware, Hawaii, Maine, Massachusetts, Michigan, Montana, New Jersey, New Mexico, Oregon, Rhode Island, Vermont, and Washington State, according to ProCon.org. In fall 2012, Washington State and Colorado were the first states to legalize a small amount of pot for personal recreational use.

In 2009, the Obama administration ordered federal prosecutors not to prioritize legal action against medical marijuana dispensaries that comply with state laws. This controversial decision has been critical to the growth of the medical marijuana industry. These conditions have combined to produce the first legal marijuana markets in modern times. This emerging market presents unique opportunities to entrepreneurs and investors as well as unique risks.

Nationally, the issue of the legality of medical marijuana dispensaries has come into greater prominence as the Justice Department recently tried to clarify its rules on when federal authorities should crack down on medicinal marijuana operations in the 20 states where voters have approved medicinal pot. Justice Department officials are scheduled to testify before the Senate Judiciary Committee in an effort to offer some clarity on how the federal government will treat the two states where marijuana is legal to all adults and the 20 where it is available only for medicinal purposes. The Drug Enforcement Agency still officially classifies marijuana as a Schedule 1 drug with "no currently accepted medical use and a high potential for abuse." In August of 2017, Deputy Attorney General James Cole wrote in a memo that the feds weren't going to be as focused on "states and local governments that have enacted laws legalizing marijuana in some form" and have "strong and effective regulatory and enforcement systems."

5.1   Key Industry Statistics

A report by marijuana analysis and investment firms ArcView Group and New Frontier, concurs and predicts $6.7 billion in legal marijuana product sales in 2017, up from $5.4 billion legal marijuana product sales nationwide in 2015. By 2019, the market could surge to $8.9 billion

The CNBC estimates that, nationwide, cannabis may be as much as a $45 billion industry in 2017.

Resources:
http://www.profitableventure.com/starting-a-medical-marijuana-dispensary/

5.2   Industry Trends

We will determine the trends that are impacting our consumers and indicate ways in which our patients' needs are changing and any relevant social, technical or other changes that will impact our target market. Keeping up with trends and reports will help management to carve a niche for our business, stay ahead of the competition and deliver products that our patients need and want

1.   Consumers are looking for more and more convenience.
2.   Mobile businesses can often reach a broader market than those that do business only in buildings.
3.   The increased personalization and customization of medical treatments.
4.   The increasing popularity of more alternative, preventative medicine and wellness spas.
5.   Continuing Medical Marijuana Dispensary process improvements.
6.   Improved use of electronic patient record and strain databases.
7.   Greater blending of a wider range of services by Medical Marijuana Dispensary providers.
8.   The government's involvement will be increasing in defining Medical Marijuana Dispensaries and its licenses, practitioners and regulations.
9.   As competition increases, business owners will be forced to run a more efficient establishment operationally, cutting unnecessary costs, tightening front desk operations, running more effectively and taking advantage of unique marketing and sales opportunities.
10.   Inclusive and alternative health programs represent the next logical step in the sequence of today's medical care.
11.   Universal Hydro said it has seen overwhelming demand in California for its new indoor hydroponics systems aimed at home growers, fueled by an increase in the number of patients looking to cultivate their own supply or marijuana as their local dispensaries close.
12.   More and more companies are developing marijuana-infused foods, desserts and beverages.
    Ex: https://mmjbusinessdaily.com/2017/03/22/qa-with-abattis-ceo-mike-withrow-on-canadian-mmj-companys-expansion-into-us/
13.   Aside from the new rules and stricter government regulations, the market began to

mature and the competition increased – meaning the weaker businesses were forced to close – while larger players began to emerge and gobble up the smaller businesses.

14. Edibles and infused products companies are using two main strategies to tap multiple markets without crossing state lines: sign licensing agreements with local manufacturers, or – depending on state laws – partner with a local cannabis business to make, sell and distribute their products.

15. Many states have given local communities the right to adopt even stricter standards than the state, including outright bans

16. There is rising desire for the federal Environmental Protection Agency to develop Pesticide Tolerance Limits for medical marijuana and industrial hemp, as they have done for every other agricultural crop produced in the United States . Even the Drug Enforcement Administration (DEA) recognizes that the U.S. government has both domestic and international responsibilities to protect the health and safety of patients and to promote the responsible development of modern medications.
Source: http://medicalmarijuana.com/experts/expert/title.cfm?artID=920

17. More medical marijuana groups are now focusing on achieving recreational expansion in several states.
Source: www.mohavedailynews.com/news/medical-marijuana-group-wants-
recreational-expansion/article_14d9e0d8-625b-11e4-8858-
a70545fbfabd.html

18. Retailers expect more patients would flock to their shops if those with chronic pain could legally use marijuana, but in many states chronic pain remains off the list of qualifying illnesses.
Source: http://www.dailyherald.com/article/20170117/business/160119045/
Resource: www.change.org

Resource:
www.benzinga.com/trading-ideas/long-ideas/17/01/8878969/top-cannabis-industry-
experts-share-17-predictions-for-mariju

5.2.1 Industry Predictions

Resource:
www.forbes.com/sites/debraborchardt/2016/12/26/here-are-the-top-2017-predictions-for-
the-marijuana-industry/#e3107c32ad84

5.3 Key Industry Terms

We will use the following term definitions to help our company to understand and speak the common language of our industry, and aid efficient communication.

Cannabis

Contains over 300 compounds. At least 66 of these are cannabinoids, which are the basis for medical and scientific use of cannabis. This presents the research problem of isolating the effect of specific compounds and taking account of the interaction of these compounds. Cannabinoids can serve as appetite

stimulants, antiemetics, antidispensarysmodics, and have some analgesic effects. Five important cannabinoids found in the cannabis plant are tetrahydrocannabinol, cannabidiol, cannabinol, β-caryophyllene, and cannabigerol.

Cannabidiol (CBD)

A major constituent of medical cannabis. CBD represents up to 40% of extracts of the medical cannabis plant. Cannabidiol has been shown to

relieve convulsion, inflammation, anxiety, cough and congestion, nausea, and inhibits cancer cell growth. Recent studies have shown cannabidiol to be as effective as atypical antipsychotics in treating schizophrenia.[89] Because cannabidiol relieves the aforementioned symptoms, cannabis strains with a high amount of CBD may benefit people withmultiple sclerosis, frequent anxiety attacks and Tourette syndrome

Cannabinol (CBN)

A therapeutic cannabinoid found in *Cannabis sativa* and *Cannabis indica*. It is also produced as a metabolite, or a breakdown product, of tetrahydrocannabinol (THC). CBN acts as a weakagonist of the CB1 and CB2 receptors, with lower affinity in comparison to THC

Cannabigerol

A compund that is not psychoactive. Cannabigerol has been shown to relieve intraoccular pressure, which may be of benefit in the treatment of glaucoma

Cannabis Clubs or Co-ops

Dispensaries sometimes call themselves cannabis clubs or co-ops, or have names denoting health, physical therapy, caregiving or the like.

Cannabis Processor

Processors take the plants grown by the producers and get them ready to turn into products for medical or recreational use.

Collectives

Dispensaries often call themselves collectives, claiming that the marijuana sold there is grown by the members, who are all patients.

Edibles

Food products made by infusing medical marijuana into oil, butter or any other fat

Indica strains

These are sedatives/relaxants and are effective for treating the symptoms of medical conditions such as anxiety, chronic pain, insomnia, muscle dispensarysms and tremors. Indicas have a higher level of cannabinoids than sativas, which results in a sedated body-type stone. Because indica strains may cause feelings of sleepiness and heaviness, many patients prefer to medicate with this type of cannabis at night.

Sativa strains
These are more of a stimulant, and are effective in appetite stimulation, relieving depression, migraines, chronic pain and nausea. Sativas have a higher level of THC than indicas, which results in a psychoactive and energetic mind-high. Because sativa strains may cause feelings of alertness and optimism, many patients prefer to medicate with this type of cannabis during the day

Tetrahydrocannabinol (THC)
This is the primary compound responsible for the psychoactive effects of cannabis. The compound is a mild analgesic, and cellular research has shown the compound has antioxidant activity. THC is believed to interfere with parts of the brain normally controlled by the endogenous cannabinoid neurotransmitter, anandamide. Anandamide is believed to play a role in pain sensation, memory, and sleep.

β-caryophyllene
Part of the mechanism by which medical cannabis has been shown to reduce
tissue inflammation is via the compound β-caryophyllene. A
cannabinoid receptor called CB2 plays a vital part in reducing inflammation in humans and other animals. β-Caryophyllene has been shown to be a selective activator of the CB2 receptor. β-Caryophyllene is especially concentrated in cannabis essential oil, which contains about 12–35% β-caryophyllene.

5.4   Industry Leaders

We plan to study the best practices of industry leaders and adapt certain selected practices to our business model concept. Best practices are those methods or techniques resulting in increased patient satisfaction when incorporated into the operation.
Source: http://www.thcbiz.com/marijuana-stocks.html

Medical Marijuana Inc. (MJNA)
Medical Marijuana Inc. reported $6 million in net income on revenue of $8.8 million in the second quarter, up significantly from $2.4 million in sales and a profit of $1.47 million a year earlier. Most of the revenue came in the form of an installment payment from a previous deal to sell inventory, licenses and other assets to CannaVest. That revenue therefore isn't part of Medical Marijuana Inc.'s core ongoing business and wasn't generated in the quarter via new sales. Without that payment, the company's sales were about $834,000, which is significantly lower than the same quarter a year earlier and the first three months of 2017.

The company experienced several setbacks, but it made notable progress in other areas. During the quarter, Medical Marijuana Inc. launched a sales and marketing arm called

HempMedsPX, which stands to play a key role in the company's future. It also acquired several new brands and products and relocated its headquarters to a larger building. The company's shares hovered around 12 cents a week ago but shot up to 23 cents on news that prominent medical expert Dr. Sanjay Gupta now publicly supports medical marijuana. The stock fluctuated significantly after MJNA released earnings before settling back down to close the day at 17 cents.

Kind Clinics   www.kindclinics.com
The primary goal of Kind Clinics is to be the best consulting group in the medical marijuana dispensary industry and to create the most compassionate, safe, and legally compliant medical marijuana dispensaries in the medical marijuana industry. They have created a business model that is risk averse, strives for equity preservation, requires less manpower to operate than your traditional dispensary and of course offers inventory management, dispensing and security. It is a consulting firm and technology retailer. They help individuals and groups obtain licenses for dispensaries and cultivation facilities in newly approved medical marijuana states and give them a competitive advantage in the application process and beyond through the use of their patented dispensing technology.

Medbox   www.medboxinc.com
Medbox is a leader in the development, sales and service of automated, biometrically controlled dispensing and storage systems for medicine and merchandise. Medbox has offices throughout the world, including New York, Arizona, Connecticut, Massachusetts, Florida, Tokyo, London and Toronto, and has their corporate headquarters in Los Angeles. Medbox provides their patented systems, software and consulting services to pharmacies, dispensaries, urgent care centers, drug rehab clinics, hospitals, prison systems, hospice facilities, and medical groups worldwide. In addition, through its wholly owned subsidiary, Vaporfection International, Inc. (www.vaporfection.com), the company offers an industry award winning medical vaporizer product. It is also a medical vending machine maker.

Puget Technologies
The company is poised to enter the fast-growing medical marijuana market through its new subsidiary, Cannabis Biotech (www.cannibusbiotech.com). Cannabis BioTech has established a research and development division to investigate alternative delivery methods to meet the growing needs of patients who desire the benefits of medical marijuana but do not want the harmful effects or stigma of smoking it. Puget Technologies is a publicly traded company on the OTCBB Market stock exchange under the ticker symbol PUGE. Headquartered in Ft. Lauderdale, Florida, Puget Technologies acquires, develops and sells leading edge consumer oriented products ready for rapid commercialization. Puget plans to become a recognized market leader in its product categories. Much of its resources are dedicated to research and development in order to provide consumers with quality options while meeting the expectations of its investors.

The Farm Co   http://thefarmco.com/
An innovative recreational cannabis dispensary in Boulder, Colorado stocking exclusively pesticide-free product. A champion of the farm-to-table movement, the Farm

Co is locally owned and produces all of its own craft cannabis through sustainable practices. In focusing on sustainable cultivation methods and placing the emphasis on chemical-free crops, the Farm Co is differentiating itself from its competition and influencing the desires of a new range of consumers.

Columbia Care   www.col-care.com

A New York based holding company with interests in the healthcare, real estate, clinical research, education and technology sectors. Columbia Care operates four dispensaries in New York State.
Source:
www.bloomberg.com/research/stocks/private/snapshot.asp?privcapId=263712791

Medicine Man

One of the largest and most successful cannabis dispensaries in the state of Colorado. With two retail locations, one in Denver and the other in Aurora, the company produced 7,000 pounds of pot and made $8 million in revenue in 2014. Cannabusinesses face extremely high taxes, in some cases exceeding 50 percent, but thanks to an efficient grow operation, which produces a gram of marijuana for the comparatively low cost of $2.50, Medicine Man has been able to slash prices for the customer while staying profitable, even after the state takes its cut. The company's margins are 30 to 40 percent.
Source: www.inc.com/will-yakowicz/best-industries-2015-legal-marijuana.html

LivWell Enlightened Health

One of Colorado's largest dispensary chains, publishes ads featuring some of the diligent-looking farmers and scientists it employs, to communicate professionalism and trustworthiness.

The Farmacy

In Los Angeles, each of its outposts in the city have a customized logo, and sell a range of products from cold remedies to beauty creams to vegan edibles and acupuncture services

Native Roots   https://nativerootsdispensary.com/

One of Colorado's most successful chain of marijuana shops. It's also one of its best designed. Industrial style reigns supreme, with graphic wallpaper, cement floors, and lots of metal.

Trulieve   www.trulieve.com

Trulieve opened its production facility in Quincy near Tallahassee. Unlike other licensees, Trulieve is a partnership between the company and two local nurseries. Trulieve has been aggressive about opening dispensaries, being the first to open one in Florida, and expanding its cannabis product line. It has three retail locations open now and five more in the works. It's also among the first in Florida to sell a flower-based cannabis product, which patients can smoke through a vaporizer. Trulieve has invested north of $15 million in the business since 2014. Delivery makes up about 60 percent of the company's business so far. Their goal is to open dispensaries in every major city in Florida, and expand its delivery operations.

5.5 Industry Resources

Change.org

A platform that more than 100,000 organizations are using to advance their causes and connect with new supporters. As an example, there is an online petition by change.org to include more medical conditions for treatment by medical marijuana dispensaries.

Denver Relief Consulting   www.denverreliefconsulting.com/

Since 2010 Denver Relief Consulting's mission has been to cultivate quality cannabis operations and progressive industry leaders committed to advancing best practices and the perception of the cannabis community. This consulting firm has referral arrangements with MJ
Freeway and Biotrack which are plant management, patient tracking, and point of sale systems. They also have a referral agreement with Cannassure, which insures medical marijuana facilities. They go through Lloyd's of London and are willing to insure not only the harvest but the final product. They also have a referral arrangement with Canna Security.

BioTrackTHC   **www.biotrackthc.com**
A turn-key medical marijuana POS software system that meets state regulations.

Canna Security   **www.cannasecurity.com/**
The leading comprehensive security solutions provider catering to businesses in the licensed cannabis industry.

Blue Line Protection Group   **www.bluelineprotectiongroup.com**
Supplies armed guards for the dispensaries and warehouses, and armored trucks to run money from the safe to pay bills, the government, and vendors.
Resource: www.denverpost.com/marijuana/ci_25965517/reluctance-banks-leaves-pot-
shops-looking-secure-practices

MMC Depot   **www.mmcdepot.com/**
The first marijuana-only packaging company in the country. A medical marijuana packaging company that specializes in wholesale marijuana containers for both medical and recreational uses.

Guardian Data Systems   **http://guardiandatasystems.com/**
A lending fund for businesses directly related to the cultivation and retail of cannabis. A leader in the development of compliant comprehensive financial management, payment, and banking solutions for the cannabis industry

Oaksterdam University in Oakland, CA   **www.oaksterdamuniversity.com**

Offers basic and advanced indoor horticulture seminars, which include four days of intensive instruction, and 26 hours of grow training from expert teach- ers. They also hold seminars across the country.

420 College   **www.420college.org**
Offers weekend seminars on how to open a dispensary, as well as workshops on cultivation training, across the US.

Cannabis University of Colorado   **www.cannabisuniversitycolorado.com**
Students can attend the All-in-One-Day class for $250, which covers everything from growing your own meds to understanding Colorado state law.

420MLS   **http://420mls.com/property-type/dispensaries/**
Lists medical dispensaries for sale.

5.6   Recap of Industry Growth Strategies

Initiative	Tactics	
Build Awareness	Advertising	
Expand Distribution	Incentives	Discounts
	Sales Reps	
Build Buying Rate	Frequent Buyer Cards	Bulk Purchase Discounts
Build Penetration	Broad Advertising	Sampling Programs
	High-value incentives	
Build Extended Usage	New Usage Ideas	
Increase Loyalty	Frequent Buyer Cards	Rebates
	Volume Discounts	Product Improvements
Strengthen In-store	Demonstrations	
Merchandising	Signage	Display Housekeeping
	Point-of-Purchase Displays	Financial Incentives
Improve Product Quality	Reduce defect rate	Add Features
	Improve Reliability	Enhance Patient Service
Decease Product Costs features	Increase production efficiency	Eliminate unnecessary
	Negotiate lower supplier costs	Utilize cheaper materials
	Realize economies of scale	Master learning curve
Introduce New Brand	Awareness	Consistency
Attract Competitor Patients	Incentive offers	Product Comparisons
	High value trail promotion	
Enter a New Market	Sampling	Incentives
	Build awareness	New application ideas
Increase Referrals	Incentives	Refer-a-friend Programs
Reposition the Brand	Packaging	Pricing
	Endorsements	Partnerships
New Distribution Channel	Online marketing	

Increase Pricing	Better image and selection.	
Strengthen Brand	Patient brand involvement	
Accelerate R & D	Develop new product development processes.	
Modular Components	Assemble into a variety of configurations	
Platform Design	Shared by a variety of products and services.	
Operations Flexibility	Reduce set-up time and costs.	
New Services	Training	Installations
	Retrofitting	Technical Support
	On-site Testing	Educational Seminars
	Field Consulting	Marketing Consulting
	Operations Consulting	Design Consulting

5.6.1   Growth Strategy

We will adopt the following growth strategies to achieve a sustainable growth pattern:

1. Schedule free informational seminars and webinars to generate a consistent string of inquiries and leads.
2. Develop annuity products from the sales of articles, books, audiotapes, workbooks, software, speeches, etc.
3. Develop a Virtual Practice Arrangement through flexible subcontractor or partner relationships.
4. Form a corporation to hire employees.
5. Raise fees to control growth and improve profitability and re-investment.
6. Enable employee telecommuting to reduce overhead expenses.
7. Utilize sales reps to open new territories.
8. Use penetration pricing tactics to enter new markets.
9. Develop new types of customized public relations programs directed at niche market segments.
10. Develop an annual rebate program to encourage patient consolidation of vendors.
11. Improve Quality by improving reliability and patient service.
12. Decease Product Costs by increasing base program standardization.
13. Introduce New Branded Image to foster awareness and remembrance.
14. Use incentives, sampling and comparisons to attract Competitor Patients
15. Increase Referrals with a structured referral program.
16. Form pre-screened alliances to reposition the brand
17. Use online affiliated websites as a New Distribution Channel.
18. Increase pricing to convey a better image
19. Accelerate R & D to develop new products and services.
20. Develop packages that can be customized with interchangeable options.
21. Develop a home party plan sales program to increase market penetration.
22. Develop a mobile unit to give demonstrations and provide a basic get acquainted service

5.7 Industry News

Nuvilex, Inc. (OTCQB: NVLX) and a host of marijuana companies are keeping a close eye on what is happening with a petition drive in Florida to get the use of medical marijuana on ballots in time for the November election. Why is Florida important? Well, for a company like Nuvilex and its medical marijuana subsidiary, Marijuana Sciences, Inc., conducting research and developing treatments using the drug are made far easier if the country moves to full acceptance, and Florida could be the domino that sets the last of the states holding out in motion.
Source: http://online.wsj.com/article/PR-CO-20180116-907654.html

The 9th U.S. Circuit Court of Appeals ruled on January 15, 2017 that three California dispensaries, their customers and their landlords are barred from using a state law allowing marijuana use with a doctor's recommendation as a shield from criminal charges and government lawsuits. All uses of marijuana are illegal under the federal Controlled Substances Act, also known as the CSA, even in states that have legalized pot.
Source: www.dailyjournal.net/view/story/f2d58d15a9e547278d93c9a8d9ea75d0/CA--
          California-Marijuana-Dispensaries-Federal-Law/#.Utgz1Ju6GMk

Certification
Patient advocacy group Americans for Safe Access (ASA) certified the first two dispensaries in the country in February of 2016, for its new nationwide program that verifies the quality and reliability of products sold at licensed medical marijuana businesses. The certifications issued today to Berkeley Patients Group and SPARC of San Francisco are based on the **Patient Focused Certification** (PFC) program, the only nonprofit, third-party certification for the medical marijuana industry based on new quality standards issued by the **American Herbal Products Association** (AHPA) and the **American Herbal Pharmacopeia** (AHP).

Further information:
     Patient Focused Certification (PFC) program: http://PatientFocusedCertification.org
     PFC brochure: http://american-safe-
     access.s3.amazonaws.com/documents/PFC_Brochure.pdf
     AHPA Standards: http://safeaccess2.org/sites/patientfocusedcertification/standards-
     development/apha-guidelines
     AHP Cannabis monograph (Abridged
     version):http://www.safeaccessnow.org/ahp_cannabis_monograph_preview
Source: http://enewspf.com/latest-news/health-and-fitness/50293-national-medical-marijuana-group-certifies-first-dispensaries-in-effort-to-bring-quality-standards-to-the-industry.html

Banking
The Justice and Treasury Departments in February of 2016 issued banks a road map for doing business with marijuana firms. The security-wary pot industry, including recreational shops in Colorado and medical marijuana operators elsewhere, welcomed the

long-awaited news, but banking industry groups made clear that the administration's tone didn't make them feel much easier about taking pot money. Under the guidance, banks must review state license applications for marijuana customers, request information about the business, develop an understanding of the types of products to be sold and monitor publicly available sources for any negative information about the business. he American Bankers Association said banks will only be comfortable serving marijuana businesses if federal prohibitions on the drug are changed in law.

Source: http://abcnews.go.com/US/wireStory/federal-guidance-pot-business-leaves-banks-wary-22530646

One of the hottest products on medical marijuana dispensary shelves and on Craigslist is a potent **hash oil** often made at home with the help of DIY YouTube clips and canisters of butane. Consumed by using discreet portable hash oil pens or water pipes heated with propane torches, butane hash oil is coveted for its quick and powerful high.

Source:

www.oregonlive.com/marijuana/index.ssf/2017/05/butane_hash_oil_overview.html
The $1.1-trillion federal spending bill approved by the Senate on Saturday, December 13, 2016, has effectively ended the longstanding federal war on medical marijuana. An amendment to the bill blocks the Department of Justice from spending money to prosecute medical marijuana dispensaries or patients that abide by state laws.

Sources:

www.mlive.com/news/grand-rapids/index.ssf/2016/12/medical_marijuana_advocates_sa_1.html

www.motherjones.com/mojo/2016/12/department-justice-congress-war-medical-marijuana

6.0 Strategy and Implementation Summary

Our sales strategy is based on serving our niche markets better than the competition and leveraging our competitive advantages. These advantages include unparalleled convenience, superior attention to understanding and satisfying patient needs and wants, creating a one-stop wraparound experience, and value pricing.

The objectives of our marketing strategy will be to recruit new patients from medical professionals, retain existing patients, get good patients to spend more and schedule visits more frequently. Establishing a loyal patient base is very important because such core patients will not only generate the most lifetime sales, but also provide valuable referrals.

We will generate word-of-mouth buzz through direct-mail campaigns, exceeding patient expectations, developing a Web site and getting involved in community events with local businesses, and donating our services at charity functions, in exchange for press release coverage. Our sales strategy will seek to convert potential and first-time patients into long-term relationships and referral agents. The combination of our competitive advantages, targeted marketing campaign and networking activities, will enable _____ (company name) to continue increasing our market share.

6.1.0 Promotion Strategy

We will depend on patient referrals, community involvement and direct mail campaigns as our primary ways to reach new patients. Our promotional strategies will also make use of the following tools:

- **Advertising**
  - Yearly anniversary parties to celebrate the success of each year.
  - Multiple bold listings in the Yellow Pages ads in the book and online.
  - Flyers promoting services with discount coupon cut-out.
  - Doorknob hangers, if not prohibited by neighborhood associations.
  - Classified ads with consultation coupons in local giveaway magazines newspapers.
- **Local Marketing / Public Relations**
  - Patient raffle for gift certificates or discount coupons
  - Participation in local civic groups.
  - Press release coverage of our sponsoring of events at the local community center for families and residents.
  - Article submissions to magazines describing the benefits of our Medical Marijuana Dispensary programs and how to select a provider.
  - Sales Brochure to convey our programs to prospective patients.
- **Local Media**
  - Direct Mail - We will send quarterly direct mailings to residents with a ___ (7?) mile radius of our center. It will contain an explanation of our Medical Marijuana Dispensary service programs and a newsletter with a

listing of open house events.

- o Radio Campaign - We will make "live on the air" presentations of our trial coupons to the disk jockeys, hoping to get the promotions broadcasted to the listening audience.
- o Newspaper Campaign - Placing several ads in local community newspapers to launch our initial campaign. We will include a trial consultation coupon in the ad to track the return on investment.
- o Website – We will collect email addresses for a monthly newsletter.

6.1.1   Grand Opening

Our Grand Opening celebration will be a very important promotion opportunity to create word-of-mouth advertising results. The primary target for our first open house event will be the doctors who will be making referrals to our dispensary.

We will do the following things to make the open house a successful event:
1.   Use a sign-in sheet to create an email/mailing list.
2.   Schedule appearances by local influencers, medical professionals, and/or celebrities like Snoop Dog.
3.   Create a festive atmosphere with balloons, beverages and music.
4.   Get the local radio station to broadcast live from the event and handout fun gifts.
5.   Offer an application fee waiver.
6.   Giveaway our logo imprinted T-shirts as a contest or door prize.
7.   Allow potential patients to view our facility and ask questions.
8.   Print promotional flyers and pay a few kids to distribute them locally.
9.   Arrange for a food truck to be available, and free beverages and snacks, such as cupcakes, for everyone.
10.   Arrange for local politician to do the official opening ceremony so all the local newspapers come to take pictures and do a feature story.
11.   Arrange that people can tour our facility on the open day in order to see our facilities, collect sales brochures and find out more about our services.
12.   Arrange the layout of all equipment in a room in order to show our home set-ups to best effect.
13.   Allocate staff members to perform specific duties, handout business cards and sales brochures and instruct them to deal with any questions or queries.
14.   Organize a drawing with everyone writing their name and phone numbers on the back of business cards and give a voucher as a prize to start a marketing list.
15.   Post ad in Facebook
        Example: www.facebook.com/trulieve/photos/rpp.202920873439434/
                409838272747692/?type=3&theater
16.   Propose a story about the Grand Opening to a local newspaper.
        Example: www.miamiherald.com/news/local/community/miami-
                dade/article145628464.html
17.   Giveaway branded accessories, such as sunglasses, lanyards, lighters, rolling

papers, T-shirts, and stickers.
Source: https://arizonamedicalmarijuanaclinic.com/7-ways-to-make-your-dispensary-event-a-success/

6.1.2   Value Proposition

Our value proposition will summarize why a consumer should use our Medical Marijuana Dispensary services. We will offer uniquely premium dispensary services, as substantiated by our program descriptions, the experience and licensing of our trained and certified staff and our community involvement. It will convince prospects that our services will add more value or better solve their need for convenient and personalized dispensary services. We will use this value proposition statement to target patients who will benefit most from using our Medical Marijuana Dispensary services. These are medical professionals who are concerned about maintaining their patient's lifestyle. Our value proposition will be concise and appeal to the patient's strongest decision-making drivers, which are convenience, personalization, safety, effectiveness, reliability and quality of personal relationships. We recognize that people are looking for a one-stop shopping experience. We plan on becoming the one service provider that will take a keen interest in their immediate needs, and help them plan for the medical marijuana services they want in the near and long-term.

Recap of Our Value Proposition:
Trust – We are known as a trusted business partner with strong patient and supplier endorsements. We have earned a reputation for quality, integrity, and delivery of successful Medical Marijuana Dispensary pain and nausea management remedies.
Quality – We offer _____ experience and extensive professional backgrounds in _____ at competitive rates.
Experience – Our ability to bring people with ____ (#) years of _____ experience with deep technical knowledge of _____ is at the core of our success.
True Vendor Partnerships – Our true vendor partnerships with _____ and _____ enable us to offer the resources of much larger organizations with greater flexibility.
Patient Satisfaction and Commitment to Success – Through partnering with our patients and delivering quality Cannabis solutions, we have been able to achieve an impressive degree of repeat and referral business. Since ____ (year), more than ____ % of our business activity is generated by existing patients. Our philosophy is that "our patient's satisfaction with our strain recommendations is our success." Our success will be measured in terms of our patient's satisfaction survey scores and testimonials.

6.1.3   Positioning Statement

It is the objective of _____ (company name) to become the local leader in quality Medical Marijuana Dispensary services in the _____ area. The educational aspect of our programs and one-stop convenience of our dispensary services will allow us to pursue a differentiation business strategy and not have to focus intently on low cost leadership.

We also plan to develop specialized services that will enable us to pursue a niche focus on specific interest based programs, such as weight control and stress management. These objectives will position us at the _____ (high-end of the market?) and will allow the company to realize a healthy profit margin in relation to its low-end, discount rivals and achieve long-term growth.

Market Positioning Recap
Price: The strategy is to offer competitive prices that are lower that the market leader, yet set to indicate value and worth. .
Quality: The Cannabis and treatment quality will have to be very good as the finished service results will be showcased in highly visible situations.
Service: Highly individualized and customized service will be the key to success in this type of business. Personal attention to the patient's pain management needs will result in higher sales and word of mouth advertising.

6.1.4   Unique Selling Proposition (USP)

Our unique selling proposition will answer the question why a patient should choose to do business with our company versus any and every other option available to them in the marketplace. Our USP will be a description of a unique important benefit that our Medical Marijuana Dispensary offers to patients, so that price is no longer the key to our sales.

Our USP will include the following:
Who our target audience is: _____
What we will do for them: _____
What qualities, skills, talents, traits do we possess that others do not: _____
What are the benefits we provide that no one else offers: _____
Why that is different from what others are offering: _____
Why that solution matters to our target audience: _____

Resources:
http://7raysmarketing.com/develop-your-medical-marijuana-brand/
https://www.entrepreneur.com/encyclopedia/unique-selling-proposition-usp

6.1.5   Distribution Strategy

_____ (company name) intends to contact individuals who will use our Medical Marijuana Dispensary through medical professional referrals in the community who recommend appropriate pain management therapies for the elderly and chronically and terminally ill. These referral sources include the attorneys, physicians, county conservators, hospital discharge planners, rehabilitation center discharge planners, day care centers, senior citizen centers, and independent case managers. We plan to mail a brochure describing our online dispensary and delivery services, along with a cover letter announcing the grand opening of our business. We will follow up with a phone call and a request for referrals. We also plan to place a continuous classified ad in the local newspaper and advertise in the yellow pages. We will gain access to many referral sources by taking advantage of the contacts made when the company owner was in an administrative position at _____ (former employer) in _____ County.

1. **Order by Phone**
   Patients can contact us 24 hours a day, 7days a week at _____.
   Our Patient Service Representatives will be available to assist patients
   Monday through Friday from ____ a.m. to ____ p.m. EST.
2. **Order by Fax**
   Patients may fax their orders to _____ anytime.
   They must provide: Account number, Billing and shipping address, Purchase order number, if applicable, Name and telephone number, Product number/description, Unit of measure and quantity ordered and Applicable sales promotion source codes.
3. **Order Online**
   Patients can order online at www._____.com.Once the account is activated, patients will be able to place orders, browse the catalog, check stock availability and pricing, check order status and view both order and transaction history.
4. **In-person**
   All patients can be serviced in person at our facilities Monday through Friday from ____ a.m. to ____ p.m. EST.

We will utilize the following distribution channels:
1. Direct Mail   using catalogs and flyers to sell directly to consumer buyers.
2. Telemarketing   selling directly to consumer buyers via phones.
3. Cybermarketing   selling directly to consumer buyers, or business-to-business services via computer networks
4. Sales Force   using independent commissioned representatives to sell services. .
5. TV and Cable   direct marketing of our services to consumers and referral agents.

We plan to pursue the following other distribution channels: (select)

		Number	Reason Chosen	Sales Costs
1.	Our own retail outlets			
2.	Independent retail outlets			
3.	Chain store retail outlets			
4.	Wholesale outlets			

5. Independent distributors _____
6. Independent commissioned sales reps _____
7. In-house sales reps _____
8. Direct mail using own catalog or flyers _____
9. Catalog broker agreement _____
10. In-house telemarketing _____
11. Contracted telemarketing call center _____
12. Cybermarketing via own website _____
13. Online sales via amazon, eBay, etc. _____
14. TV and Cable Direct Marketing _____
15. TV Home Shopping Channels _____
16. Mobile Units _____
17. Franchised Business Units _____
18. Trade Shows _____
19. Home Party Sales Plans _____
20. Fundraisers _____

6.1.6   Sales Rep Plan

The following parameters will help to define our sales rep plan:

1. In-house or Independent   _____
2. Salaried or Commissioned   _____
3. Salary or Commission Rate   _____
4. Salary Plus Commission Rate   _____
5. Special Performance Incentives   _____
6. Negotiating Parameters   Price Breaks/Added Services/
                                      _____
7. Performance Evaluation Criteria   No. of New Patients/Sales Volume/
                                      _____
8. Number of Reps   _____
9. Sales Territory Determinants   Geography/Demographics/
                                      _____
10. Sales Territories Covered   _____
11. Training Program Overview   _____
12. Training Program Cost   _____
13. Sales Kit Contents   _____
14. Primary Target Market   _____
15. Secondary Target Market   _____

Rep Name	Compensation Plan	Assigned Territory

6.2   Competitive Advantages

A **competitive advantage** is the thing that differentiates a business from its competitors. It is what separates our business from everyone else. It answers the questions: "Why do patients buy from us versus a competitor?", and "What do we offer patients that is unique?". We will make certain to include our key competitive advantages into our marketing materials. We will use the following competitive advantages to set us apart from our competitors. The distinctive competitive advantages which ___(company name) brings to the marketplace are as follows: (Note: Select only those you can support)

1.   The relaxing atmosphere in our dispensary is fused with a knowledgeable, well-trained staff.
2.   We offer a full range of Medical Marijuana Dispensary services, dispensary packages and custom remedies to meet the needs of unique individuals.
3.   Our dispensary services are part of a holistic approach to health and wellness and designed to take care of mind and body.
4.   Our dispensary services include patient education on maintaining the benefits derived from dispensary services.
5.   We maintain the highest standards of sanitation and hygiene, and only use disposable products while providing our services.
6.   We only stock all-natural, organic Cannabis plants.
7.   Employees participate in continuing education to ensure consistency and superior technique.
8.   Our Medical Marijuana Dispensary services are priced as a necessity and not a luxury.
9.   Patients can enjoy the dispensary experience online from their desired location.
10.   Personnel are trained to form personal relationships with patients.
11.   Our employees are trained to acknowledge each patient by their preferred name and to build personal relationships.
12.   We have an array of unique dispensary, and wellness services to offer patients.
13.   We provide senior discounts and referral credits.
14.   Patient education programs and handouts are offered online or printed.
15.   We have an ethnically diverse and multilingual staff, which is critical for a service-oriented business.
16.   We have the experience and ability to understand, interpret and comply with state regulations..
17.   We offer the following service guarantees: _____
18.   Alliances that enable us to provide one-stop shopping or an array of dispensary products and services through a single access point.
19.   Offer added value capabilities that are perceived as having value by patients and this has allowed us to secure higher prices.
20.   Our service providers have been carefully screened and are bonded and insured.
21.   We are a well-funded, profitable and stable company.
22.   We take pride in providing the highest quality dispensary services.
23.   We pay all employer taxes, bonding, general liability, and workers compensation insurance for our in-home certified employees.

24. We conduct pre-hire background screenings and drug testing on all individuals before they are hired.
25. We developed a specialized training program for the staff so they will be proficient at administering our specific programs.
26. Our staff has over ____ (#) years of dispensary service expertise and over ___ (#) years of _____ (technology?) savvy.
27. Our services are performed by registered Fulltime Employees, some of whom have worked for us for many years.
28. All of our bud tenders hold appropriate licenses to practice as well as professional liability insurance and have passed background and/or drug tests.
29. We use the finest products available in our treatment protocols.
30. We are the only Medical Marijuana Dispensary company with a professional Quality Assurance program.
31. We prioritized creating a well-lit area, attractive counters, attractive signage, and clean display racks that will lend a professional appearance to our store.
32. We developed detailed procedures for store security and safe cash handling.
33. We have done a thorough job of screening our vendors for consistent quality, reliability and trustworthiness.
34. We have only hired photographers that specialize in cannabis photography to portray the quality of our cannabis buds.

6.2.1   Branding Strategy

Our branding strategy involves what we do to shape what the patient immediately thinks our business offers and stands for. The purpose of our branding strategy is to reduce patient perceived purchase risk and improve our profit margins by allowing use to charge a premium for our Medical Marijuana Dispensary products and services.

We will invest $____ every year in maintaining our brand name image, which will differentiate our medical marijuana business from other companies. The amount of money spent on creating and maintaining a brand name will not convey any specific information about our products, but it will convey, indirectly, that we are in this market for the long haul, that we have a reputation to protect, and that we will interact repeatedly with our customers. In this sense, the amount of money spent on maintaining our brand name will signal to consumers that we will provide products and services of consistent quality.

We will use the following ways to build trust and establish our personal brand:
1. Build a consistently published blog and e-newsletter with informational cannabis content.
2. Create comprehensive social media profiles.
3. Contribute articles to related online cannabis publications.
4. Earn Career Certifications

Resources:
https://www.abetterlemonadestand.com/branding-guide/
www.fastcodesign.com/3024457/6-branding-lessons-from-the-pioneers-of-weed-design
www.marijuana.com/news/2016/10/brand-boosters-for-your-marijuana-business/

Our key to marketing success will be to effectively manage the building of our brand platform in the market place, which will consist of the following elements:

Brand Vision - our envisioned future of the brand is to be the regional source for Medical Marijuana Dispensary solutions to manage the complications of aging and pain management.

Brand Attributes - Partners, problem solvers, knowledgeable, progressive, responsive, innovative, Cannabis expertise, flexible and easy to work with.

Brand Essence - the shared soul of the brand, the spark of which is present in every experience a patient has with our products and services, will be "Problem Solving" and "Results Oriented." This will be the core of our organization, driving the type of people we hire and the type of behavior we expect.

Brand Image - the outside world's overall perception of our organization will be that we are Medical Marijuana Dispensary pros who are alleviating the complications of pain management, and offering more alternative natural treatments and procedures than a traditional dispensary.

Brand Promise - our concise statement of what we do, why we do it, and why patients should do business with us will be, "To Achieve a Higher Level of Pain Relief and Wellness with Fewer Side Effects".

We will use the following methodologies to implement our branding strategy:

1. Develop processes, systems and quality assurance procedures to assure the consistent adherence to our quality standards and mission statement objectives.
2. Develop business processes to consistently deliver upon our value proposition.
3. Develop training programs to assure the consistent professionalism and responsiveness of our employees.
4. Develop marketing communications with consistent, reinforcing message content.
5. Incorporate testimonials into our marketing materials that support our promises.
6. Develop marketing communications with a consistent presentation style. (Logo design, company colors, slogan, labels, packaging, stationery, etc.)
7. Exceed our brand promises to achieve consistent patient loyalty.
8. Use surveys, focus groups and interviews to consistently monitor what our brand means to our patients.
9. Consistently match our brand values or performance benchmarks to our patient requirements.
10. Focus on the maintenance of a consistent number of key brand values that are tied to our company strengths.
11. Continuously research industry trends in our markets to stay relevant to patient needs and wants.
12. Attach a logo-imprinted product label and business card to all products, marketing communications and invoices.

13. Develop a memorable and meaningful tagline that captures the essence of our brand.
14. Prepare a one page company overview and make it a key component of our sales presentation folder.
15. Hire and train employees to put the interests of patients first.
16. Develop a professional website that is updated with fresh content on a regular basis.
17. Use our blog to circulate content that establishes our niche expertise and opens a two-way dialogue with our patients.
18. Attractive and tasteful uniforms will also help our staff's morale. The branding will become complete with the addition of our corporate logo, or other trim or accessories which echo the style and theme of our establishment.
19. Create an effective slogan with the following attributes:
    a. Appeals to customers' emotions.
    b. Shows off how our service benefits customers by highlighting our customer service or care.
    c. Has 8 words or less and is memorable
    d. Can be grasped quickly by our audience.
    e. Reflects our business' personality and character.
    f. Shows sign of originality.
20. Create a Proof Book that contains before and after photos, testimonial letters, our mission statement , copies of industry certifications and our code of ethics.
21. Make effective use of trade show exhibitions, conferences and expos, and email newsletters to help brand our image.
22. Use branded wall wraps to give our shop a more official feel while creating a memorable environment for our patients and customers.
    Source:
    www.marijuana.com/news/2016/10/brand-boosters-for-your-marijuana-business/
23. Develop overtly transparent relationships with credible and vocal members of the medical community

Resources:
Cannabrand   http://cannabrand.co/
A cannabis marketing agency. The ads that Cannabrand designs typically use lifestyle-oriented images: young people hiking, frolicking with friends, sitting around campfires.
Source:
www.theatlantic.com/magazine/archive/2016/04/the-art-of-marketing-marijuana/471507/

The communications strategy we will use to build our brand platform will include the following items:
Website - featuring product line information, research, testimonials, cost benefit analysis, frequently asked questions, competitive advantages and Cannabis information. This website will be used as a tool for both our sales team and our patients.
Presentations, brochures and mailers geared to the consumer, explaining the benefits of our product and services as part of a comprehensive wellness plan.

Presentations and brochures geared to the family decision maker explaining the benefits of our programs in terms of positive outcomes, reduced costs from unforeseen complications, and reduced risk of negative survey results.

A presentation and recruiting brochure geared to prospective sales people that emphasizes the benefits of joining our organization.

Training materials that help every employee deliver our brand message in a consistent manner.

6.2.2   Brand Positioning Statement

We will use the following brand positioning statement to summarize what our brand means to our targeted market:

To _____ (target market) _____ (company name) is the brand of _____ (product/service frame of reference) that enables the patient to _____ (primary performance benefit) because _____ (company name) _____ (products/services) _____ (are made with/offer/provide) the best _____ (key attributes)

6.3   Business SWOT Analysis

Definition: SWOT Analysis is a powerful technique for understanding your Strengths and Weaknesses, and for looking at the Opportunities and Threats faced.

Strategy: We will use this SWOT Analysis to uncover exploitable opportunities and carve a sustainable niche in our market. And by understanding the weaknesses of our business, we can manage and eliminate threats that would otherwise catch us by surprise. By using the SWOT framework, we will be able to craft a strategy that distinguishes our business from our competitors, so that we can compete successfully in the market.

Strengths

What Medical Marijuana Dispensary services are we best at providing?
What unique resources can we draw upon?
1.   Experienced management team from the _____ (?) industry.
2.   Strong networking relationships with many different organizations, including _____.
3.   Excellent staff who are experienced, highly trained and very patient service oriented.
4.   Wide diversity of product/service bundled offerings.
5.   High patient loyalty.
6.   Remarkable introduction of creativity into the service delivery process.
7.   The first and only Medical Marijuana Dispensary business in the _____ area.
8.   Able to bring the dispensary experience to the patient at their chosen

location.

9. Services are responsive to the patients' hectic schedule.
10. Strong relationships with growers that offer flexibility, and response to special strain requirements.
11. Excellent well trained staff, offering personalized patient service.
12. Location: providing an easily accessible location for patients.
13. Providing an environment conducive to giving professional service in an attractive, relaxing atmosphere.
14. Offering patients a wide range of services in one setting, and extended business hours.
15. Reputation of the dispensary manager and bud tenders as providing superior personal service. ·
16. Great referral benefits for patients.
17. In-store health food and juice bar.
18. Close monitoring of industry news and legislative changes.
19. _____

Weaknesses

In what areas could we improve?
Where do we have fewer resources than others?

1. New comer to the area.
2. Lack of marketing experience.
3. The struggle to build brand equity.
4. A limited marketing budget to develop brand awareness.
5. Finding dependable and people oriented staff.
6. We need to develop the information systems that will improve our productivity.
7. Don't know the health and wellness needs of the local population.
8. Medical Marijuana Dispensaries are a new trend that needs to gain acceptance and federal government approval.
9. Low awareness of Medical Marijuana Dispensary option.
10. Traditional dispensary competitors are well established and well-known.
11. Starting business with a limited of service offerings.
12. Access to capital.
13. Cash flow will be unpredictable.
14. Have no current patient base.
15. Management expertise gaps.
16. Inadequate monitoring of competitor strategies and responses.
17. _____

Opportunities

What opportunities are there for new and/or improved services?
What trends could we take advantage of?

1. Could take market share away from existing competitors.
2. Greater need for mobile home services by time starved dual income families.

3. Growing market with a significant percentage of the target market still not aware that _____ (company name) exists.
4. The ability to develop many long-term patient relationships.
5. Expanding the range of product/service packaged offerings.
6. Greater use of direct advertising to promote our services.
7. Establish referral relationships with medical practitioners serving the same target market segment.
8. Networking with non-profit organizations.
9. The aging population will need and expect a greater range of dispensary rejuvenating services in the convenience of their own homes.
10. Increase public awareness of the importance of health and wellness matters.
11. Everything is going mobile to offer consumers greater convenience.
12. Continuing opportunity through strategic alliances for referrals and marketing activities.
13. Benefiting from high levels young professionals in the area.
14. Continuing awareness of dispensary industry and its importance to health.
15. Increasing sales opportunities beyond our 20-mile target area.
16. Internet potential for selling products to other distant markets.
17. Expansion into other markets.
19. _____

Threats

What trends or competitor actions could hurt us?
What threats do our weaknesses expose us to?
1. Another Medical Marijuana Dispensary business could move into this area.
2. Further declines in the economic forecast.
3. Inflation affecting operations for gas, labor, and other operating costs.
4. Keeping trained efficient staff and key personnel from moving on or starting their own business venture.
5. Imitation competition from similar indirect service providers.
6. Price differentiation is a significant competition factor.
7. The government could enact legislation that could affect licensing and demand.
8. We need to do a better job of assessing the strengths and weaknesses of all of our competitors.
9. Vulnerability to changes in patient priorities.
10. Shortage of qualified therapists, aestheticians and technicians.
11. Medical Marijuana Dispensaries have an unproven market.
12. There is the threat of federal involvement.
13. Competitors have superior marketing campaign resources.
14. Competition from current high profile dispensaries.
15. Salary commission structure of employees.
16. _____

Recap:

We will use the following strengths to capitalize on recognized opportunities:

1. _____
2. _____

We will take the following actions to turn our weaknesses into strengths and prepare to defend against known threats.

1. _____
2. _____

6.4.0   Marketing Strategy

Marketing in the Medical Marijuana Dispensary industry primarily depends on reputation and medical practitioner referrals. We will seek to build our reputation by having an involved commitment to those we serve. The company will rely heavily on word-of-mouth referrals for business. Marketing our services requires establishing a reputation for technical expertise and care excellence.

We will start our business with our known referral contacts and then continue our campaign to develop recognition among other professionals within the health care and dispensary service fields. We will develop and maintain a database of our contacts in the field. We will work to maintain and exploit our existing relationships throughout the start-up process and then use our marketing tools to communicate with other potential referral sources.

Our marketing strategy will also revolve around two different types of media, sales brochures and a website. These two tools will be used to make patients aware of our broad range of service offerings.

One focus of our marketing strategy will be to drive patients to our website for information about our Medical Marijuana Dispensary programs and package options.

A combination of local media and event marketing will be utilized. _____ (company name) will create an identity oriented marketing strategy with executions particularly in the local media. Our marketing strategy will utilize radio spots, print ads, press releases, yellow page ads, flyers, and newsletter distribution. We will make effective use of direct response advertising, and include coupons in all print ads. We will also place small display ads in local free magazines.

We will use comment cards, newsletter sign-up forms and surveys to collect patient email addresses and feed our patient relationship management (CRM) software system. This system will automatically send out, on a predetermined schedule, follow-up materials, such as article reprints, seminar invitations, email messages, surveys and e-newsletters. We will offset some of our advertising costs by asking our suppliers and other local merchants to place ads in our newsletter.

Current Situation

We will study the current marketing situation on a weekly basis to analyze trends and identify sources of business growth. As onsite owners, we will be on hand daily to insure patient service. Our services include products of the highest quality and a prompt response to feedback from patients. Our extensive and highly detailed financial statements, produced monthly, will enable us to stay competitive and exploit presented opportunities.

Marketing Budget

Our marketing budget will be a flexible $_____ per quarter. The marketing budget can be allocated in any way that best suits the time of year.

Marketing budget per quarter:

Newspaper Ads	$_____	Radio advertisement	$_____	
Web Page	$_____	Patient contest	$_____	
Direct Mail	$_____	Sales Brochure	$_____	
Trade Shows	$_____	Seminars	$_____	
Superpages	$_____	Google Adwords	$_____	
Giveaways	$_____	Vehicle Signs	$_____	
Business Cards	$_____	Flyers	$_____	
Labels/Stickers	$_____	Videos/DVDs	$_____	
Samples	$_____	Newsletter	$_____	
Bandit Signs	$_____	Email Campaigns	$_____	
Sales Reps Comm.	$_____	Restaurant Placemats	$_____	
Press Releases	$_____	Billboards	$_____	
Movie Theater Ads	$_____	Fund Raisers	$_____	
Infomercials	$_____	Speeches	$_____	
Postcards	$_____	Proof Books	$_____	
Social Networking	$_____	Charitable Donations	$_____	
Other	$_____			
Total:			$_____	

Our objective in setting a marketing budget has been to keep it between ____ (3?) and ____ (5?) percent of our estimated annual gross sales.

The following represents a recap of our marketing programs:
- Promotion expenses (free gifts for coming in the shop)
- Printed materials (sales brochures, pamphlets, fliers, postcards)
- Media advertisements (radio, newspapers, outdoor billboards)
- Donations (door prizes, charities)
- Referral Program Brochure
- Website Development

Marketing Mix

Patients will primarily come from word-of-mouth and our referral program. The overall market approach involves creating brand awareness through targeted advertising, public relations, co-marketing efforts with select alliance partners, direct mail, email campaigns (with constant contact.com), seminars and a website.
Resource: http://smokesignaladvertising.com/

Advertising

_____ (company name) will rely on the recommendations of satisfied patients as a means of attracting patients away from the competition. Past experience has proven that many patients come on the recommendations of others. Although word-of-mouth is an effective way of increasing market share, it is also extremely slow. To accelerate the process of expanding the patient base, the business will maintain an advertising budget of $___ for the first year. The bulk of this budget will be spent on listings in the __ (city) yellow pages, complimentary trial coupons, and direct mailings to ad respondents. We will also use home care success stories in our advertising to consumers.

Our outcall service will be marketed to a variety of target groups. We will place a basic name and telephone listing in the local telephone directory under "Medical Marijuana Dispensary". This will allow potential patients to contact us. A "Letter of Introduction" explaining our service will be sent to local medical service providers. These letters should be followed up with a phone call and/or personal visit. We will develop a referral relationship with the practice's front desk or office manager.

Resource:
www.leafly.com/news/industry/state-by-state-guide-to-cannabis-advertising-regulations

Online Website
Our dispensary will show up on every major search engine and in the phone directory. The website will have a full menu of Cannabis strains and services and eventually have the ability to schedule appointments and make purchases on-line. The dispensary software we are using will allow a user to see the schedule and make appointments without making a phone call.

Video Marketing

We will link to our website a series of YouTube.com based video clips that talk about our range of Medical Marijuana Dispensary products and services, and demonstrate our expertise with certain strains. We will create business marketing videos that are both entertaining and informational, and improve our search engine rankings. For each video, we will be sure to include our business keyword in the title and at least once in the description section.

The video will include:
>   **Patient testimonials** - We will let our best patients become our instant sales force because people will believe what others say about us more readily than what we

say about ourselves.

Product Demonstrations - We will train and pre-sell our potential patients on our most popular products and services just by talking about and showing them. Often, our potential patients don't know the full range and depth of our Medical Marijuana Dispensary products and services because we haven't taken the adequate time to tell them.

Include Business Website Address

Conduct video tour of our facilities.

Post commercial created for Cable TV or DVD sales presentation.

Owner Interview: Include company mission statement and Unique Selling Proposition

Record Frequently Asked Questions Session - We will answer questions that we often get, and anticipate objections we might get and give great reasons to convince potential patients that we are the best Medical Marijuana Dispensary in the area.

Include a Call to Action - We have the experience and the know-how to dramatically improve your self-esteem. So call us, right now, and let's get started.

Seminar - Include a portion of a seminar on how the medical benefits of Cannabis.

Comment on industry trends and product news - We will appear more in-tune and knowledgeable in our market if we can talk about what's happening in our Medical Marijuana Dispensary industry and marketplace.

Resources:

www.businessvideomarketing.tv

www.hotpluto.com

www.hubspot.com/video-marketing-kit

www.youtube.com/user/mybusinessstory

Analytics Report

http://support.google.com/youtube/bin/static.py?hl=en&topic=1728599&guide=1 714169&page=guide.cs

Example:

www.youtube.com/watch?v=-W8EoEs3KPY

Top 11 places where we will share our videos online:

YouTube   **www.youtube.com**

This very popular website allows you to log-in and leave comments and ratings on the videos. You can also save your favorite videos and allows you to tag posted videos. This makes it easier for your videos to come up in search engines.

Google Video   **http://video.google.com/**

A video hosting site. Google Video is not just focused on sharing videos online, but this is also a market place where you can buy the videos you find on this site using Google search engine.

Yahoo! Video   **http://video.yahoo.com/**

Uploading and sharing videos is possible with Yahoo Video!. You can find several types of videos on their site and you can also post comments and ratings for the videos.

Revver   **http://www.revver.com/**

This website lets you earn money through ads on your videos and you will have a 50/50 profit split with the website. Another great deal with Revver is that your fans who posted your videos on their site can also earn money.

Blip.tv   **http://blip.tv/**

Allows viewers to stream and download the videos posted on their website. You can also use Creative Commons licenses on your videos posted on the website. This allows you to decide if your videos should be attributed, restricted for commercial use and be used under specific terms.

Vimeo   **http://www.vimeo.com/**

This website is family safe and focuses on sharing private videos. The interface of the website is similar to some social networking sites that allow you to customize your profile page with photos from Flickr and embeddable player. This site allows users to socialize through their videos.

Metacafe   **http://www.metacafe.com/**

This video sharing site is community based. You can upload short-form videos and share it to the other users of the website. Metacafe has its own system called VideoRank that ranks videos according to the viewer reactions and features the most popular among the viewers.

ClipShack   **http://www.clipshack.com/**

Like most video sharing websites you can post comments on the videos and even tag some as your favorite. You can also share the videos on other websites through the html code from ClipShack and even sending it through your email.

Veoh   **http://www.veoh.com/**

You can rent or sell your videos and keep the 70% of the sales price. You can upload a range of different video formats on Veoh and there is no limit on the size and length of the file. However when your video is over 45 minutes it has to be downloaded before the viewer can watch it.

Jumpcut   **http://download.cnet.com/JumpCut/3000-18515_4-10546353.html**

Jumpcut allows its users to upload videos using their mobile phones. You will have to attach the video captured from your mobile phone to an email. It has its own movie making wizard that helps you familiarize with the interface of the site.

DailyMotion   **www.dailymotion.com**

As one of the leading sites for sharing videos, Dailymotion attracts over 114 million unique monthly visitors (source: comScore, May 2017) 1.2 billion videos views worldwide (source: internal). Offers the best content from users, independent content creators and premium partners. Using the most advanced technology for both users and content creators, provides high-quality and HD video in a fast, easy-to-use online service that also automatically filters infringing material as notified by content owners.

Offering 32 localized versions, their mission is to provide the best possible entertainment experience for users and the best marketing opportunities for advertisers, while respecting content protection.

Networking

Networking will be a key to success because referrals and alliances formed can help to improve our community image and keep our business growing. We will strive to build long-term mutually beneficial relationships with our networking contacts and join the following types of organizations:

1. We will form a LeTip Chapter to exchange business leads.
2. We will join the local BNI.com referral exchange group.
3. We will join the Chamber of Commerce to further corporate relationships.
4. We will join the Rotary Club, Kiwanis Club, Church Groups, etc.
5. We will become an active member of the National Association for the Education of Young Children and the Child Care Action Campaign.
6. We will do volunteer work for the American Cancer Society.
7. We will join the Medical Marijuana Network (http://www.medicalcannabis.net/) and the Cannabis Activist Network (http://cannabisactivistnetwork.com/) and the Holistic Cannabis Network (http://holisticcannabisnetwork.com/)

The Medical Cannabis Network is a leading provider of marketing and business solutions for the medical marijuana industry. As a network MCN represents some the industry's largest web properties, which include MarijuanaDoctors.com, Potlocator.com, StrainBrain.com, 420Petition.com, Cheeba.com and many others to come.

Cannabis Activist Network was started in 2010. It is a grassroots news site that seeks to inform cannabis activists worldwide with the latest news relevant to the cause. Their mission to spread information to a global audience.

The Holistic Cannabis Network® (HCN) is a cannabis education, training, and business-building platform for holistic-minded practitioners about medical marijuana and its integration with other healing modalities.

We will use our metropolitan _____ (city) Chamber of Commerce to target prospective medical practice contacts. We will mail letters to each prospect describing our Medical Marijuana Dispensary services. We will follow-up with phone calls.

Newsletter

We will develop a monthly e-newsletter to stay in touch with our patients and use it to market to local businesses. We will include the following types of information:

1. Success case studies
2. New Service Introductions/ Staff Changes
3. Featured employee/patient of the month.
4. Medical Marijuana Dispensary industry trends.
5. Patient endorsements/testimonials.
6. Classified ads from local sponsors and suppliers.
7. Nutrition / recipes.
8. Announcements / Upcoming events.

Resource: Microsoft Publisher

Examples:
https://weedmaps.com/newsletters
https://nativerootsdispensary.com/

HelloMD **https://www.hellomd.com/**

This newsletter originally contained articles from medical professionals, but recently expanded to include the perspective of cannabis brands as well.

We will adhere to the following newsletter writing guidelines:
1. We will provide content that is of real value to our subscribers.
2. We will provide solutions to our subscriber's problems or questions, and the status of status medical marijuana state laws.
3. We will communicate regularly on a weekly basis.
4. We will create HTML Messages that look professional and allow us to track how many people click on our links and/or open our emails.
5. We will not pitch our business opportunity in our Ezine very often.
6. We will focus our marketing dollars on building our Ezine subscriber list.
7. We will focus on relationship building and the conveying of useful information, and not the conveying of a sales message.
8. We will vary our message format with videos, articles, checklists, quotes, pictures and charts.
9. We will recommend occasionally affiliate products in some of our messages to help cover our marketing costs.
10. We will consistently follow the above steps to build a database of qualified prospects and customers.

Resources:
www.constantcontact.com
www.mailchimp.com
http://lmssuccess.com/10-reasons-online-business-send-regular-newsletter-customers/
www.smallbusinessmiracles.com/how/newsletters/
www.fuelingnewbusiness.com/2010/06/01/combine-email-marketing-and-social-media-
    for-ad-agency-new-business/
www.allbud.com/

Examples:
http://www.harborsidehealthcenter.com/community/newsletter.html
https://buddepotdispensary.com/boulder-dispensary-news
http://apothecariumsf.com/
https://essencevegas.com/#subscribe

Vehicle Signs

We will place magnetic and vinyl signs on our vehicles and include our company name, phone number, company slogan and website address, if possible. We will create a cost-effective moving billboard with high-quality, high-resolution vehicle wraps. We will wrap a portion of the vehicle or van to deliver excellent marketing exposure.
Resource: http://www.fastsigns.com/

Design Tips:
1. Avoid mixing letter styles and too many different letter sizes.
2. Use the easiest to recognize form of your logo.
3. The standard background is white.
4. Do not use a background color that is the same as or close to your vehicle color.
5. Choose colors that complement your logo colors.
6. Avoid the use too many colors.
7. Use dark letter colors on a light background or the reverse.
8. Use easy to read block letters in caps and lower case.
9. Limit content to your business name, slogan, logo, phone number and website-address.
10. Include your license number if required by law.
11. Magnetic signs are ideal for door panels (material comes on 24" wide rolls).
12. Graphic vehicle window wraps allow the driver to still see out.
13. Keep your message short so people driving by can read it at a glance.
14. Do not use all capital letters.
15. Be sure to include your business name, phone number, slogan and web address.

DVD Presentation

We plan to create a DVD that will provide testimonials from some our satisfied patients and record a seminar presentation on the potential of cannabis remedies. We will include this DVD in our sales presentation folder and direct mail package.

Advertising Wearables

We will give all preferred club members an eye-catching T-shirt or sweatshirt with our company name and logo printed across the garment to wear about town. We will also give them away as a thank you for patient referral activities. We will also ask all employees to wear our logo-imprinted shirts in the play area and at sponsored events. We will also sell the garments in our facility at cost.

Sales Promotion/Information Package Kit

Our promotional sales presentation kit will contain the following items:

- Owner/Key Staff Resumes	- Rate Sheet/Payment Policies
- Article Reprints	- Business Forms
- DVD Presentation	- Sales Brochure
- FAQs	- Business Card
- Press Release Clippings	- Community Service Awards
- Testimonials	- Policy Statement
- Sample Contract	- Medical/Emergency Form
- Referral Program Form	- Patient Satisfaction Survey

Stage Events

We will stage events to become known in our community. This is essential to attracting referrals. We will schedule regular events, such as seminar talks, workshops, business expos, cooking demonstrations, catered open house events and fundraisers. We will use event registration forms, our website and an event sign-in sheet to collect the names and email addresses of all attendees. This database will be used to feed our automatic patient relationship follow-up program and newsletter service.

Our director of medical education will offer monthly patient orientations that are free and open to patients, prospective patients, health care professionals and anyone else interested.

Workshop Examples:
1. The Health Benefits of Medical Marijuana: Science and Case Applications
2. How to prevent medical marijuana from contributing to youth substance abuse.
3. Medical Marijuana and Delivery Devices 101,
4. Know Your Medical Marijuana Rights and The Law
5. Cooking with Medical Marijuana
6. What You need to Know About Terpenes

We will hold medical marijuana educational fairs where experts will be onsite to answer questions about state regulations. alternative health and wellness programs and medical marijuana products. There will also be free food, raffles and massage therapy for community members.

Example: Cooking Demonstration
Organizers estimated that several hundred people attended an expo Sunday sponsored by the three medical marijuana dispensaries currently operating in Lake County. The event was designed to be an opportunity for those looking to learn about medical marijuana and it was also hoped, organizers said, that current users would be able to connect with dispensaries, product vendors and researchers in an informal setting.
Source:
www.chicagotribune.com/suburbs/mundelein/news/ct-vhr-medical-marijuana-expo-tl-
      0810-20170807-story.html

Example: Community Cleanup
Anyone lucky enough to be in Maine over the weekend had a chance to get free weed for cleaning up trash. Thanks to Summit Medical Marijuana, the town of Gardiner, Maine is looking a whole lot cleaner—and weed smokers are a whole lot happier.
Source:
https://www.greenrushdaily.com/get-free-weed-for-cleaning-up-trash/

Examples:
https://essencevegas.com/events/

Resources:
www.eventbrite.com
www.leafly.com/news/industry/7-ways-make-dispensary-event-success

Sales Brochures

Our sales brochure will include the following contents and become a key part of our direct mail package:

- Contact Information
- Patient Testimonials
- Competitive Advantages
- Trial Coupon
- Referral Doctors

- Company Description
- List of Products/Services/Benefits
- Owner Resume
- Grower Vendor List

Resources:

Educational Brochures   https://www.projectcbd.org/educational-brochures

Sales Brochure Design

1. Speak in Terms of Our Prospects/Patients Wants and Interests.
2. Focus on all the Benefits, not Just Features.
3. Put the company logo and Unique Selling Proposition together to reinforce the fact that your company is different and better than the competition.
4. Include a special offer, such as a discount, a free report, a sample, or a free trial to increase the chances that the brochure will generate sales.

We will incorporate the following Brochure Design Guidelines:

1. Design the brochure to achieve a focused set of objectives (marketing of programs) with a target market segment (residential vs. commercial).
2. Tie the brochure design to our other marketing materials with colors, logo, fonts and formatting.
3. List capabilities and how they benefit patients.
4. Demonstrate what we do and how we do it differently.
5. Define the value proposition of our engineering installing services
6. Use a design template that reflects your market positioning strategy.
7. Identify your key message (unique selling proposition)
8. List our competitive advantages.
9. Express our understanding of patient needs and wants.
10. Use easy to read (scan) headlines, subheadings, bullet points, pictures, etc.
11. Use a logo to create a visual branded identity.
12. The most common and accepted format for a brochure is a folded A3 (= 2 x A4), which gives 4 pages of information.
13. Use a quality of paper that reflects the image we want to project.
14. Consistently stick to the colors of our corporate style.
15. Consider that colors have associations, such as green colors are associated with the environment and enhance an environmental image.
16. Illustrations will be appropriate and of top quality and directly visualize the product assortment, product application and production facility.
17. The front page will contain the company name, logo, the main application of your product or service and positioning message or Unique Selling Proposition.
18. The back page will be used for testimonials or references, and contact details.

Sales Presentation Folder Contents

1.	Resumes	2.	Cannabis Photos
3.	Contract/Application	4.	Frequently Asked Questions
5.	Sales Brochure	6.	Business Cards
7.	Testimonials/References	8.	Program Descriptions
9.	Informative Articles	10.	Referral Program
11.	Company Overview	12.	Operating Policies
13.	Article Reprints	14.	Press Releases

Brochure distribution will include;

1.	Local businesses	2.	Medical Clinics
3.	Assisted Living Facilities	4.	College administrators
5.	Hospitals	6.	Physicians
7.	Medical Specialists	8.	Lawyers
9.	Libraries	10.	Counselors
11.	Psychiatrists	12.	Psychologists
13.	Weight Watchers	14.	Hospices

Coupons

We will use coupons with limited time expirations to get prospects to try our service programs. We will also accept the coupons of our competitors to help establish new patient relationships. We will run ads directing people to our Web site for a $___ coupon certificate for free consultations. This will help to draw in new patients and collect e-mail addresses for the distribution of a monthly newsletter. We will use "dollars off" and not "discount" percentages, as patients are not impressed with "10 to 20 percent off" coupons today. They are very impressed with "$10 off a $50 value" or one free week or the waiving of the registration fee. Research indicates that we can use our coupons to spark online searches of our website and drive sales. This will help to draw in new patients and collect e-mail addresses for the distribution of a monthly newsletter. We will include a coupon with each sale, or send them by mail to our mailing list.

Resources:
https://weedmaps.com/deals
https://www.mainstreet.com/article/discount-marijuana-top-7-cannabis-coupon-sites
Examples:
http://www.weedpons.com/
https://www.cannasaver.com/

We will use coupons selectively to accomplish the following:
1. To introduce a new product or service.
2. To attract loyal patients away from the competition
3. To prevent patient defection to a new competitor.
4. To help celebrate a special event.
5. To thank patients for a large order and ensure a repeat order within a certain limited time frame.

Types of Coupons:
1.   Courtesy Coupons   Rewards for repeat business
2.   Cross-Marketing Coupons   Incentive to try other products/services.
3.   Companion Coupon   Bring a friend incentive.

Websites like Groupon.com, LivingSocial, Eversave, and BuyWithMe sell discount vouchers for services ranging from custom _____ to ____ consultations. Best known is Chicago-based Groupon. To consumers, discount vouchers promise substantial savings — often 50% or more. To merchants, discount vouchers offer possible opportunities for price discrimination, exposure to new patients, online marketing, and "buzz." Vouchers are more likely to be profitable for merchants with low marginal costs, who can better accommodate a large discount and for patient merchants, who place higher value on consumers' possible future return visits.

Premium Giveaways
We will distribute logo-imprinted promotional products at events, also known as giveaway premiums, to foster top-of-mind awareness (www.promoideas.org). These items include logo-imprinted T-shirts, business cards with magnetic backs, mugs with contact phone number and calendars that feature important date reminders.

Samples
We will give away Goodie Bags of sample products with our business labels adhered to these products as referral rewards.

Local Newspaper Ads
We will use these ads to announce the opening of our business and get our name established. We will include a listing of the Medical Marijuana Dispensary services we provide. We will include a coupon to track results in zoned editions.

Our newspaper ads will utilize the following design tips:
1.   We will start by getting a media kit from the publisher to analyze their demographic information as well as their reach and distribution.
2.   Don't let the newspaper people have total control of our ad design, as we know how we want our company portrayed to the market.
3.   Make sure to have 1st class graphics since this will be the only visual distinction we can provide the reader about our business.
4.   Buy the biggest ad we can afford, with full-page ads being the best.
5.   Go with color if affordable, because consumers pick color ads over black 82% of the time.
6.   Ask the paper if they have specific days that more of our type of buyer reads their paper.
7.   If we have a hit ad on our hands, we will make it into a circular or door-hanger to extend the life of the offer.
8.   Don't change an ad because we are getting tired of looking at it.
9.   We will start our headline by telling our story to pull the reader into the ad.

10. We will use "Act Now" to convey a sense of urgency to the reader.
11. We will use our headline to tell the reader what to do: enhance beauty and wellness.
12. The headline is a great place to announce a free offer, such as a free consultation.
13. We will write our headline as if we were speaking to one person, and make it personal.
14. We will use our headline to either relay a benefit or intrigue the reader into wanting more information.
15. Use coupons giving a dollar amount off, not a percentage, as people hate doing the math.

Local Publications

We will place low-cost classified ads in neighborhood publications to advertise our medical marijuana dispensary. We will also submit public relations and informative articles to improve our visibility and establish our cannabis expertise and trustworthiness. These publications include the following:

1. Neighborhood Newsletters and Church Bulletins
2. Local Restaurant Association Newsletter
3. Local Chamber of Commerce Newsletter
4. Realtor Magazines
5. Homeowner Association Newsletters

Resource:

Hometown News   www.hometownnews.com
Pennysaver   www.pennysaverusa.com

Publication Type	Ad Size	Timing	Circulation	Section	Fee

Magazine Ads

We plan on purchasing the names of local subscribers to national lifestyle themed magazines and seniors magazines, and make a direct mailing based on zip codes. We will use these display ads to get our name in front of our likely prospects and track the return on investment to determine if we should expand or restrict this marketing strategy.

Publication Type	Ad Size	Timing	Circulation	Section	Fee

Journal Display Ads

We will consider placing display ads in business and trade journals read by professionals, such as physicians and attorneys, and possibly rent a list of their local subscribers for a planned direct mailing. The mailing will describe our Medical Marijuana Dispensary programs and servicing methods. We will use empirical data to prove how our programs can actually foster lifestyle and health improvements. We will also pursue the writing of

news stories by their journalists.
Example:
www.bizjournals.com/baltimore/news/2017/10/06/federal-hill-is-getting-a-medical-
    marijuana.html

Resource: The Business Journals http://www.bizjournals.com/
The premier media solutions platform for companies strategically targeting business
decision makers. Delivers a total business audience of over 10 million people via their
 42 websites, 62 publications and over 700 annual industry leading events. Their media
products provide comprehensive coverage of business news from a local, regional and
national perspective.

Publication Type	Ad Size	Timing	Circulation	Section	Fee

Trade Shows
We will exhibit at as many local trade shows per year as possible. These include Home
and Garden Shows, Health Fairs and Clinics, Medical Conferences, County Fairs,
Business Expos, open exhibits in shopping malls, business spot-lights with our local
Chamber of Commerce, and more. The objective is to get our company name and service
out to as many people as possible. We will do our homework and ask other stores where
they exhibit their products and services. When exhibiting at a trade show, we will put our
best foot forward and represent ourselves as professionals. We will be open, enthusiastic,
informative and courteous. We will exhibit our services with sales brochures, logo-
imprinted giveaways, sample products, a photo book for people to browse through and a
computer to run our video presentation through. We will use a 'free drawing' for a gift
basket prize and a sign-in sheet to collect names and email addresses. We will also
develop a questionnaire or survey that helps us to assemble an ideal patient profile and
qualify the leads we receive. We will train our booth attendants to answer all type of
questions and to handle objections. We will also seek to present educational seminars at
the show to gain increased publicity, and name and expertise recognition. Most
importantly, we will develop and implement a follow-up program to stay-in-touch with
prospects.

Resources:	www.tsnn.com	www.expocentral.com
	www.acshomeshow.com/	www.EventsInAmerica.com
	www.Biztradeshows.com	www.commerce.gov
	www.newpa.com	www.sba.gov/international
	www.expoworld.net	www.biztradeshows.gov
	www.eventseye.com	www.trade-show-advisor.com
	www.fita.org	www.tscentral.com
Example:	http://medicalfarmersmarket.com/	

Article Submissions
We will pitch articles to consumer magazines, local newspapers, business magazines and

internet articles directories to help establish our specialized cannabis expertise and improve our visibility. Hyperlinks will be placed within written articles and can be clicked on to take the patient to another webpage within our website or to a totally different website. These clickable links or hyperlinks will be keywords or relevant words that have meaning to our Medical Marijuana Dispensary. We will create keyword-rich article titles that match the most commonly searched keywords for our topic. In fact, we will create a position whose primary function is to link our Medical Marijuana Dispensary with opportunities to be published in local publications.

We will write a 1,000 word piece on a topic that reflects our Medical Marijuana Dispensary consulting expertise, and submit it for publication in the Sunday opinion section of our local newspaper and the _____ (*New York Times?*). We will also submit articles or post to blogs or email newsletters that were created around a Medical Marijuana Dispensary theme. We will do extensive research to find the blogger or other "thought leaders" out there who have a sway over discussion in our specific field of pain management and their own audience. We will reach out to these influential bloggers, because they will provide a very powerful way to promote our Medical Marijuana Dispensary. Their audience may be smaller, but it is much more concentrated and passionate about Medical Marijuana Dispensary treatments, and will thus take action in much higher numbers. Our objective will be to locate a single-author blog with a large audience that is highly focused, and the author favors or endorses our approach to health and wellness. We will then seek to build a long-term, mutually beneficial relationship with the author. We will attempt to make friends with them and show them that our methodology is sound and relevant to their audience, so that they will confidently and actively promote our methods and _____ to their followers. In fact, we will take the following approach:

1. We will focus on a relevant idea to the alternative medicine theme of the blog and endeavor to add value to the selected blog over time.
2. We will leave some thoughtful comments on their blog, highlighting certain helpful ideas from our Medical Marijuana Dispensary consulting approach.
3. We will forward interesting articles with a different perspective on the blogger's position or focus, to add content value from the blogger's perspective.
4. We will pose questions in our cover letter like; "do you think maybe this might be interesting to your audience?."

Publishing requires an understanding of the following publisher needs:

1.	Review of good work.	2.	Editor story needs.
3.	Article submission process rules	4.	Quality photo portfolio
5.	Exclusivity requirements.	6.	Target market interests

Our Article Submission Package will include the following:

1.	Well-written materials	2.	Good Drawings
3.	High-quality Photographs	4.	Well-organized outline.

Examples of General Publishing Opportunities:

1.	Document a new solution to old problem	2.	Publish a research study
3.	Mistake prevention advice	4.	Present a different viewpoint

5.	Introduce a local angle on a hot topic.	6.	Reveal a new trend.
7.	Share specialty niche expertise.	8.	Share wine health benefits

Specific Article Titles:

Examples: New Trends in Medical Marijuana Dispensary Services.
Tips for Choosing a Good Medical Marijuana Dispensary Service.
How to Avoid Medical Marijuana Dispensary Scams.
Resolutions to Improve Life and Health.
Medical Marijuana Dispensaries: Where Recreation Meets Healing
How to Compare Medical Marijuana Dispensaries
How to Choose a Medical Marijuana Dispensary
Six Fabulous Reasons For Visiting A Medical Marijuana Dispensary
Medical Marijuana Dispensaries: Catering to Contemporary Health Needs
Medical Marijuana Dispensaries: Combining Alternative Treatment Plans
with Recreational Pursuits.
How to Get A Medical Marijuana Card in _____ (state) in 4 Easy Steps.

Write Articles With a Closing Author Resource Box or Byline

1.	Author Name with credential titles.	2.	Explanation of area of expertise.
3.	Mention of a special offer.	4.	A specific call to action
5.	A Call to Action Motivator	6.	All possible contact information
7.	Helpful Links	8.	Link to Firm Website.

Article Objectives:

Article Topic	Target Audience	Target Date

Article Tracking Form

SubjectPublication	Target Audience	Business Development	Resources Needed	Target Date

Possible Magazines to submit articles include:

Aging Parents	Off Our Rockers	Senior Savvy
Caregiver	Options at 50 Plus	Senior Times
Fifty~Plus News	Prime Season	Senior Times
For My Grandchild	Reader's Digest	Senior Travel Tips
Friends Magazine	Retired Living	Senior World Online
Generation Over 50	The Rubins	Seniors Magazine
Silver Threads	Good Life	Seasoned Citizen
Third Age	Grand Times	Senior Golfer
Today's Grandparent	Guide to Retirement Living	Senior Journal
Today's Senior	Life After 55	Senior Lifestyle
Today's Seniors	Lifeline Magazine	Senior Living Online

Vintage Magazine	Modern Maturity	Senior One Source
NetWatch Top Ten	Senior Pages	Wyndsong
Men's Health	Women's Health	

Resources:

| Writer's Market | www.writersmarket.com |
| Directory of Trade Magazines | www.techexpo.com/tech_mag.html |

Sampling of Internet article directories include:

http://ezinearticles.com/	http://www.mommyshelpercommunity.com
http://www.wahm-articles.com	http://www.ladypens.com/
http://www.articlecity.com	http://www.amazines.com
http://www.articledashboard.com	http://www.submityourarticle.com/articles
http://www.webarticles.com	http://www.articlecube.com
http://www.article-buzz.com	http://www.free-articles-zone.com
www.articletogo.com	http://www.content-articles.com
http://article-niche.com	http://superpublisher.com
www.internethomebusinessarticles.com	http://www.site-reference.com
http://www.articlenexus.com	www.articlebin.com
http://www.articlefinders.com	www.articlesfactory.com
http://www.articlewarehouse.com	www.buzzle.com
http://www.easyarticles.com	www.isnare.com
http://ideamarketers.com/	//groups.yahoo.com/group/article_announce
http://clearviewpublications.com/	www.ebusiness-articles.com
http://www.goarticles.com/	www.authorconnection.com/
http://www.webmasterslibrary.com/	www.businesstoolchest.com
http://www.connectionteam.com	www.digital-women.com/submitarticle.htm
http://www.MarketingArticleLibrary.com	www.searchwarp.com
http://www.dime-co.com	www.articleshaven.com
http://www.reprintarticles.com	www.articles411.com
http://www.articlestreet.com	www.articleshelf.com
http://www.articlepeak.com	www.articlesbase.com
http://www.simplysearch4it.com	www.articlealley.com
http://www.valuablecontent.com	www.articleavenue.com
http://www.article99.com	www.virtual-professionals.com

Free Classified Ad Placements

The following free classified ad sites, will enable our business to thoroughly describe the benefits of our Medical Marijuana Dispensary products and services:

1.	**Craigslist.org**	2.	Ebay Classifieds
3.	Classifieds.myspace.com	4.	KIJIJI.com
5.	//Lycos.oodle.com	6.	Webclassifieds.us
7.	USFreeAds.com	8.	www.oodle.com
9.	Backpage.com	10.	stumblehere.com
11.	Classifiedads.com	12.	gumtree.com

13.	Inetgiant.com	14.	www.sell.com
15.	Freeadvertisingforum.com	16.	Classifiedsforfree.com
17.	www.olx.com	18.	www.isell.com
19.	Base.google.com	20.	www.epage.com
21.	Chooseyouritem.com	22.	www.adpost.com
23.	Adjingo.com	24.	Kugli.com
25.	global-free-classified-ads.com	26.	free4uclassifieds.com
27.	www.Salespider.com	28.	www.adsonmap.com
29.	www.usnetads.com	30.	Sawitonline.com
31.	www.freeclassifieds.com	32.	www.openclassifiedsads.com
33.	www.jwiz.com	34.	www.ClassifiedsGiant.com
35.	http://klondajk.us		

Cannabis Specific Classified Ads:

1. http://mjcircle.com/
2. https://mmpconnect.com/get-started/browse-ads/10/dispensaries/
3. www.weedtrader.com/
4. www.bigherbs.com/
5. https://budbay.com/
6. http://jivetree.com/
7. http://cannabisclassifieds.com/
8. https://www.themjdirectory.com/classifieds
9. http://thepotdot.com/classifieds

Sample CraigsList.org Classified Ads

_____ (company name) provides patients with the best Medical Marijuana Dispensary treatment options in the _____ Area! Free consultations, affordable prices, quality organic product infused ingredients and personalized service. We offer the complete range of Medical Marijuana Dispensary products and services, including ___ (#) medical grade marijuana strains. Call _____. or e-mail _____ for further info or to schedule an appointment. References are available upon request. Visit our website _____ for our patients' reviews.

Two-Step Direct Response Classified Advertising

We will use 'two-step direct response advertising' to motivate readers to take a step or action that signals that we have their permission to begin marketing to them in step two. Our objective is to build a trusting relationship with our prospects by offering a free unbiased, educational report in exchange for permission to continue the marketing process. This method of advertising has the following benefits:

1.	Shorter sales cycle.	2.	Eliminates need for cold calling.
3.	Establishes expert reputation.	4.	Better qualifies prospects
5.	Process is very trackable.	6.	Able to run smaller ads.

Sample Two-Step Lead Generating Classified Ad:

FREE Report Reveals "The Secrets to Working With the Best Medical Marijuana Dispensary Service"

or…" How to Plan the Most Rewarding Medical Marijuana Dispensary Visit".
Call 24 hour recorded message and leave your name and address or visit our website at
_____ and enter your contact information. Your report will be sent out immediately.

Note: The respondent has shown they have an interest in our Medical Marijuana
Dispensary services. We will send this lead the report with excellent and impartial
advice. We will also include a section in the report on our complete range of organic
products and contact information, along with a coupon for a free product sampling, initial
consultation and a sales brochure.

Seminars

Seminars present the following marketing and bonding opportunities:
1.   Signage and branding as a presenting sponsor.
2.   Opportunity to provide logo imprinted handouts.
3.   Media exposure through advertising and public relations.
4.   The opportunity for one-on-one interaction with a targeted group of consumers to
        demonstrate an understanding of their needs and our matching expert solutions.
5.   Use of sign-in sheet to collect names and email addresses for database build.
6.   Present opportunity to sell products, such as workbooks.
Resource:
https://sites.google.com/site/420college/curriculum-1/advanced-seminar

Website notice:
Join our Preferred Patients List and Receive Emails on Upcoming Seminars

Possible seminar funding sources:
1.   Small registration fee to cover the cost of hand-outs and refreshments.
2.   Get sponsorship funding from partner/networking organizations.
3.   Sponsorship classified ads in the program guide or handouts.

**We will establish our expertise and trustworthiness by offering free seminars on the
following topics:**
1.   How to Locate and Evaluate Medical Marijuana Dispensaries
2.   How to Plan for Successful Medical Marijuana Dispensary Treatments
3.   The Latest Advances in Medical Marijuana Dispensary Services
5.   How a Medical Marijuana Dispensary Can Help to Melt Away Stress and Years
        of Hard Living
6.   The Secrets to Homeopathic Weight Loss
7.   Medical Marijuana 101
8.   Using Cannabis to Treat Cancer in a Safe and Natural Way

Examples:
https://thehealingclinic.org/medical-marijuana-education/

Seminar target groups include the following:
1.   Traditional Dispensary Owners   2.   Women's Club Members

3.	Physicians	4.	Working Professionals
5.	Health Consultants	6.	Realtors
7.	Health Club Members	8.	Country Club Members
9.	Medical Practitioners		

Possible Seminar Handouts:

1.	Article Reprints	2.	Graphs/Charts
3.	Worksheets	4.	Research Studies
5.	Resource Lists	6.	Summary Report
7.	Presentation Outline	8.	Feedback Surveys
9.	Sales Brochures	10.	Business Cards

Seminar marketing approaches include:

1. Posting to website and enabling online registrations.
2. Email blast to in-house database using www.constantcontact.com
3. Include seminar schedule in newsletter and flyer.
4. Classified ads using craigslist.org

Seminar Objectives:

Seminar Topic	Target Audience	Handout	Target Date

Webinars

A webinar is a presentation, lecture, workshop or seminar that is transmitted over the Web. A key feature of a Webinar is its interactive elements -- the ability to give, receive and discuss information. Webinars will be used as an effective vehicle for communicating a message, building awareness and buy-in about a particular topic, and offering an interactive educational experience.

Our Webinars will be educational in nature and allow our clinic to demonstrate the value of our Medical Marijuana Dispensary services and expertise, directly to prospects or existing patients without spending money to meet with them. Webinars allow prospects to listen to experts discuss uses, benefits and demand for certain products and services while gleaning insights about the unique benefits businesses provide. Webinars, like other forms of content marketing, should convey succinct messages and focus on one topic of interest. Webinars tend to run an hour, including Q&A time. Webinars are generally in the form of slide decks. While webinar marketing is a great tool for lead generation, the webinars, themselves, must be informative and cater to the learning needs of patients or prospects. Pairing webinars with blog posts and other website content, as well as placing calls to action at the end of the presentations, can direct prospects through conversion funnels.

Sample Webinar
Title: How to Best Deal with Nausea and Migraines
As a result of the webinar participants will:

Learn better pain management procedures.

Prerequisite: none

Target Audience: Cancer Patients.

Resources: www.gotomeeting.com/fec/webinar/secure_webinar_software
www.webex.com/WebEx-Meetings-Purchase-FAQ.html?TrackID=
1030070&hbxref=&goid=webex-meetings-FAQ

Yellow Page Ads

Research indicates that the use of the traditional Yellow Page Book is declining, but that new residents or people who don't have many personal acquaintances will look to the Yellow Pages to establish a list of potential businesses to call upon. Even a small 2" x 2" boxed ad can create awareness and attract the desired target patient, above and beyond the ability of a simple listing. We will use the following design concepts:

1. We will use a headline to sell people on what is unique about our Medical Marijuana Dispensary.
2. We will include a service guarantee to improve our credibility.
3. We will include a coupon offer and a tracking code to monitor the response rate and decide whether to increase or decrease our ad size in subsequent years.
4. We will choose an ad size equal to that of our competitors, and evaluate the response rate for future insertion commitments.
5. We will include our hours of operation, motto or slogan and logo.
6. We will list some of the most popular benefits of using our services.
7. We will include our competitive advantages, specialties and years in business.
8. We will borrow the best features of our competitor ads.
9. We will offer a free consultation and discount coupon.

Resource: www.superpages.com   www.yellowpages.com

Ex: http://www.yellowpages.com/paramount-ca/medical-cannabis-dispensaries

Ad Information:

Book Title: _____   Coverage Area: _____

Yearly Fee: $_____   Ad Size: _____ page

Renewal date: _____   Contact: _____

Cable Television Advertising

Cable television will offer us more ability to target certain market niches or demographics with specialty programming. We will use our marketing research survey to determine which cable TV channels our patients are watching. It is expected that many watch the Home & Garden TV channel, and that people with surplus money for remodeling projects watch the Golf Channel and the Food Network. Our plan is to choose the audience we want, and to hit them often enough to entice them to take action. We will also take advantage of the fact that we will be able to pick the specific areas we want our commercial to air. Ad pricing will be dependent upon the number of households the network reaches, the ratings the particular show has earned, and the supply and demand for a particular network.

Resources:

Spot Runner	www.spotrunner.com
Television Advertising	http://televisionadvertising.com/faq.htm
Comcast Spotlight	https://www.comcastspotlight.com/how-to-start/intake

Ad Information:

Length of ad "spot": ___ seconds   Development costs: $____ (onetime fee)

Length of campaign: __ (#) mos.   Runs per month: Three times per day

Cost per month.: $_____   Total campaign cost: $_____.

Radio Advertising

Warnings:

Radio advertising is highly restrictive, especially when it comes to controlled substances. As such, advertising for cannabis products and services over the radio is illegal.......... but is also slowly evolving.

Source:

www.marijuanadoctors.com/blog/medical-marijuana/marijuana-advertising-policies

While we expect that some stations may be running some ads for legal dispensaries, we urge any station considering it to give great thought to the issue and the practices in other industries and make a legally-informed decision before proceeding.

Source:

www.broadcastlawblog.com/2016/02/articles/the-murky-state-of-rules-on-broadcast-advertising-of-marijuana-products-in-states-which-have-legalized-its-sale-or-use/

We will use non-event based radio advertising. This style of campaign is best suited for non-promotional retail sales businesses, such as our Medical Marijuana Dispensary. We will utilize a much smaller schedule of ads on a consistent long-range basis (48 to 52 weeks a year) with the objective of continuously maintaining top-of-mind-awareness. This will mean maintaining a sufficient level of awareness to be either the number one or number two choice when a triggering-event, such as a nausea condition, moves the consumer into the market for services and forces "a consumer choice" about which Medical Marijuana Dispensary in the consumer's perception might help them the most. This consistent approach will utilize only one ad each week day (260 days per year) and allow our company to cost-effectively keep our message in front of consumers once every week day. The ad copy for this non-event campaign, called a positioning message, will not be time-sensitive. It will define and differentiate our business' "unique market position" , and will be repeated for a year.

Note: On the average, listeners spend over 3.5 hours per day with radio.

2Radio will give us the ability to target our audience, based on radio formats, such as news-talk, classic rock and the oldies. Radio will also be a good way to get repetition into our message, as listeners tend to be loyal to stations and parts of the day.

1.   We will use radio advertising to direct prospects to our Web site, advertise a limited time promotion or call for an informational Medical Marijuana Dispensary brochure.

2. We will try to barter our services for radio ad spots.
3. We will use a limited-time offer to entice first-time patients to use our services.
4. We will explore the use of on-air community bulletin boards to play our public announcements about community sponsored events.
5. We will also make the radio station aware of our expertise in the Medical Marijuana Dispensary field and our availability for interviews.
6. Our choice of stations will be driven by the market research information we collect via our surveys.
7. We will capitalize on the fact that many stations now stream their programming on the internet and reach additional local and even national audiences, and if online listeners like what they hear in our streaming radio spot, they can click over to our website.
8. Our radio ads will use humor, sounds, compelling music or unusual voices to grab attention.
9. Our spots will tell stories or present situations that our target audience can relate to, such as how to read skin care product labels for the real story.
10. We will make our call to action, a website address or vanity phone number, easy to remember and tie it in with our company name or message.
11. We will approach radio stations about buying their unsold advertising space for deep discounts. (Commonly known at radio stations' as "Run of Station")
    On radio, this might mean very early in the morning or late at night. We will talk to our advertising representatives and see what discounts they can offer when one of those empty spaces comes open.

Resources: Radio Advertising Bureau   www.RAB.com
                Radio Locator   www.radio-locator.com
                Radio Directory   www.radiodirectory.com

Ad Information:

    Length of ad "spot": ___ seconds   Development costs: $____ (onetime fee)
    Length of campaign: __ (#) mos.   Runs per month: Three times per day
    Cost per month.: $_____   Total campaign cost: $_____.

Script Resources:

www.voices.com/documents/secure/voices.com-commercial-scripts-for-radio-and-
    television-ads.pdf

http://smallbusiness.chron.com/say-30second-radio-advertising-spot-10065.html

https://voicebunny.com/blog/5-tips-make-radio-ads-grab-attention-sell/

Blog Talk Radio

National Public Radio (www.NPR.org) plays host to a radio program called _____.
The program features _____ (type of experts) who talk and blog about Medical Marijuana Dispensary treatment tips. This will help to establish our _____ expertise and build the trust factor with potential patients. Even if we can't get our own nationally syndicated talk show, we will try to make guest appearances and try our hand with podcasting by using apps like Spreaker or joining podcasting communities like BlogTalkRadio.

Resources:

National Public Radio   www.npr.org
Spreaker   http://www.spreaker.com/
Blog Talk Radio   http://www.blogtalkradio.com/

With BlogTalkRadio, people can either host their own live talk radio show with any phone and a computer or listen to thousands of new shows created daily.
Examples:
www.blogtalkradio.com/cannabis-times-
www.blogtalkradio.com/sjb340/2010/12/21/entrepreneurs-r-us

E-mail Marketing

We will use the following email marketing tips to build our mailing list database, improve communications, boost patient loyalty and attract new and repeat business.

1. Define our objectives as the most effective email strategies are those that offer value to our subscribers: either in the form of educational content or promotions. To drive sales, a promotional campaign is the best format. To create brand recognition and reinforce our expertise in our industry we will use educational newsletters.

2. A quality, permission-based email list will be a vital component of our email marketing campaign. We will ask patients and prospects for permission to add them to our list at every touch-point or use a sign-in sheet.

3. We will listen to our patients by using easy-to-use online surveys to ask specific questions about patients' preferences, interests and satisfaction.

4. We will send only relevant and targeted communications.

5. We will reinforce our brand to ensure recognition of our brand by using a recognizable name in the "from" line of our emails and including our company name, logo and a consistent design and color scheme in every email.

Resources:
https://cbtnews.com/8-tips-drive-successful-email-marketing-campaign/
https://www.inman.com/2017/06/05/4-tips-for-effective-email-marketing/
https://due.com/blog/ways-take-good-care-email-list/

Every ____ (five?) to ____ (six?) weeks, we will send graphically-rich, permission-based, personalized, email marketing messages to our list of patients who registered on our website, or at an event. The emails will alert patients in a ____ (50?)-mile radius to promotions as well as other local events sponsored by our company. This service will be provided by either ExactTarget.com or ConstantContact.com. The email will announce a special promotional event and contain a short sales letter. The message will invite recipients to click on a link to our website to checkout more information about the event, then print out the page and bring it with them to the event. The software offered by these two companies will automatically personalize each email with the patient's name. The software also provides detailed click-through behavior reports that will enable us to evaluate the success of each message. The software will also allow us to dramatically scale back its direct mail efforts and associated costs. Our company will send a promotional e-mail about a promotion that the patient indicated was important to them in their preferred membership application. Each identified market segment will get notified of new products, specials and offers based on past buying patterns and what they've clicked on in our previous e-newsletters or indicated on their surveys. The objective is to tap the right patient's need at the right time, with a targeted subject line and targeted content. Our general e-newsletter may appeal to most patients, but targeted mailings that reach out to our various audience segments will build even deeper relationships, and drive higher sales.

Resources:

www.constantcontact.com/pricing/email-marketing.jsp

Google Reviews

We will use our email marketing campaign to ask people for reviews. We will ask people what they thought of our cannabis business or services and encourage them to write a Google Review if they were impressed. We will incorporate a call to action (CTA) on our email auto signature with a link to our Google My Review page.

Source:

https://superb.digital/how-to-ask-your-clients-for-google-reviews/

Resources:

https://support.google.com/business/answer/3474122?hl=en

https://support.google.com/maps/answer/6230175?co=GENIE.Platform
        %3DDesktop&hl=en

Example:

Tell your customers to:

1.   Go to https://www.google.com/maps
2.   Type in your business name, select the listing
3.   There's a "card" (sidebar) on the left-hand side. At the bottom, they can click 'Be the First to Write a Review' or 'Write a Review' if you already have one review.

Source:

https://www.reviewjump.com/blog/how-do-i-get-google-reviews/

Facebook.com

We will use Facebook to move our businesses forward and stay connected to our patients in this fast-paced world. Content will be the key to staying in touch with our patients and keeping them informed. The content will be a rich mix of information, before and after photos, interactive questions, current trends and events, industry facts, education, promotions and specials, humor and fun. We will use the following step system to get patients from Facebook.com:

1.   We will open a free Facebook account at Facebook.com.
2.   We will begin by adding Facebook friends. The fastest way to do this is to allow Facebook to import our email addresses and send an invite out to all our patients.
3.   We will post a video to get our patients involved with our Facebook page. We will post a video called "How to Plan a Successful Medical Marijuana

Dispensary Visit." The video will be first uploaded to YouTube.com and then simply be linked to our Facebook page. Video will be a great way to get people active and involved with our Facebook page.

4.   We will send an email to our patients base that encourages them to check out the new video and to post their feedback about it on our Facebook page. Then we will provide a link driving patients to our Facebook page.

5.   We will respond quickly to feedback, engage in the dialogue and add links to our response that direct the author to a structured mini-survey.

6.   We will optimize our Facebook profile with our business keyword to make it an invaluable marketing tool and become the "go-to" expert in our industry

7.   On a monthly basis, we will send out a message to all Facebook fans with a special offer, as Fan pages are the best way to interact with patients and potential patients on Facebook,

8.   We will use Facebook as a tool for sharing success stories and relate the ways in which we have helped our patients.

9.   We will use Facebook Connect to integrate our Facebook efforts with our regular website to share our Facebook Page activity. This will also give us statistics about our website visitors, and add social interaction to our site.

The Official and Unofficial Facebook Policies:
Facebook's advertising policies state that it will deny paid posts that "constitute, facilitate, or promote illegal products, services or activities"—including marijuana. "Anyone can report content to us if they think it violates our standards. Our teams review these reports rapidly and will remove the content if there is a violation."

Facebook also says it makes an exception for ads advocating the legalization of marijuana. And its policy is silent on advertising by equipment makers, such as vaporizers and grinders. Some advertisers substitute "herb" and other pot synonyms to avoid the appearance they're encouraging marijuana use. Facebook also makes a distinction between posts on a company's own Facebook page, which are usually treated more leniently, and ads or "boosted" posts that companies have paid to put in front of more users, which appear to get more scrutiny.
Source:
www.bostonglobe.com/business/2017/03/01/for-marijuana-advertisers-options-are-
        limited/bNLDg38KHaqRvP4lwFggJN/story.html

Resources:
http://www.facebook.com/advertising/
http://www.socialmediaexaminer.com/how-to-set-up-a-facebook-page-for-business/
http://smallbizsurvival.com/2009/11/6-big-facebook-tips-for-small-business.html
http://themarijuanamarketer.com/10-tips-on-how-to-use-social-media-to-market-your-
        dispensary/

Examples:
https://www.facebook.com/essencevegas
www.facebook.com/pages/Kind-Clinics-Medical-Marijuana-Dispensaries/

102526376486538

Facebook Profiles represent individual users and are held under a person's name. Each profile should only be controlled by that person. Each user has a wall, information tab, likes, interests, photos, videos and each individual can create events.

Facebook Groups are pretty similar to Fan Pages but are usually created for a group of people with a similar interest and they are wanting to keep their discussions private. The members are not usually looking to find out more about a business - they want to discuss a certain topic.

Facebook Fan Pages are the most viral of your three options. When someone becomes a fan of your page or comments on one of your posts, photos or videos, that is spread to all of their personal friends. This can be a great way to get your information out to lots of people...and quickly! In addition, one of the most valuable features of a business page is that you can send "updates" about new products and content to fans and your home building brand becomes more visible.

Facebook Live lets people, public figures and Pages share live video with their followers and friends on Facebook.
Source:
https://live.fb.com/about/
Resources:
https://www.facebook.com/business/a/Facebook-video-ads
http://smartphones.wonderhowto.com/news/facebook-is-going-all-live-video-streaming-your-phone-0170132/

Small Business Promotions
This group allows members to post about their products and services and is a public group designated as a Buy and Sell Facebook group.
Source: https://www.facebook.com/groups/smallbusinesspronotions/
Resource:
https://contently.com/strategist/2017/03/23/hazy-world-cannabis-marketing/
https://www.facebook.com/business/a/local-business-promotion-ads
https://www.facebook.com/business/learn/facebook-create-ad-local-awareness
www.socialmediaexaminer.com/how-to-use-facebook-local-awareness-ads-to-target-customers/

Facebook Ad Builder
https://waymark.com/signup/db869ac4-7202-4e3b-93c3-80acc5988df9/?partner=fitsmallbusiness

Facebook Business Page
Resources:
https://www.facebook.com/business/learn/set-up-facebook-page
https://www.pcworld.com/article/240258/how_to_make_a_facebook_page_for_your_

small_business.html
https://blog.hubspot.com/blog/tabid/6307/bid/5492/how-to-create-a-facebook-business-page-in-5-simple-steps-with-video.aspx

Best social media marketing practices:
1. Assign daily responsibility for Facebook to a single person on your staff with an affinity for dialoguing .
2. Set expectations for how often they should post new content and how quickly they should respond to comments – usually within a couple hours.
3. Follow and like your followers when they seem to have a genuine interest in your area of health and wellness expertise.
4. Post on the walls of not only your own Facebook site, but also on your most active, influential posters with the largest networks.
5. Periodically post a request for your followers to "like" your page.
6. Monitor Facebook posts to your wall and respond every two hours throughout.

We will use Facebook in the following ways to market our Medical Marijuana Dispensary:
1. Promote our blog posts on our Facebook page
2. Post a video of our service people in action.
3. Create a Welcome tab to display a video message from our owner.
    Resource: Pagemodo.
4. Support a local charity by posting a link to their website.
5. Thank our patients while promoting their businesses at the same time.
6. Describe milestone accomplishments and thank patients for their role.
7. Ask patients to contribute stories about positive outcomes.
8. Use the built-in Facebook polling application to solicit feedback.
9. Use the Facebook reviews page to feature positive comments from patients, and to respond to negative reviews.
10. Introduce patients to our staff with resume and video profiles.
11. Create a photo gallery to showcase our expertise.
Resource:
https://mmjbusinessdaily.com/2017/04/15/cheryl-shuman-top-12-cannabis-marketing-
    tips-for-facebook-success/

We will also explore location-based platforms like the following:
- FourSquare   - GoWalla
- Facebook Places   - Google Latitude

As a Medical Marijuana Dispensary serving a local community, we will appreciate the potential for hyper-local platforms like these. Location-based applications are increasingly attracting young, urban influencers with disposable income, which is precisely the audience we are trying to attract. People connect to geo-location apps primarily to "get informed" about local happenings.

Foursquare.com

A web and mobile application that allows registered users to post their location at a venue ("check-in") and connect with friends. Check-in requires active user selection and points are awarded at check-in. Users can choose to have their check-ins posted on their accounts on Twitter, Facebook, or both. In version 1.3 of their iPhone application, foursquare enabled push-notification of friend updates, which they call "Pings". Users can also earn badges by checking in at locations with certain tags, for check-in frequency, or for other patterns such as time of check-in.]
Resource:
https://foursquare.com/business/
Example:
https://foursquare.com/revivameddispensary

Instagram

Instagram.com is an online photo-sharing, video-sharing and social networking service that enables its users to take pictures and videos, apply digital filters to them, and share them on a variety of social networking services, such as Facebook, Twitter, Tumblr and Flickr. A distinctive feature is that it confines photos to a square shape, similar to Kodak Instamatic and Polaroid images, in contrast to the 16:9 aspect ratio now typically used by mobile device cameras. Users are also able to record and share short videos lasting for up to 15 seconds.

Instagram Cannabis Policy:

Instagram does not allow people or organizations to use the platform to advertise or sell marijuana, regardless of the seller's state or country. This is primarily because most federal laws, including those of the United States, treat marijuana as either an illegal substance or highly regulated good. Our policy prohibits any marijuana seller, including dispensaries, from promoting their business by providing contact information like phone numbers, street addresses, or by using the "contact us" tab in Instagram Business Accounts. We do however allow marijuana advocacy content as long as it is not promoting the sale of the drug. Dispensaries can promote the use and federal legalization of marijuana provided that they do not also promote its sale or provide contact information to their store.

Resources:
http://www.wordstream.com/blog/ws/2015/01/06/instagram-marketing

We will use Instagram in the following ways to help amplify the story of our brand, get people to engage with our content when not at our store, and get people to visit our store or site:
1.   Let our customers and fans know about specific product availability.
2.   Tie into trends, events or holidays to drive awareness.
3.   Let people know we are open and our selection and ambiance are spectacular.
4.   Run a monthly contest and pick the winning hashtagged photograph
        to activate our customer base and increase our exposure.

5.   Encourage the posting and collection of happy onsite or offsite customer photos.

Examples:
https://www.instagram.com/essence_vegas/
http://www.jennysdispensary.com/instagram.html

Note: Commonly found in tweets, a hashtag is a word or connected phrase (no spaces) that begins with a hash symbol (#). They're so popular that other social media platforms including Facebook, Instagram and Google+ now support them. Using a hashtag turns a word or phrase into a clickable link that displays a feed (list) of other posts with that same hashtag. For example, if you click on #medicalmarijuana in a tweet, or enter #medicalmarijuana in the search box, you'll see a list of tweets all about medical marijuana.

Snapchat.com

This is a photo messaging app for iPhone and Android mobile devices. Users can take a picture or video and add text, drawings, and a variety of filters. They set a designated time limit, 1-10 seconds, and send to selected contacts from their list. Users can also set a "story" – a Snap that pins to their profile and is viewable for 24 hours after posting. Snapchat photos display for a maximum of 10 seconds (for 24 hours, in the case of a snap story) before becoming permanently inaccessible. The user may choose to save their snaps, but this will only save it to their local device. If the receiver uses the screenshot function on their phone, or chooses to replay a snap, the sender is notified. The point of Snapchat is to be fun and quirky, enticing and engaging your contacts with visual snippets of whatever you are doing. Teen and millennial users enjoy using Snapchat where they would traditionally send a text message. In many cases it's easier and more stimulating to send a quick clip of the property you are viewing, for example, than it would be to send a text description.

Snapchat is not useful as a lead generating tool, but it is exceptionally useful for client engagement and retention. When we meet with a client and exchange mobile contact information, we will ask if they use Snapchat and if we can add them to keep them updated on event schedules. The beauty of the Snap is that is draws the client into the environment and makes them want to see or learn more. We will use this limitation to our advantage and make our client feel compelled to request and attend more demonstrations and classes . Snapchat is also a phenomenal tool to engage with existing clients. It will make customers feel connected to the budmaster and the strain searching process, which is conducive to converting sales and retaining these clients in the future. While the primary user demographic is in the millennial age range, the app is popular with many adults as well. Incorporating Snapchat into our client communication strategy will aid our ability to form long term client relationships.

Resources:
https://www.highsnobiety.com/2016/08/17/snapchat-accounts-weed/
https://blog.hootsuite.com/smart-ways-to-use-snapchat-for-business/

http://smallbiztrends.com/2014/10/how-businesses-can-use-snapchat.html
http://nymag.com/selectall/2016/04/the-snapchat-101-the-best-coolest-smartest-weirdest-accounts.html

Examples:
https://www.snapchat.com/add/essencevegas

Alternative Cannabis Centric Social Media Sites
MassRoots   **www.massroots.com/**
This is like a cannabis-centric Facebook, allowing users and companies to create profiles, following trending news, share images and other media, and advertise. They also offer how-to guides with useful information and step-by-step tutorials. MassRoots also has an extensive repository of strains with information about strain type, THC and CBD levels, aroma, flavor, effects and more.

Duby   **https://www.duby.co/**
This app operates like an Instagram for cannabis culture, allowing users to circulate image-based posts referred to as "dubys."

Social High   **http://socialhigh.com/**
Markets itself as "Facebook for the Cannabis Community," and it has amassed a small but growing community of users in 50 states and 65 countries. Powered by a third-party cannabis database known as Leafly, users can share their passion for cannabis, and converse over and compare various marijuana strains.
Source:
http://fortune.com/2016/03/02/cannabis-companies-turn-to-pot-friendly-social-media/

Adistry   **https://adistry.com/**
This Colorado-based firm has accumulated a network of hundreds of publications and event organizers that will accept marijuana ads. The firm also helps scrub its clients' social media pages of images or language that might trigger a Facebook review. Adistry has also figured a workaround to Facebook's controls by paying "influencers" with large online followings to post ads on their pages. Adistry has streamlined all of the grunt work involved and made the entire media selling process easy like it should be.

LinkedIn.com
LinkedIn ranks high in search engines and will provide a great platform for sending event updates to business associates. To optimize our LinkedIn profile, we will select one core keyword. We will use it frequently, without sacrificing consumer experience, to get our profile to skyrocket in the search engines. Linkedin provides options that will allow our detailed profile to be indexed by search engines, like Google. We will make use of these options so our business will achieve greater visibility on the Web. We will use widgets to integrate other tools, such as importing your blog entries or Twitter stream into your profile, and go market research and gain knowledge with Polls. We will answer questions

in Questions and Answers to show our expertise, and ask questions in Questions and Answers to get a feel for what patients and prospects want or think. We will publish our LinkedIn URL on all our marketing collateral, including business cards, email signature, newsletters, and web site. We will grow our network by joining industry and alumni groups related to our business. We will update our status examples of recent work, and link our status updates with our other social media accounts. We will start and manage a group or fan page for our product, brand or business. We will share useful articles that will be of interest to patients, and request LinkedIn recommendations from patients willing to provide testimonials. We will post our presentations on our profile using a presentation application. We will ask our first-level contacts for introductions to their contacts and interact with LinkedIn on a regular basis to reach those who may not see us on other social media sites. We will link to articles posted elsewhere, with a summary of why it's valuable to add to our credibility and list our newsletter subscription information and archives. We will post discounts and package deals. We will buy a LinkedIn direct ad that our target market will see. We will find vendors and contractors through connections.

Examples:
www.linkedin.com/company/young-medical-dispensary
www.linkedin.com/showcase/medical-marijuana-dispensary/

Podcasting

Our podcasts will provide both information and advertising. Our podcasts will allow us to pull in a lot of patients. Our monthly podcasts will be heard by ___ (#) eventual subscribers. Podcasts can now be downloaded for mobile devices, such as an iPod. Podcasts will give our company a new way to provide information and an additional way to advertise. Podcasting will give our business another connection point with patients. We will use this medium to communicate on important issues, what is going on with a planned event, and other things of interest to our health conscious patients. The programs will last about 10 minutes and can be downloaded for free on iTunes. The purpose is not to be a mass medium. It is directed at a niche market with an above-average educational background and very special interests. It will provide a very direct and a reasonably inexpensive way of reaching our targeted audience with relevant information about our Medical Marijuana Dispensary products and services.

Resources:
www.apple.com/itunes/download/.
www.cbc.ca/podcasting/gettingstarted.html
Examples:
www.podbean.com/podcast-detail?pid=44775
http://www.cannabisradio.com/
Resource:
https://itunes.apple.com/us/podcast/the-medical-pot-guide/id1121882880?mt=2
Directory:
https://player.fm/podcasts/Dispensary

Blogging

We will use our blog to keep patients and prospects informed about products, events and services that relate to our Medical Marijuana Dispensary business, new releases, contests, and specials. Our blog will show readers that we are a good source of expert information that they can count on. With our blog, we can quickly update our patients anytime our company releases a new product, the holding of a contest or are placing items on special pricing. We will use our blog to share patient testimonials and meaningful success stories. We will use the blog to supply advice on creative cosmetology, skin care and massage techniques. Our visitors will be able to subscribe to our RSS feeds and be instantly updated without any spam filters interfering. We will also use the blog to solicit product usage recommendations and future service addition suggestions. Additionally, blogs are free and allow for constant ease of updating.

Our blog will give our company the following benefits:
1. An cost-effective marketing tool.
2. An expanded network.
3. A promotional platform for new Medical Marijuana Dispensary services.
4. An introduction to people with similar interests.
5. Builds credibility and expertise recognition.

We will use our blog for the following purposes:
1. To share patient testimonials, experiences and meaningful success stories.
2. Update our patients anytime our company releases a new service.
3. Supply advice on nausea treatment options.
4. Discuss research findings.
5. To publish helpful content.
6, To welcome feedback in multiple formats.
7. Link together other social networking sites, including Twitter.
8. To improve Google rankings.
9. Make use of automatic RSS feeds.

We will adhere to the following blog writing guidelines:
1. We will blog at least 2 or 3 times per week to maintain interest.
2. We will integrate our blog into the design of our website.
3. We will use our blog to convey useful information and not our advertisements.
4. We will make the content easy to understand.
5. We will focus our content on the needs of our targeted audience.

Our blog will feature the following on a regular basis:
1. Useful articles and assessment coupons.
2. Give away of a helpful free report in exchange for email addresses
3. Helpful information for our professional referral sources, as well as patients, and online and offline community members.
5. Use of a few social media outposts to educate, inform, engage and drive people back to our blog for more information and our free report.

To get visitors to our blog to take the next action step and contact our firm we will do the following:

1. Put a contact form on the upper-left hand corner of our blog, right below the header.
2. Put our complete contact information in the header itself.
3. Add a page to our blog and title it, "Become My Patient.", giving the reader somewhere to go for the next sign-up steps.
4. At the end of each blog post, we will clearly tell the reader what to do next; such as subscribe to our RSS feed, or to sign up for our newsletter mailing list.

Resources: www.blogger.com   www.blogspot.com
              www.wordpress.com   www.tumblr.com
              www.typepad.com

Examples:
https://essencevegas.com/blog/
www.timelessmeddispensaryutah.com/blog/
www.emergemedicaldispensarys.com/blog/

Twitter

We will use 'Twitter.com' as a way to produce new business from existing patients and generate prospective patients online. Twitter is a free social networking and micro-blogging service that allows its users to send and read other users' updates (otherwise known as tweets), which are text-based posts of up to 140 characters in length. Updates are displayed on the user's profile page and delivered to other users who have signed up to receive them. The sender can restrict delivery to those in his or her circle of friends, with delivery to everyone being the default. Users can receive updates via the Twitter website, SMS text messaging, RSS feeds, or email. Twitter will give us the ability to have ongoing two-way conversations with our patients, which will allow us to get better at what we do and offer, while giving us the ability to express our own unique 'personality'. We will use our Twitter account to respond directly to questions, distribute news, solve problems, post updates, circulate information about fundraisers, hold trivia question contests for a chance to win a gift certificate and offer special discounts, known as 'Tweet Deals', on selected products and services. Our posts on Twitter will include our URL (address), our new product offers, skin care tips and new service offerings. On a long-term basis, using Twitter consistently and efficiently will help push our website up the rankings on Google. The intangible, that will only have a positive effect, are the hundreds of impressions that each tweet will get, not to mention the positive statements that will be posted about our service, staff, selection and product knowledge. Using TweetReach, we expect our special promotional offers to receive thousands of impressions. We will also add our website, company logo, personal photo and/or blog on our profile page.

We will build a targeted Twitter following through Twitter lists such as Mashable's Twitter List Directory, and third-party programs such as TweetAdder. In addition to our own blog's content, we will be sure to supplement our Twitter posts with resources from others that are of help to our target audience. In addition to Twitter being a broadcasting tool, it will also be utilized as a networking tool to turn content awareness into relationships. We will also use third-party Twitter tools like CoTweet and HootSuite to minimize our time and maximize the effectiveness of our Twittering. We will incorporate our business keywords into our bio to facilitate searches.

We will use a Twitter directory to find potential patients. Twitter directories such as WeFollow.com and Twellow.com are among the fastest growing directories online, and can help narrow down the field of tweeters based on keywords such as '_____', but also by location. The location search feature is the best ways to narrow down the field and find prospective guests. When we have found them, we will follow them and wait for them to follow us back.

We will provide the following instructions to register as a 'Follower' of _____ (company name) on Twitter:
1.   In your Twitter account, click on 'Find People' in the top right navigation bar, which will redirect to a new page.
2.   Click on 'Find on Twitter' which will open a search box that says 'Who are you looking for?'
3.   Type '_____ (company name) / _____ (owner name)' and click 'search'. This will bring up the results page.
4.   Click the blue '_____' name to read the bio or select the 'Follow' button.

Examples:
https://twitter.com/essencevegas
http://twitter.com/#!/ThriveMedDispensary

Press Release Overview
We will use market research surveys to determine the media outlets that our demographic patients read and then target them with press releases. We will draft a cover letter for our media kit that explains that we would like to have the newspaper print a story about the start-up of our new local Medical Marijuana Dispensary business or a milestone that we have accomplished. And, because news releases may be delivered by feeds or on news services and various websites, we will create links from our news releases to content on our website. These links which will point to more information or a special offer, will drive our patients into the sales process. They will also increase search engine ranking on our site. We will follow-up each faxed package to the media outlet with a phone call to the lifestyle or health section editor.

Media Kit
We will compile a media kit with the following items:
1.   A pitch letter introducing our company and relevant impact newsworthiness for their readership.
2.   A press release with helpful newsworthy story facts.
3.   Biographical fact sheet or sketches of key personnel.

4. Listing of product and service features and benefits to patients.
5. Photos and digital logo graphics
6. Copies of media coverage already received.
7. FAQ
8. Patient testimonials
9. Sales brochure
10. Media contact information
11. URL links to these online documents instead of email attachments.
12. Our blog URL address.

Public Relations Opportunities

The following represents a partial list of some of the reasons we will issue a free press release on a regular basis:
1. Announce Grand Opening Event and the availability of Medical Marijuana Dispensary services.
2. Planned Open House Event
3   Addition of new product release or service line.
4. Support for a Non-profit Cause or other local event.
5. Presentation of a free maintenance seminar or workshop on varicose veins.
6. Report Survey Results
7. Publication of an article on Medical Marijuana Dispensary industry trends.
8. Addition of a new staff member.
9. Notable Successes/Case Studies/Awards Received
10. Other Milestone Accomplishments.

Examples:

https://essencevegas.com/press/
www.vcstar.com/news/2017/jun/16/medical-dispensary-owner-earns-ucc-award/

We will use the following techniques to get our press releases into print:

1. Find the right contact editor at a publication, that is, the editor who specializes in health and wellness issues.
2. Understand the target publication's format, flavor and style and learn to think like its readers to better tailor our pitch.
3. Ask up front if the journalist is on deadline.
4. Request a copy of the editorial calendar--a listing of targeted articles or subjects broken down by month or issue date, to determine the issue best suited for the content of our news release or article.
5. Make certain the press release appeals to a large audience by reading a couple of back issues of the publication we are targeting to familiarize ourselves with its various sections and departments.
6. Customize the PR story to meet the magazine's particular style.
7. Avoid creating releases that look like advertising or self-promotion.
8. Make certain the release contains all the pertinent and accurate information the journalist will need to write the article and accurately answer the questions "who, what, when, why and where".

9.   Include a contact name and telephone number for the reporter to call for more information.

PR Distribution Checklist

We will send copies of our press releases to the following entities:

1.   Send it to patients to show accomplishments.
2.   Send to prospects to help prospects better know who you are and what you do.
3.   Send it to vendors to strengthen the relationship and to influence referrals.
4.   Send it to strategic partners to strengthen and enhance the commitment and support to our firm.
5.   Send it to employees to keep them in the loop.
6.   Send it to Employees' contacts to increase the firm's visibility exponentially.
7.   Send it to elected officials who often provide direction for their constituents.
8.   Send it to trade associations for maximum exposure.
9.   Put copies in the lobby and waiting areas.
10.   Put it on our Web site, to enable visitors to find out who we are and what our firm is doing, with the appropriate links to more detailed information.
11.   Register the Web page with search engines to increase search engine optimization.
12.   Put it in our press kit to provide members of the media background information about our firm.
13.   Include it in our newsletter to enable easy access to details about company activities.
14.   Include it in our brochure to provide information that compels the reader to contact our firm when in need of legal counsel.
15.   Hand it out at trade shows and job fairs to share news with attendees and establish credibility.

Media List

Journalist	Interests	Organization	Contact Info

Distribution:	www.1888PressRelease.com	www.ecomwire.com	
	www.prweb.com	www.WiredPRnews.com	
	www.PR.com	www.eReleases.com	
	www.24-7PressRelease.com	www.NewsWireToday.com	
	www.PRnewswire.com	www.onlinePRnews.com	
	www.PRLog.org		
	www.businesswire.com	www.marketwire.com	
	www.primezone.com	www.primewswire.com	
	www.xpresspress.com/	www.ereleases.com/index.html	
	www.Mediapost.com		
Journalist Lists:	www.mastheads.org	www.easymedialist.com	
	www.helpareporter.com		
Media Directories			
Bacon's –	www.bacons.com/	AScribe –	www.ascribe.org/

Newdispensarypers – www.newdispensarypers.com/   Gebbie Press – www.gebbieinc.com/

Support Services
          PR Web -   http://www.prweb.com
          Yahoo News –   http://news.yahoo.com/
          Google News –   http://news.google.com/

Resource:
HARO ("Help A Reporter Out")   www.helpareporter.com/
An online platform that provides journalists with a robust database of sources for upcoming stories. It also provides business owners and marketers with opportunities to serve as sources and secure valuable media coverage.

Professional Relations

We will place greater emphasis on professional education and networking. We will use education forums to address the needs, misconceptions and concerns of health care professionals about the benefits of Medical Marijuana Dispensary services. We will use the opportunity to translate Medical Marijuana Dispensary services into the benefits needed by health care professionals and patients.

Postcards

1.   We will use personalized postcards to stay-in-touch with prior patients.
2.   Postcards will offer cheaper mailing rates, staying power and attention grabbing graphics, but require repetition, like most other advertising methods.
3.   We will develop an in-house list of potential patients for routine communications from open house events, seminar registrations, direct response ads, etc.
4.   We will use postcards to encourage users to visit our website, and take advantage of a special offer.
5.   We will grab attention and communicate a single-focus message in just a few words.
6.   The visual elements of our postcard (color, picture, symbol) will be strong to help get attention and be directly supportive of the message.
7.   We will facilitate a call to immediate action by prominently displaying our phone number and website address.
8.   We will include a clear deadline, expiration date, limited quantity, or consequence of inaction that is connected to the offer to communicate immediacy and increase response.

Resources:
www.Postcardmania.com
https://www.pinterest.com/pin/77053843608633105/
https://www.tanagramdesign.com/silverpeak?lightbox=i11ocn

Flyers

1.   We will seek permission to post flyers on the bulletin boards in local businesses,

community centers, doctor and clinic waiting rooms, housing development offices and local schools.

2. We will also insert flyers into our direct mailings.
3. We will use our flyers as part of a handout package at open house events.
4. The flyers will feature a discount or free consultation coupon.
5. We will circulate flyers to the following local agencies and organizations:
   - Churches and Synagogues   - Parent Support Groups
   - Nat'l Council of Jewish Women   - National Org. for Women
6. We will seek to tie our flyers to upcoming holiday celebrations and civic events.
7. We will use flyers to promote the items we have on sale and upcoming events.
8. We will use colored paper to grab the reader's attention.
9. We will write a compelling and memorable headline that includes some of the following proven words: Discover, Exclusive, Free, The Only, At Last, Amazing, How to, etc.

Resource:

https://99designs.com/postcard-flyer-design/contests/grand-opening-flyer-marijuana-dispensary-guest-hosts-718308

Referral Program

We understand the importance of setting up a formal referral program with the following characteristics:

1. Give a premium reward based simply on people giving referral names.
2. Send an endorsed testimonial letter from a loyal patient to the referred prospect.
3. Include a separate referral form as a direct response device.
4. Provide a space on the response form for leaving positive comments that can be used to build a testimonial letter, that will be sent to each referral.
5. We will clearly state our incentive rewards, and terms and conditions.
6. We will distribute a newsletter to stay in touch with our patients and include articles about our referral program success stories.

Resources:

http://themarijuanamarketer.com/5-tips-winning-customer-referral-program/

Sources:

1. Referrals from other retailers, particularly those of other niche specialties.
2. Give speeches on a complicated niche area that other practitioners may feel is too narrow for them to handle, thus triggering referrals.
3. Structured Patient Referral Program.
4. Newsletter Coupons.

Methods:

1. Always have ready a 30-second elevator speech that describes what you do and who you do it for.
2. Use a newsletter to keep our name in front of referrals sources.
3. Repeatedly demonstrate to referral sources that we are also thinking about their

practice or business.

4. Regularly send referrals sources articles on unique yet important topics that might affect their businesses.
5. Use Microsoft Outlook to flag our contacts to remind us it is time to give them some form of personal attention.
6. Ask referral sources for referrals.
7. Get more work from a referral source by sending them work.
8. Immediately thank a referral source, even for the mere act of giving his name to a third party for consideration.
9. Remember referral sources with generous gift baskets and gift certificates.
10. Schedule regular lunches with former school classmates and new contacts.

We will offer an additional donation of $ _____ to any organization whose member use a referral coupon to become a patient. The coupon will be paid for and printed in the organization's newsletter.

Referral Tracking Form

Referral Source Name	Presently Referring Yes/No	No. of Patients Referred	Anticipated Revenue	Actions to be Taken	Target Date

Sample Medical Marijuana Dispensary Referral Program

We want to show our appreciation to established patients and business network partners for their kind referrals to our business. ____ (company name) wants to reward our valued and loyal patients who support our Medical Marijuana Dispensary Programs by implementing a new referral program. Ask any of our team members for referral cards to share with your family and friends to begin saving towards your next service. We will credit your account $___ (10?) for each new patient you refer to us as well as give them 10% off their first visit. When they come for their first visit, they should present the card upon arrival. We will automatically set you up a referral account.

The Referral Details Are As Follows:

1. You will receive a $__ (50?) credit for every patient that you refer for _____ services. Credit will be applied to your referral account on their initial visit.
2. We will keep track of your accumulated reward dollars and at any time we can let you know the amount you have available for use in your reward account.
3. Each time you visit ____ Medical Marijuana Dispensary, you can use your referral dollars to pay up to 50% of your total charge that day
4. Referral dollars are not applicable towards the purchase of products.

Resources:

http://brightsmack.com/marketing-strategies/37-referral-ideas-to-grow-your-business/
http://www.nisacards.com/Business-Referral-Marketing-Cards.aspx
https://www.referralsaasquatch.com/resources/
https://www.referralcandy.com/blog/47-referral-programs/

www.consultingsuccess.com/10-referral-strategies-to-grow-your-consulting-business

Resources:
Referral Program Software Packages
  www.invitebox.com
  www.referralsaasquatch.com/
  www.referralcandy.com/
  www.getambassador.com/

Statistics that support referral programs include:
92% of consumers trust peer recommendations, 40% trust advertising in search results, 36% trust online video ads, 36% trust sponsored ads on social networking sites and 33% trust online banner ads.

The average value of a referred customer is at least 16% higher than that of a non-referred customer with similar demographics and time of acquisition.

Referral Coupon Template
Company Name: _____
Address: _____
Phone: _____ Website: _____
Print and present this coupon with your first order and the existing patient who referred you will receive a credit for $_____ .

Current patient	**Referred patient**
Name: _____	Name: _____
Address: _____	Address: _____
Phone: _____	Phone: _____
Email: _____	Email: _____
Date referred:	

Office use only
Credit memo number:_____
Credit issued date: _____   Credit applied by: _____

Example: As part of patient appreciation month, throughout the month of _____, _____ Medical Marijuana Dispensary will offer a $_____ (10?) referral bonus for all current members when a referring new patient comes to the Medical Marijuana Dispensary for a service of $_____ (300?) or more. This will be a great way to really recognize our existing patients and the value they bring to our Medical Marijuana Dispensary.

Invite-A-Friend
We will setup an aggressive invite-a-friend referral program. We will encourage new members or newsletter subscribers, during their initial registration process, to upload and send an invitation to multiple contacts in their email address books. We will encourage them by providing an added incentive, such as a free _____.

Google Maps

We will first make certain that our business is listed in Google Maps. We will do a search for our business in Google Maps. If we don't see our business listed, then we will add our business to Google Maps. Even if our business is listed in Google Maps, we will create a Local Business Center account and take control of our listing, by adding more relevant information. Consumers generally go to Google Maps for two reasons: Driving Directions and to Find a Business.

Resource: http://maps.google.com/

Bing Maps   www.bingplaces.com/

This will make it easy for customers to find our business.

Apple Maps

A web mapping service developed by Apple Inc. It is the default map system of iOS, macOS, and watchOS. It provides directions and estimated times of arrival for automobile, pedestrian, and public transportation navigation.

Resources:

http://www.stallcupgroup.com/2012/09/19/three-ways-to-make-your-pawn-business-
        more-profitable-and-sellable/

http://www.apple.com/ios/maps/

https://en.wikipedia.org/wiki/Apple_Maps

Google Places

Google Places helps people make more informed decisions about where to go for Medical Marijuana Dispensary services under the 'Alternative Medicine' category. Place Pages connect people to information from the best sources across the web, displaying photos, reviews and essential facts, as well as real-time updates and offers from business owners. We will make sure that our Google Places listing is up to date to increase our online visibility. Google Places is linked to our Google Maps listing, and will help to get on the first page of Google search page results when people search for a Medical Marijuana Dispensary in our area.

Resources:

www.google/com/places

http://searchengineland.com/get-medical-marijuana-dispensary-google-places-190832

Yelp.com

We will use Yelp.com to help people find our local business. Yelp allows a business to be categorized as a "Cannabis Clinic." Visitors to Yelp write local reviews, over 85% of them rating a business 3 stars or higher In addition to reviews, visitors can use Yelp to find events, special offers, lists and to talk with other Yelpers. As business owners, we will setup a free account to post offers, photos and message our patients. We will also buy ads on Yelp, which will be clearly labeled "Sponsored Results". We will also use the Weekly Yelp, which is available in 42 city editions to bring news about the latest business openings and other happenings.

Examples:
www.yelp.com/list/top-medical-marijuana-dispensarys-san-francisco
www.yelp.com/biz/green-blossom-medical-cannabis-dispensary-huntington-beach-2

Epinions.com

This site helps people make informed buying decisions. It is a premier consumer reviews platform on the Web and a reliable source for valuable consumer insight, unbiased advice, in-depth product evaluations and personalized recommendations. Epinions is a service of Shopping.com, Inc., a leading provider of comparison shopping services. Shopping.com's mission is to help consumers anywhere use the power of information to find, compare and buy anything.

Manta.com

Manta is the largest free source of information on small companies, with profiles of more than 64 million businesses and organizations. Business owners and sales professionals use Manta's vast database and custom search capabilities to quickly find companies, easily connect with prospective patients and promote their own services. Manta.com, founded in 2005, is based in Columbus, Ohio.
Examples:
www.manta.com/c/mmsvbqp/new-life-medical-dispensary-corp

Pay-Per-Click Advertising

Google AdWords, Yahoo! Search Marketing, and Microsoft adCenter are the three largest network operators, and all three operate under a bid-based model. Cost per click (CPC) varies depending on the search engine and the level of competition for a particular keyword. Google AdWords are small text ads that appear next to the search results on Google. In addition, these ads appear on many partner web sites, including NYTimes.com (The New York Times), Business.com, Weather.com, About.com, and many more. Google's text advertisements are short, consisting of one title line and two content text lines. Image ads can be one of several different Interactive Advertising Bureau (IAB) standard sizes. Through Google AdWords, we plan to buy placements (ads) for specific search terms through this "Pay-Per-Click" advertising program. This PPC advertising campaign will allow our ad to appear when someone searches for a keyword related to our business, organization, or subject matter. More importantly, we will only pay when a potential patient clicks on our ad to visit our website. For instance, since we operate a Medical Marijuana Dispensary in ___ (city), _____ (state), we will target people using search terms such as "Medical Marijuana Dispensary, nausea remedy, pot, health, dispensary, legal weed, cannabis in ____ (city), ___ (state)". With an effective PPC campaign our ads will only be displayed when a user searches for one of these keywords. In short, PPC advertising will be the most cost-effective and measurable form of advertising for our Medical Marijuana Dispensary business.

Resources:
http://adwords.google.com/support/aw/?hl=en
www.wordtracker.com

Yahoo Local Listings

We will create our own local listing on Yahoo. To create our free listing, we will use our web browser and navigate to http://local.yahoo.com. We will first register for free with Yahoo, and create a member ID and password to list our business. Once we have accessed http://local.yahoo.com, we will scroll down to the bottom and click on "Add/Edit a Business" to get onto the Yahoo Search Marketing Local Listings page. In the lower right of the screen we will see "Local Basic Listings FREE". We will click on the Get Started button and log in again with our new Yahoo ID and password. The form for our local business listing will now be displayed. When filling it out, we will be sure to include our full web address (http://www.companyname.com). We will include a description of our Medical Marijuana Dispensary products and services in the description section, but avoid hype or blatant advertising, to get the listing to pass Yahoo's editorial review. We will also be sure to select the appropriate business category and sub categories.

Examples:
https://local.yahoo.com/info-159386741-bloom-dispensary-phoenix?csz=Phoenix%2C+
        AZ&stx=Alternative+Medicine+Retailers
Resource:
http://finance.yahoo.com/news/meet-yelp-medical-marijuana-dispensaries-
        200000053.html

Billboards

Research indicates that billboards have emerged as one of the few marijuana-friendly advertising venues. We will use billboard advertising to create brand awareness and strong name recognition. We will design Billboards that are eye-catching and informative, and use easy to read fonts like Verdana. We will include our business name, location, a graphic, standout border and no more than eight words. In designing the billboard we will consider the fact that the eye typically moves from the upper left corner to the lower right corner of a billboard. We will use colors that can be viewed by color blind people, such as yellow, black and blue, and pictures to contrast with the sky and other surroundings. We will keep the layout uncluttered and the message simple, and include a direct call to action. Depending on the billboards size and location, the cost will range from $1,000 to $5,000 per month. We will try to negotiate a discount on a long-term contract.

Resources:
Outdoor Advertising Association of America   www.oaaa.org
EMC Outdoor, Inc.   www.emcoutdoor.com

Article:
"Why Wait for Better Health"
www.boston.com/news/business/2017/10/06/first-billboard-ads-for-a-marijuana-
    dispensary-will-go-up-monday

Theater Advertising

Theater advertising is the method of promoting our business through in-theatre promotions. The objective of theater advertising is to expose the movie patron to our advertising message in various ways throughout the theater. Benefits include; an engaged audience that can't change the channel, an audience that is in a quiet environment, an audience that is in a good mood and receptive, advertising that is targeted to our local geographic area, full color video advertising on a 40 foot screen, and a moving and interactive ad with music and voiceover.

Resources:

Velocity Cinema Advertising	www.movieadvertising.com/index.html
NCM	www.nationalcinemedia.com/intheatreadvertising/
ScreenVision	www.screenvision.com
AMC Theaters	www.amctheatres.com
Regal Entertainment Group	www.regmovies.com

Advertorials

An advertorial is an advertisement written in the form of an objective article, and presented in a printed publication—usually designed to look like a legitimate and independent news story. We will use quotes as testimonials to back up certain claims throughout our copy and break-up copy with subheadings to make the material more reader-friendly. We will include the "call to action" and contact information with a 24/7 voicemail number and a discount coupon. The advertorial will have a short intro about a patient's experience with our Medical Marijuana Dispensary services and include quotes, facts, and statistics. We will present helpful information about therapeutic massage benefits.

Affiliate Marketing

We will create an affiliate marketing program to broaden our reach. We will first devise a commission structure, so affiliates have a reason to promote our business. We will give them ___ (10)% of whatever sales they generate. We will go after event planner bloggers or webmasters who get a lot of web traffic for our keywords. These companies would then promote our Medical Marijuana Dispensary products/services, and they would earn commissions for the sales they generated. We will work with the following services to handle the technical aspects of our program.

ConnectCommerce	https://www.connectcommerce.com/
Commission Junction	https://members.cj.com
ShareASale	http://www.shareasale.com/
Share Results	
LinkShare	https://cli.linksynergy.com/cli/publisher/registration/
Affiliate Scout	http://affiliatescout.com/

Affiliate Seeking   http://www.affiliateseeking.com/

Clix Galore   http://www.clixgalore.com/

Ex: http://entrepotneurmagazine.com/marijuana-affiliate-programs/

HotFrog.com

HotFrog is a fast growing free online business directory listing over 6.6 million US businesses. HotFrog now has local versions in 34 countries worldwide.

Anyone can list their business in HotFrog for free, along with contact details, and products and services. Listing in HotFrog directs sales leads and enquiries to your business. Businesses are encouraged to add any latest news and information about their products and services to their listing. HotFrog is indexed by Google and other search engines, meaning that patients can find your HotFrog listing when they use Google, Yahoo! or other search engines.

Resource:

http://www.hotfrog.com/AddYourBusiness.aspx

Examples:

http://www.hotfrog.com/business/co/empire/medical-marijuana-dispensary-winter-park

Local.com

Local.com owns and operates a leading local search site and network in the United States. Its mission is to be the leader at enabling local businesses and consumers to find each other and connect. To do so, the company uses patented and proprietary technologies to provide over 20 million consumers each month with relevant search results for local businesses, products and services on Local.com and more than 1,000 partner sites. Local.com powers more than 100,000 local websites. Tens of thousands of small business patients use Local.com products and services to reach consumers using a variety of subscription, performance and display advertising and website products.

Resource:

http://corporate.local.com/mk/get/advertising-opportunities

Autoresponder

An autoresponder is an online tool that will automatically manage our mailing list and send out emails to our patients at preset intervals. We will write a short article that is helpful to potential Medical Marijuana Dispensary buyers. We will load this article into our autoresponder. We will let people know of the availability of our article by posting to newsgroups, forums, social networking sites etc. We will list our autoresponder email address at the end of the posting so they can send a blank email to our autoresponder to receive our article and be added to our mailing list. We will then email them at the interval of our choosing with special offers. We will load the messages into our autoresponder and set a time interval for the messages to be mailed out.

Resource: www.aweber.com

Corporate Incentive/ Employee Rewards Program

Our Employee Rewards Program will motivate and reward the key resources of local corporations, that is, the people who make their business a success. We will use independent sales reps to market these programs to local corporations. It will be a versatile program, allowing the corporate patient to customize it to best suit the following goals:

1. Welcome New Hires
2. Introduce an Employee Discount Program for our Medical Marijuana Dispensary services.
3. Reward increases in sales or productivity with an Employee Incentive Program
4. Thank Retirees for their service to the company
5. Initiate a Loyalty Rewards Program geared towards the patients of our corporate patients or their employees.

Database Marketing

Database marketing is a form of direct marketing using databases of patients or potential patients to generate personalized communications in order to promote a product or service for marketing purposes. The method of communication can be any addressable medium, as in direct marketing. As marketers trained in the use of database marketing tools, we will be able to carry out patient nurturing, which is a tactic that attempts to communicate with each patient or prospect at the right time, using the right information to meet that patient's need to progress through the process of identifying a problem, learning options available to resolve it, selecting the right solution, and making the purchasing decision. As marketers we will use our databases to learn more about patients, select target markets for specific campaigns, through patient segmentation, compare patients' value to the company, and provide more specialized offerings for patients based on their transaction histories and surveyed needs and wants.

We will use sign-in sheets, coupons, surveys and newsletter subscriptions to collect the following information from our patients:

1. Name
2. Telephone Number
3. Email Address
4. Home Address
5. Birth Date
6. Cannabis Strain Preferences
7. Known Allergies
8. Medical Condition

We will utilize the following types of contact management software to generate leads and stay in touch with patients to produce repeat business and referrals:

1. Act   www.act.com
2. Front Range Solutions   www.frontrange.com
3. The Turning Point   www.turningpoint.com
4. Acxiom   www.acxiom.com/products_and_services/

Speaking Engagements

We will develop at least one core presentation and adapt it to each audience. We will consider a "problem/solution" format where we describe a challenge and tell how our expertise achieved an exceptional solution. We will use speaking engagements as an opportunity to expose our areas of expertise to prospective patients. By speaking at conferences and forums put together by professional and industry trade groups, we will increase our firm's visibility, and consequently, its prospects for attracting new business. Public speaking will give us a special status, and make it easier for our speakers to meet prospects. Attendees expect speakers to reach out to the audience, which gives speakers respect and credibility. We will identify speaking opportunities that will let us reach our targeted audience. We will designate a person who is responsible for developing relationships with event and industry associations, submitting proposals and, most importantly, staying in touch with contacts. We will tailor our proposals to the event organizers' preferences.

Speaking Proposal Package:
1.   Speech Topic/Agenda/Synopsis
2.   Target Audience: Community and Civic Groups
3.   Speaker Biography
4.   List of previous speaking engagements
5.   Previous engagement evaluations

Possible Speaking Topics:
1.   The Most Effective Medical Marijuana Dispensary Stress Relief Techniques.
2.   How to Evaluate and Compare Medical Marijuana Dispensary Service Companies
3.   How to Plan a Home Medical Marijuana Dispensary Sales Party
4.   Therapeutic Dispensary Services for Cancer Patients and Survivors
5.   The Latest Pain Management Treatments

Examples:
Sex and Cannabis: Can Cannabis Help with Human Sexuality?
Source:
https://inhalemd.com/book-dr-tishler-speaking-engagement-appearance/

Possible Targets:
1.   AARP Groups
2.   Churches
3.   Health Professionals
4.   Concierges
5.   Support Groups
6.   Corporations
7.   Health Event Planners
8.   Medical Trade Associations

Handout Materials:
1.   Presentation Outline
2.   Company Brochure
3.   Business Cards
4.   Survey

Speech Tracking Form

Group/Class	Subject/ Topic	Business Development Potential	Resources Needed	Target Date

We will use the following techniques to leverage the business development impact of our speaking engagements:

1. Send out press releases to local papers announcing the upcoming speech. We will get great free publicity by sending the topic and highlights of the talk to the newspaper.

2. Produce a flyer with our picture on it, and distribute it to our network.

3. Send publicity materials to our prospects inviting them to attend our presentation.

4. Whenever possible, get a list of attendees before the event. Contact them and introduce yourself before the talk to build rapport with your audience. Arrive early and don't leave immediately after your presentation.

5. Always give out handouts and a business card. Include marketing materials and something of value to the recipient, so that it will be retained and not just tossed away. You might include tips or secrets you share in your talk.

6. Give out an evaluation form to all participants. This form should request names and contact information. Offer a free consultation if it's appropriate. Follow up within 72 hours with any members of the audience who could become ideal patients.

7. Have a place on the form where participants can list other groups that might need speakers, along with the name of the program chairperson or other contact person.

8. Offer a door prize as incentive for handing in the evaluation. When you have collected all of the evaluations, you can select a winner of the prize.

9. Meet with audience members, answer their questions and listen to their concerns. Stay after your talk and mingle with the audience. Answer any questions that come up and offer follow-up conversations for additional support.

10. Request a free ad in the group's newsletter in exchange for your speech.

11. Send a thank-you note to the person who invited you to speak. Include copies of some of the evaluations to show how useful it was.

Speaking Engagement Package

1.	Video or DVD of prior presentation.	2.	Session Description
3.	Learning Objectives	4.	Takeaway Message
5.	Speaking experience	6.	Letters of recommendation
7.	General Biography	8.	Introduction Biography

Resource: www.toastmasters.com

Meet-up Group

We will form a meet-up group to encourage people to participate in our information sharing programs on medical marijuana health benefits.

Resource:

www.meetup.com/create/

Examples:

http://medical-dispensary-savings.meetup.com/

http://www.meetup.com/HighNY/

Marketing Associations/Groups

We will set up a marketing association comprised of complementary businesses. We will market our Medical Marijuana Dispensary as a member of a group of complementary companies. Our marketing group will include a physical therapist, a weight loss center, massage therapist and a physician. Any business that provides event services will be a likely candidate for being a member of our marketing group. The group will joint advertise, distribute joint promotional materials, exchange mailing lists, and develop a group website. The obvious benefit is that we will increase our marketing effectiveness by extending our reach.

BBB Accreditation

We will apply for BBB Accreditation to improve our perceived trustworthiness. BBB determines that a company meets BBB accreditation standards, which include a commitment to make a good faith effort to resolve any consumer complaints. BBB Accredited Businesses pay a fee for accreditation review/monitoring and for support of BBB services to the public. BBB accreditation does not mean that the business' products or services have been evaluated or endorsed by BBB, or that BBB has made a determination as to the business' product quality or competency in performing services. We will place the BBB Accreditation Logo in all of our ads.
Examples:
www.bbb.org/oregon/business-reviews/dispensary-medical-marijuana/the-medmar-
clinic-in-beaverton-or-22726520

Sponsor Events

The sponsoring of events, such as golf tournaments, will allow our company to engage in what is known as experiential marketing, which is the idea that the best way to deepen the emotional bond between a company and its patients is by creating a memorable and interactive experience. We will ask for the opportunity to prominently display our company signage and the set-up of a booth from which to handout sample products and sales literature. We will also seek to capitalize on networking, speech giving and workshop presenting opportunities

Patch.com

A community-specific news and information platform dedicated to providing comprehensive and trusted local coverage for individual towns and communities. Patch makes it easy to: Keep up with news and events, Look at photos and videos from around town, Learn about local businesses, Participate in discussions and Submit announcements, photos, and reviews.
Examples:
http://woodbridge.patch.com/groups/politics-and-elections/p/woodbridge-medical-
marijuana-dispensary-given-green-light-to-grow

Mobile iPhone Apps

We will use new distribution tools like the iPhone App Store to give us unprecedented direct access to consumers, without the need to necessarily buy actual mobile *ads* to reach people. Thanks to Apple's iPhone and the App Store, we will be able to make cool mobile apps that may generate as much goodwill and purchase intent as a banner ad. We will research Mobile Application Development, which is the process by which application software is developed for small low-power handheld devices, such as personal digital assistants, enterprise digital assistants or mobile phones. These applications are either pre-installed on phones during manufacture, or downloaded by patients from various mobile software distribution platforms. iPhone apps make good marketing tools. The bottom line is iPhones and smartphones sales are continually growing, and people are going to their phones for information. Apps will definitely be a lead generation tool because it gives potential patients easy access to our contact and business information and the ability to call for more information while they are still "hot". Our apps will contain: directory of staffers, publications on relevant issues, office location, videos, etc.

We will especially focus on the development of apps that can accomplish the following:

1. **Mobile Reservations:** Customers can use this app to access mobile reservations linked directly to your in-house calendar. They can browse open slots and book appointments easily, while on the go.

2. **Appointment Reminders:** You can send current customers reminders of regular or special appointments through your mobile app to increase your yearly revenue per customer.

3. **Style Libraries**
   Offer a style library in your app to help customers to pick out a _____ style. Using a simple photo gallery, you can collect photos of various styles, and have customers browse and select specific _____.

4. **Customer Photos**
   Your app can also have a feature that lets customers take photos and email them to you. This is great for creating a database of customer photos for testimonial purposes, advertising, or just easy reference.

5. **Special Offers**
   Push notifications allow you to drive activity on special promotions, deals, events, and offers. If you ever need to generate revenue during a down time, push notifications allow you to generate interest easily and proactively.

6. **Loyalty Programs**
   A mobile app allows you to offer a mobile loyalty program (buy ten ___, get one free, etc.). You won't need to print up cards or track anything manually – it's all done simply through users' mobile devices.

7. **Referrals**
   A mobile app can make referrals easy. With a single click, a user can post to a social media account on Facebook or Twitter about their experience with your business. This allows you to earn new business organically through the networks of existing customers.

8. **Product Sales**
   We can sell ____ products through our mobile app. Customers can browse products, submit orders, and make payments easily, helping you open up a new revenue stream.

Resources: http://www.apple.com/iphone/apps-for-iphone/
                               http://iphoneapplicationlist.com/apps/business/
Software Development: http://www.mutualmobile.com/
                               http://www.avenuesocial.com/mob-app.php#
                               http://www.biznessapps.com/

Resources:

Dispensary Mobile   **www.dispensarymobile.com/**

This app enables the user to build customer loyalty, increase sales, adapt to customer demands, and become an innovative leader in your industry.

Weed Maps   **https://weedmaps.com/**

MassRoots   **http://massroots.com/landing-desktop**

A mobile platform for "discovering cannabis." The app is featured under a mandatory geolocation system, meaning that only people living in the 23 states that have legalized marijuana will be able to access to the app. The app's users can share photos and connect over a mutual interest in cannabis. The app's creators have also incorporated their strong advocacy of marijuana legalization into MassRoots, encouraging businesses to become involved with its network.

Examples:

https://app.massroots.com/user/essencevegas

https://itunes.apple.com/us/app/la-medical-marijuana-dispensaries/id379861603?mt=8

Eaze app   **www.eazeup.com/#/home**

Works with local distributors and couriers to deliver prescriptions on a fast and efficient basis. The Eaze app confirms the eligibility of the user within five minutes of signing up, which means if you don't have a prescription and can't legally obtain the stuff yourself then you won't be able to place an order. The Eaze app will provide elderly and differently disabled individuals the ability to obtain prescriptions on a delivery basis like other medications, to make the system that much more efficient.

Blazenow   **www.blazenow.com/**

A mobile app used to locate dispensaries, delivery services, doctor's offices, and accessories.

Transit Ads

According to the Metropolitan Transportation Authority, MTA subways, buses and railroads provide billions of trips each year to residents. Marketing our medical marijuana dispensary in subway cars and on the walls of subway stations will be a great way to advertise our business to a large, captive audience.

Examples:

www.nydailynews.com/new-york/medical-marijuana-ad-campaign-pops-city-subways-
        article-1.3186542

Restroom billboard advertising (Bathroom Advertising)

We will target a captive audience by placing restroom billboard advertising in select high-traffic venues with targeted demographics. A simple, framed ad on the inside of a bathroom stall door or above a urinal gets at least a minute of viewing, according to several studies. The stall door ads are a good choice for venues with shorter waiting times, such as small businesses, while large wall posters are well-suited to airports or movie theatres where people are more likely to be standing in line near the entrance or exit. Many new restroom based ad agencies that's specialize in restroom advertisement have also come about, such as; Zoom Media, BillBoardZ , Flush Media , Jonny Advertising, Insite Advertising, Inc, Wall AG USA, ADpower, NextMedia, and Alive Promo (American Restroom Association, 9/24/2009).

Resources:

http://www.indooradvertising.org/

http://www.stallmall.com/

http://www.zoommedia.com/

Tumblr.com

Tumblr will allow us to effortlessly share anything. We will be able to post text, photos, quotes, links, music, and videos, from our browser, phone, desktop, email, or wherever we happen to be. We will be able to customize everything, from colors, to our theme's HTML.

Examples:

https://www.tumblr.com/tagged/medical-cannabis

https://www.tumblr.com/tagged/dispensaries

Patient Reward / Loyalty Program

As a means of building business by word-of-mouth, patients will be encouraged and rewarded as repeat patients. This will be accomplished by offering a discounted bottle of wine to those patients who sign-up for our frequent buyer card and purchase $____ of cannabis products and services within a ____ (#) month period.

Examples:

http://thesourcenv.com/loyalty-rewards-program/

http://www.nlcannabis.com/loyalty-program/

Resource:

http://greenstarpaymentsolutions.com/customer-loyalty-program/

Frequent Buyer Program Types:

1.	Punch Cards	Receive something for free after ? Purchases.
2.	Dollar-for-point Systems	Accrue points toward a free product.
3.	Percentage of Purchase	Accrue points toward future purchases.

Resources:

http://www.refinery29.com/best-store-loyalty-programs

https://thrivehive.com/customer-retention-and-loyalty-programs/
http://blog.fivestars.com/5-companies-loyalty-programs/
www.americanexpress.com/us/small-business/openforum/articles/10-cool-mobile-apps-
    that-increase-customer-loyalty/
https://squareup.com/loyalty
www.consumerreports.org/cro/news/2013/10/retailer-loyalty-rewards-
    programs/index.htm

thumbtack.com
A directory for finding and booking trustworthy local services, which is free to consumers.
Resource: www.thumbtack.com/postservice
Examples:
www.thumbtack.com/Medical-Marijuana-Dispensary-Clinic-Long-Beach-
    CA/service/378657
www.thumbtack.com/ca/san-francisco/doctors/medical-marijuana-clinic

Publish e-Book
Ebooks are electronic books which can be downloaded from any website or FTP site on the Internet. Ebooks are made using special software and can include a wide variety of media such as HTML, graphics, Flash animation and video. We will publish an e-book to establish our Medical Marijuana Dispensary expertise, and reach people who are searching for ebooks on how to make better use our products and/or services. Included in our ebook will be links back to our website, product or affiliate program. Because users will have permanent access to it, they will use our ebook again and again, constantly seeing a link or banner which directs them to our site. The real power behind ebook marketing will be the viral aspect of it and the free traffic it helps to build for our website.
ebook directories include:
        www.e-booksdirectory.com/
        www.ebookfreeway.com/p-ebook-directory-list.html
        www.quantumseolabs.com/blog/seolinkbuilding/top-5-free-ebook-directories-
            subscribers/
Resource: www.free-ebooks.net/
Examples:
www.goodreads.com/book/show/18271842-medical-marijuana-delivery-business-guide-
    ebook
www.vitalsource.com/products/the-cannabis-manifesto-steve-deangelo

e-books are available from the following sites:

Amazon.com	Createspace.com
Lulu.com	Kobobooks.com
BarnesandNoble.com	Scribd.com
AuthorHouse.com	

Business Card Exchanges

We will join our Chamber of Commerce or local retail merchants association and volunteer to host a mixer or business card exchange at our store. We will take the opportunity to invite social and business groups to our store to enjoy beer and wine tastings, and market to local businesses that will be looking for employee and patient holiday gifts in the coming months. We will also build our email database by collecting the business cards of all attendees.

Storefront Banner Advertising

We will use banners as an affordable way to draw attention to our business. We will place one on the side or front of our building, or on a prominent building and have it point to ours. We will use colorful storefront banners with catchy phrases to grab the attention of local foot and vehicle traffic.

Resource: http://www.bobs-signs.com/

Ex: "Free Healthy Herb Cooking Classes with Dispensary Membership"

Hubpages.com

HubPages has easy-to-use publishing tools, a vibrant author community and underlying revenue-maximizing infrastructure. Hubbers (HubPages authors) earn money by publishing their Hubs (content-rich Internet pages) on topics they know and love, and earn recognition among fellow Hubbers through the community-wide HubScore ranking system. The HubPages ecosystem provides a search-friendly infrastructure which drives traffic to Hubs from search engines such as Google and Yahoo, and enables Hubbers to earn revenue from industry-standard advertising vehicles such as Google AdSense and the eBay and Amazon Affiliates program. All of this is provided free to Hubbers in an open online community.

Resources: http://hubpages.crabbysbeach.com/blogs/
                http://hubpages.com/learningcenter/contents
                http://medical-dispensary-md.hubpages.com/hub/PR-Marketing-Tips-For-
                    Medical-Dispensarys-Laser-Clinics

Pinterest.com

The goal of this website is to connect everyone in the world through the 'things' they find interesting. They think that a favorite book, toy, or recipe can reveal a common link between two people. With millions of new pins added every week, Pinterest is connecting people all over the world based on shared tastes and interests. What's special about Pinterest is that the boards are all visual, which is a very important marketing plus. When users enter a URL, they select a picture from the site to pin to their board. People spend hours pinning their own content, and then finding content on other people's boards to "re-pin" to their own boards. We will use Pinterest for remote personal shopping appointments. When we have a patient with specific needs, we will create a board just for them with items we sell that would meet their needs, along with links to other tips and content. We will invite our patient to check out the board on Pinterest, and let them know we created it just for them.

Resources:
www.copyblogger.com/pinterest-marketing/

www.shopify.com/infographics/pinterest
www.pinterest.com/entmagazine/retail-business/
www.pinterest.com/brettcarneiro/ecommerce/
www.pinterest.com/denniswortham/infographics-retail-online-shopping/
www.cio.com/article/3018852/e-commerce/how-to-use-pinterest-to-grow-your-
    business.html

Examples:
http://www.pinterest.com/marijuanaedible/

Pinterest usage recommendation include:
1.   Hold a contest allowing fans of the brand to create photos of looks they like, with prizes for the most creative, or simply feature patient suggestions for herbal treatments.
2.   Conduct market research by showing photos of potential products or test launches, asking the patient base for feedback.
3.   Personalize the brand by showcasing style and what makes the brand different, highlighting new and exciting things through the use of imagery.
4.   Add links from Pinterest photos to the company webstore, putting price banners on each photo and providing a link where users can buy the products directly.

Topix.com
Topix is the world's largest community news website. Users can read, talk about and edit the news on over 360,000 of our news pages. Topix is also a place for users to post their own news stories, as well as comment about stories they have seen on the Topix site. Each story and every Topix page comes with the ability to add your voice to the conversation.
Example:
www.topix.com/state/de/2017/11/opening-of-new-delaware-medical-marijuana-
    dispensary-delayed?fromrss=1

Survey Marketing
We will conduct a door-to-door survey in our target area to illicit opinions to our proposed business. This will provide valuable feedback, lead to prospective patients and serve to introduce our Medical Marijuana Dispensary business, before we begin actual operations.

'Green' Marketing
We will target environmentally friendly patients to introduce new patients to our business and help spread the word about going "green". We will use the following 'green' marketing strategies to form an emotional bond with our patients:
1.   We will use clearly labeled 'Recycled Paper' and Sustainable Packaging, such as receipts and storage containers.
2.   We will use "green", non-toxic cleaning supplies.
3.   We will install 'green' lighting and heating systems to be more eco-friendly.

4. We will use web-based Electronic Mail and Social Media instead of using paper advertisements.
5. We will find local suppliers to minimize the carbon footprint that it takes for deliveries.
6. We will use products that are made with organic ingredients and supplies.
7. We will document our 'Green' Programs in our sales brochure and website.
8. We will be a Certified Energy Star Partner.
9. We will install new LED warehouse lighting, exit signs, and emergency signs.
10. We will install motion detectors in low-traffic areas both inside and outside of warehouses.
11. We will implement new electricity regulators on HVAC units and compressors to lower energy consumption.
12. We will mount highly supervised and highly respected recycling campaigns.
13. We will start a program for waste product to be converted into sustainable energy sources.
14. We will start new company-wide document shredding programs.
15. We will use of water-based paints during the finishing process to reduce V.O.C.'s to virtually zero.
16. Use of solar panels for non-critical sections and facilities in the complex.
17. Use of only hybrid or electric vehicles.

Sticker Marketing

Low-cost sticker, label and decal marketing will provide a cost-effective way to convey information, build identity and promote our company in unique and influential ways. Stickers can be affixed to almost any surface, so they can go and stay affixed where other marketing materials can't; opening a world of avenues through which we can reach our target audience. Our stickers will be simple in design, and convey an impression quickly and clearly, with valuable information or coupon, printed optionally as part of its backcopy. Our stickers will handed out at trade shows and special events, mailed as a postcard, packaged with product and/or included as part of a mailing package. We will insert the stickers inside our product or hand them out along with other marketing tools such as flyers or brochures. Research has found that the strongest stickers are usually less than 16 square inches, are printed on white vinyl, and are often die cut. Utilizing a strong design, in a versatile size, and with an eye-catching shape, that is, relevant to our business, will add to the perceived value of our promotional stickers.

Resources:
http://www.cafepress.com/+medical-marijuana-dispensary+stickers
https://www.stickergiant.com/custom-marijuana-stickers
https://www.redbubble.com/shop/dispensary+stickers

We will adhere to the following sticker design tips:
1. We will strengthen our brand by placing our logo on the stickers and using company colors and font styles.
2. We will include our phone number, address, and/or website along with our logo

to provide patients with a call to action.

3. We will write compelling copy that solicits an emotional reaction.

4. We will use die-cut stickers using unusual and business relevant shapes to help draw attention to our business.

5. We will consider that size matters and that will be determined by where they will be applied and the degree of desired visibility to be realized.

6. We will be aware of using color on our stickers as color can help create contrast in our design, which enables the directing of prospect eyes to images or actionable items on the stickers.

7. We will encourage patients to post our stickers near their phones, on yellow page book covers, on party invitations, on notepads, on book covers, on gift boxes and product packaging, etc.

8. We will place our stickers on all the products we sell.

USPS Every Door Direct Mail Program

Every Door Direct Mail from the U.S. Postal Service® is designed to reach every home, every address, every time at a very affordable delivery rate. Every business and resident living in the _____ zip code will receive an over sized post card and coupon announcing the _____ (company name) grand opening 7-days before the grand opening:

Price – USPS Marketing Mail™ Flats up to 3.3 oz
EDDM Retail® USPS Marketing Flats $0.177 per piece
EDDM BMEU USPS Marketing Mail at $0.156 per piece

Resource:
https://www.usps.com/business/every-door-direct-mail.htm
https://eddm.usps.com/eddm/customer/routeSearch.action

Note: The Postal Service has said post offices cannot actually refuse to deliver publications with pot ads. Instead, a spokesman said, workers must refer the material to "the responsible law enforcement agencies for investigation if appropriate.
Source:
www.bostonglobe.com/business/2017/03/01/for-marijuana-advertisers-options-are-limited/bNLDg38KHaqRvP4lwFggJN/story.html

ZoomInfo.com

Their vision is to be the sole provider of constantly verified information about companies and their employees, making our data indispensible — available anytime, anywhere and anyplace the patient needs it. Creates just-verified, detailed profiles of 65 million businesspeople and six million businesses. Makes data available through powerful tools for lead generation, prospecting and recruiting.

Zipslocal.com

Provides one of the most comprehensive ZIP Code-based local search services, allowing visitors to access information through our online business directories that cover all ZIP Codes in the United States. Interactive local yellow pages show listings and display relevant advertising through the medium of the Internet, making it easy for everyone to find local business information.

Hold Biggest Fan Contest

Do you love _____ (company name)? Do you have a great story about how the team at ____ (company Name) helped you "get there" to achieve your goals? Well, then ____ (company name) wants to hear from you! _____ (company name) has launched the "Biggest Fan Contest" on its Facebook Page at the beginning of ____ (month), inviting current and former patients to share why they are _____'s (company name) "Biggest Fan." Participants are eligible to win a number of prizes including: _____.
To enter, visit www.facebook.com/_____ (company name), "like" the page, and click the "Biggest Fan Contest" tab on the right hand side. Participants are then asked to write a short blurb or upload a photo sharing why they love _____ (company name). If you have a story to tell or photo to share, enter today. Contest ends _____ (date). See contest tab for full details.

BusinessVibes   www.businessvibes.com/about-businessvibes

A growing B2B networking platform for global trade professionals. BusinessVibes uses a social networking model for businesses to find and connect with international partner companies. With a network of over 5000+ trade associations, 20 million companies and 25,000+ business events across 100+ major industries and 175 countries, BusinessVibes is a decisive source to companies looking for international business partners, be they clients, suppliers, JV partners, or any other type of business contact.
Examples:
https://www.businessvibes.com/companyprofile/Medical-Marijuana-Dispensary-llc

Testimonial Marketing

We will either always ask for testimonials immediately after a completed project or contact our clients once a quarter for them. We will also have something prepared that we would like the client to say that is specific to a service we offer, or anything relevant to advertising claims that we have put together. For the convenience of the client we will assemble a testimonial letter that they can either modify or just sign off on. Additionally, testimonials can also be in the form of audio or video and put on our website or mailed to potential clients in the form of a DVD or Audio CD. A picture with a testimonial is also excellent. We will put testimonials directly on a magazine ad, slick sheet, brochure, or website, or assemble a complete page of testimonials for our sales presentation folder.

Examples:
https://essencevegas.com/testimonials/
https://weedmaps.com/dispensaries/mindful-medical-marijuana-dispensary
www.westword.com/news/medical-marijuana-dispensary-review-pure-medical-
        dispensary-in-north-denver-5859398

We will collect customer testimonials in the following ways:
1.   Our website – A page dedicated to testimonials (written and/or video).

2.   Social media accounts – Facebook fan pages offer a review tab, which makes it easy to receive and display customer testimonials.
3.   Google+ also offers a similar feature with Google+ Local.
4.   Local search directories – Ask customers to post more reviews on Yelp and Yahoo Local.
5.   Customer Satisfaction Survey Forms

We will pose the following questions to our customers to help them frame their testimonials:
1. What was the obstacle that would have prevented you from buying this product?
2. "What was your main concern about buying this product?"
3. What did you find as a result of buying this product?
4. What specific feature did you like most about this product?
5. What would be three other benefits about this product?
6. Would you recommend this product? If so, why?
7. Is there anything you'd like to add?

Resource:
https://smallbiztrends.com/2016/06/use-customer-testimonials.html

Reminder Service
We will use a four-tier reminder system in the following sequence: email, postcard, letter, phone call. We will stress the importance of staying in touch in our messages and keeping their profile updated with their activities. We will also try to determine the reason for the non-response or inactivity and what can be done to reactivate the client. The reminder service will also work to the benefit of regular clients, that want to be reminded of an agreed upon special date or coming event.
Resource:
http://www.easyivr.com/reminder-service.htm

Business Logo
Our logo will graphically represent who we are and what we do, and it will serve to help brand our image. It will also convey a sense of uniqueness and professionalism. The logo will represent our company image and the message we are trying to convey. Our business logo will reflect the philosophy and objective of the liquor store business. Our logo will incorporate the following design guidelines:
1.   It will relate to our industry, our name, a defining characteristic of our company or a competitive advantage we offer.
2.   It will be a simple logo that can be recognized faster.
3.   It will contain strong lines and letters which show up better than thin ones.
4.   It will feature something unexpected or unique without being overdrawn.
5.   It will work well in black and white (one-color printing).
6.   It will be scalable and look pleasing in both small and large sizes.
7.   It will be artistically balanced and make effective use of color, line density and shape.

8.   It will be unique when compared to competitors.
9.   It will use original, professionally rendered artwork.
10.   It can be replicated across any media mix without losing quality.
11.   It appeals to our target audience.
12.   It will be easily recognizable from a distance if utilized in outdoor advertising.

Resources: www.freelogoservices.com/   www.hatchwise.com
                      www.logosnap.com   www.99designs.com
                      www.fiverr.com   www.freelancer.com
                      www.upwork.com

Logo Design Guide:
www.bestfreewebresources.com/logo-design-professional-guide
www.creativebloq.com/graphic-design/pro-guide-logo-design-21221

Examples:
https://99designs.com/blog/creative-inspiration/cannabis-branding-weed-logos-
       marijuana-packaging-ideas/

Resource:
www.qualitylogoproducts.com/blog/straight-dope-marketing-marijuana-promotional-
       products/

Fundraisers

Community outreach programs involving charitable fundraising and showing a strong interest in the local school system will serve to elevate our status in the community as a "good corporate citizen" while simultaneously increasing store traffic. We will execute a successful fundraising program for our liquor store and build goodwill in the community, by adhering to the following guidelines:

1.   Keep It Local
       When looking for a worthy cause, we will make sure it is local so the whole neighborhood will support it.
2.   Plan It
       We will make sure that we are organized and outline everything we want to accomplish before planning the fundraiser.
3.   Contact Local Media
       We will contact the suburban newspapers to do stories on the event and send out press releases to the local TV and radio stations.
4.   Contact Area Businesses
       We will contact other businesses and have them put up posters in their stores and pass out flyers to promote the event.
5.   Get Recipient Support
       We will make sure the recipients of the fundraiser are really willing to participate and get out in the neighborhood to invite everyone into our store for the event, plus help pass out flyers and getting other businesses to put up the posters.

6. Give Out Bounce Backs
   We will give a "bounce-back" coupon that allows for both a discount and an additional donation in exchange for customer next purchase. (It will have an expiration date of two weeks to give a sense of urgency.)
7. Be Ready with plenty of product and labor on hand for the event.

Fundraiser Action Plan Checklist:
1. Choose a good local cause for your fundraiser.
2. Calculate donations as a percentage for normal sales.
3. Require the group to promote and support the event.
4. Contact local media to get exposure before and after the event.
5. Ask area businesses to put up flyers and donate printing of materials.
6. Use a bounce-back coupon to get new customers back.
7. Be prepared with sufficient labor and product.

Resource:
www.thefundraisingauthority.com/fundraising-basics/fundraising-event/

Online Directory Listings

The following directory listings use proprietary technology to match patients with industry professionals in their geographical area. The local search capabilities for specific niche markets offer an invaluable tool for the patient. These directories help member businesses connect with purchase-ready buyers, convert leads to sales, and maximize the value of patient relationships. Their online and offline communities provide a quick and easy low or no-cost solution for patients to find a liquor store quickly. We intend to sign-up with all no cost directories and evaluate the ones that charge a fee.

1. https://weedmaps.com/?ss=dispensary
2. http://www.leafly.com/medical-marijuana/browse/or/salem
3. http://thecannabisindustry.org/members
4. http://www.thcfinder.com/
5. http://medical-marijuana-dispensaries.findthebest.com/
6. http://canorml.org/medical-marijuana/California-collectives-and-dispensaries-guide
7. https://www.marijuanadoctors.com/
8. http://national-bud-directory.com/marijuana/MedicalMarijuanaDispensary
9. http://www.shabong.com/
10. http://www.findlocalweed.com/
11. www.dopedirectory.com

Others:
☐ 420Medicated.com
☐ ChiTownDispensaries.com
☐ LiftCannabis.ca
☐ THCBiz.com
☐ 420scan.com
☐ allbud.com

☐ BestMedicalMarijuanaDoctors.com
☐ LegalMarijuanaFinder.com
☐ MMJPR.ca
☐ WeedReader
☐ 502maps.com
☐ alternative-medicine.inseattle.us

- alternativeresourcesdirectory.com
- bud.ninja
- budvibes.com
- cannabis.net
- cannabisrevu.com
- cannmarket.io
- dispensaryfinder.net
- greenlightwashington.com
- headshopfinder.com
- live420md.com
- mobiwana.com
- potshops.directory
- stingysmoker.com
- theweed.market
- weeddepot.com
- yourlocalbudstore.com
- bonglocal.com
- buddhub.com
- yourlocalbudstore.com
- cannabisadventures.guru
- cannapages.com
- directory.medicalmarijuana411.com
- ganjagps.com
- greentripz.com
- herbscout.com
- metaweed.com
- potmy.com
- stickyshops.com
- thesocialweed.com
- washington.statecannabisguide.com
- weedsta.com

Source:

http://www.localseoguide.com/the-top-marijuana-directories-citation-sources/

Other General Directories Include:

Listings.local.yahoo.com
YellowPages.com
Bing.com/businessportal
Yelp.com
InfoUSA.com
Localeze.com
YellowBot.com
InsiderPages.com
CitySearch.com
Profiles.google.com/me
Jigsaw.com
Whitepages.com
Judysbook.com
Google.com
Infogroup.com

Switchboard Super Pages
MerchantCircle.com
Local.com
BrownBook.com
iBegin.com
Bestoftheweb.com
HotFrog.com
MatchPoint.com
YellowUSA.com
Manta.com
LinkedIn.com
PowerProfiles.com
Company.com
Yahoo.com

Get Listed   http://getlisted.org/enhanced-business-listings.aspx
Universal Business Listing   https://www.ubl.org/index.aspx
                        www.UniversalBusinessListing.org

Universal Business Listing (UBL) is a local search industry service dedicated to acting as a central collection and distribution point for business information online. UBL provides business owners and their marketing representatives with a one-stop location for broad distribution of complete, accurate, and detailed listing information.

MyMarijuanaCommunity.com

A leader in geographically targeted advertising for the medical marijuana community. The site - which is a 100-percent veteran- and disabled-owned business - maintains the largest business listing database of dispensaries, doctors, legal services and hydroponics shops on the Internet. Its approximately 4,000 listings include street-level interactive maps, consumer reviews and a verification system.

Google+

We will pay specific attention to Google+, which is already playing a more important role in Google's organic ranking algorithm. We will create a business page on Google+ to achieve improved local search visibility. Google+ will also be the best way to get access to Google Authorship, which will play a huge role in SEO. Aside from having all the necessary information like hours and contact information, quality photos and visuals will be essential on our Google+ local page. To go above the basics, we will have a local Google photographer visit and create a virtual tour.

Resources:

https://plus.google.com/pages/create

http://www.google.com/+/brands/

https://www.google.com/appserve/fb/forms/plusweekly/

https://plus.google.com/+GoogleBusiness/posts

http://marketingland.com/beyond-social-benefits-google-business-73460

Examples:

https://plus.google.com/+OasisMedicalCannabisLasVegas

https://plus.google.com/+UrbangreenhouseUGD/about

Inbound Marketing

Inbound marketing is about pulling people in by sharing relevant medical marijuana information, creating useful content, and generally being helpful. It involves writing everything from buyer's guides to blogs and newsletters that deliver useful content. The objective will be to nurture customers through the buying process with unbiased educational materials that turn consumers into informed buyers.

Resource:

www.Hubspot.com

Google My Business Profile   www.google.com/business/befound.html

We will have a complete and active Google My Business profile to give our medical marijuana dispensary company a tremendous advantage over the competition, and help potential customers easily find our company and provide relevant information about our business.

Reddit.com

An online community where users vote on stories. The hottest stories rise to the top, while the cooler stories sink. Comments can be posted on every story, including stories about startup medical marijuana companies.

Examples:

www.reddit.com/r/mildlyinteresting/comments/2d6gph/the_inside_view_of_a_medical_
marijuana_dispensary/

Exterior Signage

We will make effective use of the following types of signage: (select)

1. **Channel Letter**

    Channel letters can be illuminated by LED or neon and come in a variety of colors and sizes. Front-lit signs are illuminated from the letter face, while reverse-lit signs are lit from behind the sign. Open-face channel letters lit by exposed neon work well to create a night presence.

2. **Monument Signs**

    Monument signs are usually placed at the entrance to a parking lot or a building. This sign can easily be installed on a median or lawn. The size for a monument sign is typically based on city regulations for the specific location. These signs can be illuminated or non-illuminated, single- or double-sided.

3. **Pylon Signs**

    Also known as pole signs, they soar high above a business location to set the business apart from other businesses. They get attention from highway motorists who are still a distance away.

4. **Cabinet Signs**

    Commonly called "wall" or "box" signs, they are a traditional form of signage. They effectively use a large copy area and eye-popping graphics. This type of signage can highlight our business day or night because we have the option to add illumination. The background can be the element that lights up, and the copy can be lit or non-lit.

5. **Sandwich Signs**

    This sign will be placed on the sidewalk in front of our business to attract foot traffic.

6. **Vehicle Roof-top and Side-panel Signage**

6.4.1   Strategic Alliances

We will form strategic alliances to accomplish the following objectives:

1. To share marketing expenses.
2. To realize bulk buying power on wholesale purchases.
3. To engage in barter arrangements.
4. To collaborate with industry experts.
5. To set-up mutual referral relationships.

We will develop strategic alliances with the following service providers by conducting introductory 'cold calls' to their offices and making them aware of our capabilities by distributing our brochures and business cards. Our objective is to establish a working relationship with nearby businesses that serve the same target audience. To make it a win-win arrangement, we will create an offer/incentive. For example, our offer extended by the wedding photographer to his patients might be: "A certificate for a chemical peel from this leading medi-dispensary is included when you purchase a Picture Package (of $-value or more)".

We will pursue referrals from the following types of businesses:
1.	Family Physicians	2.	Hospitals
3.	Attorneys	4.	Weight Management/Watchers
5.	Fitness Clubs/Gyms	6.	Dermatologists
7.	Chiropractors	8.	Nutritionists
9.	Optometrists	10.	Hospices

We will assemble a sales presentation package that includes sales brochures, business cards, and a DVD seminar presentation. We will print coupons that offer a discount or other type of introductory deal. We will ask to set-up a take-one display for our sales brochures at the business registration counter. We will give the referring business any one or combination of the following reward options:
1. Referral fees
2. Free services
3. Mutual referral exchanges

We will monitor referral sources to evaluate the mutual benefits of the alliance and make certain to clearly define and document our referral incentives prior to initiating our referral exchange program.

6.4.2 Monitoring Marketing Results

To monitor how well _____ (company name) is doing, we will measure how well the advertising campaign is working by taking patient surveys. What we would like to know is how they heard of us and how they like and dislike about our services. In order to get responses to the surveys, we will be give discounts as thank you rewards.

Response Tracking Methods
Coupons: ad-specific coupons that easily enable tracking
Landing Pages: unique web landing pages for each advertisement
800 Numbers: unique 1-800-# per advertisement
Email Service Provider: Instantly track email views, opens, and clicks

Our financial statements will offer excellent data to track all phases of sales. These are available for review on a daily basis. _____ (company name) will benchmark our objectives for sales promotion and advertising in order to evaluate our return on invested marketing dollars, and determine where to concentrate our limited advertising dollars to realize the best return. We will also strive to stay within our marketing budget.

Key Marketing Metrics
We will use the following two marketing metrics to evaluate the cost-effectiveness of our marketing campaign:

1.   The cost to acquire a new patient: The average dollar amount invested to get one new patient. Example: If we invest $3,000 on marketing in a single month and end the month with 10 new patients, our cost of acquisition is $300 per new   patient.
2.   The lifetime value of the average active patient. The average dollar value of an average patient over the life of their business with you. To calculate this metric for a given period of time, we will take the total amount of revenue our business generated during the time period and divide it by the total number of patients we had from the beginning of the time period.
3.   We will track the following set of statistics on a weekly basis to keep informed of the progress of our Medical Marijuana Dispensary service business:
    A.   Number of total referrals.
    B.   Percentage increase of total referrals (over baseline).
    C.   Number of new referral sources.
    D.   Average number of sessions per patient.
    E.   Average transaction amount per session.
    F.   Percentage decrease in number of sessions (under baseline).

Key Marketing Metrics Table
We've listed some key metrics in the following table. We will need to keep a close eye on these, to see if we meet our own forecasted expectations. If our numbers are off in too many categories, we may, after proper analysis, have to make substantial changes to our marketing efforts.

Key Marketing Metrics	2017	2018	2019
Revenue			
Leads			
Leads Converted			
Avg. Transaction per Patient			
Avg. Dollars per Patient			
Number of Referrals			
Number of PR Appearances			
Number of Testimonials			
Number of New Club Members			
Number of Returns			
Number of BBB Complaints			
Number of Completed Surveys			
Number of Blog readers			
Number of Twitter followers			
Number of Facebook Fans			

Metric Definitions

1. Leads: Individuals who step into the store to consider a purchase.
2. Leads Converted: Percent of individuals who actually make a purchase.
3. Average Transactions Per Patient: Number of purchases per patient per month. Expected to rise significantly as patients return for more and more _____ items per month
4. Average $ Per Patient: Average dollar amount of each transaction. Expected to rise along with average transactions.
5. Referrals: Includes patient and business referrals
6. PR Appearances: Online or print mentions of the business that are not paid advertising. Expected to be high upon opening, then drop off and rise again until achieving a steady level.
7. Testimonials: Will be sought from the best and most loyal patients. Our objective is ___ (#) per month) and they will be added to the website. Some will be sought as video testimonials.
8. New Loyalty Club Members: This number will rise significantly as more patients see the value in repeated visits and the benefits of club membership.
9. Number of Returns/BBB Complaints: Our goal is zero.
10. Number of Completed Surveys: We will provide incentives for patients to complete patient satisfaction surveys.

6.4.3   Word-of-Mouth Marketing

We plan to make use of the following techniques to spur word-of-mouth advertising:

1. Repetitive Image Advertising
2. Provide exceptional patient service.
3. Make effective use of loss leaders.
2. Schedule in-store activities, such as demonstrations or special events.
3. Make trial easy with a coupon or introductory discount.
4. Initiate web and magazine article submissions
5. Utilize a sampling program
6. Add a forward email feature to our website.
7. Share relevant and believable testimonial letters
8. Publish staff bios.
9. Make product/service upgrade announcements
10. Hold contests or sweepstakes
12. Have involvement with community events.
13. Pay suggestion box rewards
14. Distribute a monthly newsletter
15. Share easy-to-understand information (via an article or seminar).
16. Make personalized marketing communications.
17. Structure our referral program.
18. Sharing of Community Commonalities
19. Invitations to join our community of shared interests.
20. Publish Uncensored Patient Reviews

21. Enable Information Exchange Forums
22. Provide meaningful comparisons with competitors.
23. Clearly state our user benefits.
24. Make and honor ironclad guarantees
25. Provide superior post-sale support
26. Provide support in the pre-sale decision making process.
27. Host Free Informational Seminars or Workshops
28. Get involved with local business organizations.
29. Issue Press Release coverage of charitable involvements.
30. Hold traveling company demonstrations/exhibitions/competitions.
31. Stay in touch with inactive patients.

6.4.4   Patient Satisfaction Survey

We will design a patient satisfaction survey to measure the "satisfaction quotient" of our Medical Marijuana Dispensary patients. By providing a detailed snapshot of our current patient base, we will be able to generate more repeat and referral business and enhance the profitability of our medical marijuana dispensary company.

Our Patient Satisfaction Survey will including the following basics:
1. How do our patients rate our business?
2. How do our patients rate our competition?
3. How well do our patients rate the value of our products or services?
4. What new patient needs and trends are emerging?
5. How loyal are our patients?
6. What can be done to improve patient loyalty and repeat business?
7. How strongly do our patients recommend our business?
8. What is the best way to market our business?
9. What new value-added services would best differentiate our business from that of our competitors?
10. How can we encourage more referral business?
11. How can our pricing strategy be improved?

Our patient satisfaction survey will help to answer these questions and more. From the need for continual new products and services to improved patient service, our satisfaction surveys will allow our business to quickly identify problematic and underperforming areas, while enhancing our overall patient satisfaction.

Resources:
http://mmjpatients.org/survey-your-patients/
http://patientsurvey.com/
http://www.uclamedicalmarijuanaresearch.com/node/3
https://www.survata.com/
https://www.google.com/insights/consumersurveys/use_cases

Survey Monkey www.surveymonkey.com
http://www.smetoolkit.org/smetoolkit/en/content/en/6708/Patient-Satisfaction-Survey-
    Template-
http://smallbusiness.chron.com/common-questions-patient-service-survey-1121.html

We will also try to collect the following kinds of information from our patient surveys:

1. Demographic Profile
    - Age   - Sex
    - Income   - Lifestyle
    - Household purchase penetration   - Education
    - Ethnicity   - Zipcode
    - Occupation
2. Purchase decision-making criteria.
3. Frequency of purchase
4. Pattern of purchase
5. Related purchases
6. Planned or Unplanned purchase
7. Promotional materials exposed to.
8. Brand loyalty
9. Buyer switching patterns.
10. Type of cannabis strain preferred
11. Price range preferred
12. Where most frequently buy this product or service
13. How and for what conditions consumers buy this product.
14. Loyalty factor
15. Learning about growing and extraction methods
16. How much they want to learn.
17. Purchase decision influences.

6.4.5   Marketing Training Program

Our Marketing Training Program will include both an initial orientation and training, as well as ongoing continuing education classes. Initial orientation will be run by the owner until an HR manager is hired. For one week, half of each day will be spent in training, and the other half shadowing the operations manager.
Training will include:
   Learning the entire selection of Medical Marijuana Dispensary products and services.
   Understanding our Mission Statement, Value Proposition, Position Statement and
      Unique Selling Proposition.
   Appreciating our competitive advantages.
   Understanding our core message and branding approach.
   Learning our store's policies; returns processing, complaint handling, etc.
   Learning our patient services standards of practice.

Learning our patient and business referral programs.
Learning our Membership Club procedures, rules and benefits.
Becoming familiar with our company website, and online ordering options.
Service procedures specific to the employee's role.

Ongoing workshops will be based on patient feedback and problem areas identified by mystery buyers, which will better train employees to educate patients. These ongoing workshops will be held _____ (once?) a month for _____ (three?) hours.

6.5   Sales Strategy

The development of our sales strategy will start by developing a better understanding of our patient needs. To accomplish this task we will pursue the following research methods:

1.   Join the associations that our target patients belong to.
2.   Contact the membership director and establish a relationship to understand their member's needs, challenges and concerns.
3.   Identify non-competitive suppliers who sell to our patient to learn their challenges and look for partnering solutions.
4.   Work directly with our patient and ask them what their needs are and if our business may offer a possible solution.

Sales in our business will result from quality patient service and utmost satisfaction from referring professionals and hotel facilities. Our sales strategy is based on the selling of the following service benefits:

1.   Excellent quality of service
2.   Trustworthiness
3.   Effective Interpersonal Relationships
4.   Superior Convenience

Our focus will be on making the services we offer of the highest possible quality. Only when those services are well-established, will we consider expanding our range of services offered.

We will become a one-stop shop for Medical Marijuana Dispensary services, and specialized program offerings. We will also be very active in the community, building a solid reputation with professionals and community leaders.

Our patients will be primarily obtained through word-of-mouth referrals, but we will also advertise introductory offers, such as the waiving of the travel fee, to introduce people to our programs. The combination of the perception of higher quality, exceptional technical support and the recognition of superior value should turn referral leads into satisfied patients.

The company's sales strategy will be based on the following elements:

Advertising in the Yellow Pages - two inch by three inch ads describing our services will be placed in the local Yellow Pages.

Placing classified advertisements in the regional editions of health and home magazines.

Word of mouth referrals - generating sales leads in the local community through patient referrals.

Our basic sales strategy is to:

Develop a website for lead generation by _____ (date).

Provide exceptional patient service.

Accept payment by all major credit cards, cash, PayPal and check.

Survey our patients regarding services they would like to see added.

Sponsor charitable and other community events.

Motivate employees with a pay-for-performance component to their straight salary compensation package, based on profits and patient satisfaction rates.

Build long-term patient relationships by putting the interests of patients first.

Establish mutually beneficial relationship with local businesses serving the needs of children and seniors.

6.5.1   Patient Retention Strategy

We will use the following techniques to improve patient retention and the profitability of our business:

1. Keep our facility and vehicle sparkling clean and well-organized.
2. Use only well-trained therapists and technicians, and the highest quality equipment and personal care supplies.
3. Ask the patients for feedback and promptly act upon their inputs.
4. Tell patients how much you appreciate their business.
5. Call regular patients by their first names.
6. Send thank you notes.
7. Offer free new product and service samples.
8. Change displays and sales presentations on a regular basis.
9. Practice good phone etiquette
10. Respond to complaints promptly.
11. Reward referrals.
12. Publish a monthly opt-in direct response newsletter with customized content, dependent on recipient stated information preferences .
13. Develop and publish a list of frequently asked questions.
14. Issue Preferred Patient Membership Cards.
15. Hold informational seminars and workshops.
16. Run contests.
17. Develop service contracts.
18. Provide an emergency hotline number.
19. Publish code of ethics and our service guarantees.

20. Publish all patient reviews.
21. Help patients to make accurate competitor comparisons
22. Build a stay-in-touch (drip marketing) communications calendar.
23. Keep marketing communications focused on our competitive advantages.
24. Offer repeat user discounts and incentives.
25. Be supportive and encouraging, and not judgmental.
26. Measure patient retention and look at recurring revenue and patient surveys.
27. Build a community of shared interests by offering a website forum or discussion group for professionals and patients to allow sharing of knowledge.
28. By creating forums around certain health concerns, targeted messages and promotions can be sent to a relevant group.
29. Offer benefits above and beyond those of our competitors.
30. Selective product discounts and special product offers from our partners.
31. Reminder emails and holiday gift cards.

We will also consider the following Patient Retention Programs:

Type of Program	Patient Rewards
Frequency Purchase Loyalty Program	Special Discounts
	Free Product or Services
Rebate Loyalty Programs	Credit Based on Percent of
	Incremental Sales from Prior Period.
'Best Patient' Program	Special Recognition/Treatment/Offers
Auto-Knowledge Building Programs	Purchase Recommendations based
	On Past Transaction History
Profile Building Programs	Recommendations Based on Stated
	Patient Profile Information.

6.5.2   Sales Forecast

Our sales projections are based on the following:
1. Actual sales volumes of local competitors.
2. Interviews with Medical Marijuana Dispensary owners and managers.
3. Observations of Medical Marijuana Dispensary sales and traffic at competitor establishments.
4. Government and industry trade statistics.
5. Local population demographics and projections.
6. Discussions with suppliers.

Our sales forecast is an estimated projection of expected sales over the next three years, based on our chosen marketing strategy, government reimbursement rates and assumed competitive environment. Sales are expected to be below average during the first year, until a regular patient base has been established. It has been estimated that it takes the average Medical Marijuana Dispensary business a minimum of two years to establish a significant patient base. After the patient base is built, sales will grow at an accelerated rate from word-of-mouth referrals and continued networking efforts.

We expect sales to steadily increase as our marketing campaign, employee training programs and contact management system are executed. By using advertising, especially discounted introductory coupons, as a catalyst for this prolonged process, _____ (company name) plans to attract more patients sooner.

Throughout the first year, it is forecasted that sales will incrementally grow until profitability is reached toward the end of year _____ (one?). Year two reflects a conservative growth rate of _____ (20?) percent. Year three reflects a growth rate of _____ (25?) percent. We expect to be open for business on _____ (date), and start with an initial enrollment of _____ (#) students. With our unique product and service offerings, along with our thorough and aggressive marketing strategies, we believe that sales forecasts are actually on the conservative side.

In our first year of operation, we plan to net more than $_____ (700,000?), assuming _____ (1.6?) ounces per patient per month and a price of $_____ (4,800?) per pound. Projected revenue is $_____ (9.8 million?) for 2018, reaching $_____ (19?) million by 2019. The dispensary plans to reach a peak patient level of _____ (3,200?) in _____ (2019?).

Table: Sales Forecast	Annual Sales		
Sales	**2017**	**2018**	**2019**
Cannabis Sales			
Edible Sales			
Seminars/Workshops			
Consulting			
Weight/Stress Programs			
Health/Wellness Coaching			
Miscellaneous			
Total Unit Sales			
Direct Cost of Sales:			
Cannabis Sales			
Edible Sales			
Seminars/Workshops			
Consulting			
Weight/Stress Programs			
Health/Wellness Coaching			
Miscellaneous			
Subtotal Direct Cost of Sales			

6.6 Merchandising Strategy

Merchandising is that part of our marketing strategy that is involved with promoting the sales of our merchandise, as by consideration of the most effective means of selecting, pricing, displaying, and advertising items for sale in our child care business.

We will develop a merchandising strategy to sell health related products to our patients. We will strive to feature merchandise that is not found in competitor stores and use proper and informative signage to help sell merchandise. We plan to group similar types of merchandise together for maximum visual appeal. Product presentation will be designed to lead the patients through the entire display area.

We will monitor our sales figures and data to confirm that products in demand are well-stocked and slow moving products are phased-out. We will improve telephone skills of employees to boost phone orders.

To illustrate our cost competitiveness on selected educational products, we will use signs to compare our prices to those of the local discount store. This will also help to develop the patient's trust in the competitive pricing of all of our products and services.

We will create merchandising displays that will attract patients by:
   Choosing market appropriate merchandise.
   Strategically positioning, designing and mapping displays.
   Inventory tracking and control.
   Working with vendors to promote their products in-house.
   Training our staff to cross-sell and up-sell products.
   Setting the retail stage to encourage impulse sales
   Planning our displays to convey a branded message.
   Using lighting as a key accent factor.
   Organizing the retail products into themed groupings.
   Developing the visual layout and design of the retail area
   Selecting attractive and informative signage.
   Using the right mix of packaging, displays, POP media, and couponing.

We will encourage impulse purchases with the use of descriptive adjectives in our signage. We will attach our own additional business labels to all products to promote our line of services and location.

6.7 Pricing Strategy

Our pricing strategy will take into view the following factors:
1.   Our firm's overall marketing and positioning objectives
2.   Patient demand
3.   Service quality attributes
4.   Competitor's Pricing
5.   Market and Economic Trends.

6. Level of Operating Expenses
7. Desired Profit Margin
8. Number of Regional Dispensaries
9. Prices in Local Black Markets.

Research indicates that a pound of "pharmaceutical-grade" marijuana costs about $1,000 to produce and sells for $7,500 at retail prices.

All of our top shelf house favorites will be just $80 per 1/4 ounce or $160 per 1/2 ounce. Plus, members will get an additional $10 off middle shelf 1/4 ounces.

Sample Price Lists and Menus
1. http://www.rivercityphoenix.info/menu
2. http://www.thecliniccolorado.com/menus/caphill-menu

The company estimates that each of the patients it expects to serve will consume an ounce per month, at an estimated cost of $_____ (325?) per ounce, though it also expects to provide significant hardship discounts to ____ (20?) percent of its customer base.

The price of the marijuana — $_____ (5,200?) per pound — is designed to roughly match the black market, thus presumably reducing the temptation for people to resell it. The company anticipates needing ____ (700?) pounds in the first year and ____ (1600) pounds in the second, basing that on attracting _____ (1,550?) patients in its first year of operation and _____ (3,000?) by the second. By year three, the company expects to have _____ (3,800?) patients, or ____ (1?) percent of the population in its target region of _____ County).

We will consider the following basic pricing strategies:

Quantity Discounts:	Bulk purchase breaks to increase sales volume.
Bundling Discounts:	Additive deal sweetners to differentiate product offering.
Version Pricing:	Degree of functionality pricing, from Basic to Premium
Loss Leaders	Attract first-time patient deals
Competitive Pricing	Reference point for product positioning.
Targeted Special Discounts:	For seniors, active military and students.
Time of Day/Week Discounts	Dependant on slow time of day or day of the week.
Continuity Discounts	Monthly automatic purchase plans for members.
Automatic Price Reductions	Monthly automatic markdowns of unsold merchandise.

Price List Comparison

Competitor	Service/Product	Our Price	Competitor Price	B/(W) Competitor

Resources:

Price of Weed	www.priceofweed.com

BudShark   www.budshark.com

A website dedicated to being the first medical marijuana price comparison engine. Utilizing public domain data, BudShark aims to provide its audience of medical marijuana patients with the ability to search by price, quantity, and proximity.

Pricing Options

The objective of our Medical Marijuana Dispensary pricing strategy is to achieve success by finding the price point where we can maximize sales and profits. We will use a variety of pricing strategies, depending upon our own unique marketing goals and objectives, product life cycle and competitor responses. We will consider the following pricing strategies:

1. **Premium Pricing**

   Premium pricing strategy will establish a price higher than our competitors. It's a strategy that will be effectively used when there is something unique about the service, or when a product is first to market and the business has a distinct competitive advantage. Premium pricing will be a good strategy when entering the market with a new exclusive product or service and hoping to maximize revenue during the early stages of the product's life cycle.

2. **Penetration Pricing**

   A penetration pricing strategy will be designed to capture market share by entering the market with a low price relative to our competition to attract buyers. The idea is that the business will be able to raise awareness and get people to try the product. Even though penetration pricing may initially create a loss for our company, the hope is that it will help to generate word-of-mouth and create awareness amid a crowded market category.

3. **Price Skimming**

   Only businesses that have a significant competitive advantage can enter the market with a price skimming strategy designed to gain maximum revenue advantage before other competitors begin offering similar products or service alternatives. This will be appropriate if we can develop a unique new service, such as at home Medical Marijuana Dispensary services.

4. **Psychological Pricing**

   Psychological pricing will be a commonly used strategy in the prices we establish for our products and services. For instance, $99 is psychologically "less" in the minds of consumers than $100. It's a minor distinction that can make a big difference.

We will adopt the following pricing guidelines:

1..   We must insure that our price plus service equation is perceived to be an exceptional value proposition.
2.   We must refrain from competing on price, but always be price competitive.
3.   We must develop value-added services, and bundle those with our products to create offerings that cannot be easily price compared.
4.   We must focus attention on our competitive advantages.
5.   Development of a pricing strategy based on our market positioning strategy, which is _____ (mass market value leadership/exceptional premium niche value?)

6.	Our pricing policy objective, which is to _____ (increase profit margins/ achieve revenue maximization to increase market share/lower unit costs).
7.	We will use marketplace intelligence and gain insights from competitor pricing strategy comparisons.
8.	We will solicit pricing feedback from patients using surveys and informal interviews.
9.	We will utilize limited time pricing incentives to penetrate niche markets
10.	We will conduct experiments at prices above and below the current price to determine the price elasticity of demand. (Inelastic demand or demand that does not decrease with a price increase, indicates that price increases may be feasible.)
11.	We will keep our offerings and prices simple to understand and competitive, based on market intelligence.

Determining the costs of servicing business is the most important part of covering our expenses and earning profits. We will factor in the following pricing formula:

Materials + Overhead + Labor + Profit = Price
Materials are those items consumed in the delivering of the service.
Overhead costs are the variable and fixed expenses that must be covered to stay in business. Variable costs are those expenses that fluctuate including vehicle expenses, rental expenses, utility bills and supplies. Fixed costs include the purchase of equipment, service ware, marketing and advertising, and insurance. After overhead costs are determined, the total overhead costs are divided among the total number of transactions forecasted for the year.
Labor costs include the costs of performing the services. Also included are Social Security taxes (FICA), vacation time, retirement and other benefits such as health or life insurance. To determine labor costs per hour, keep a time log. When placing a value on our time, we will consider the following: 1) skill and reputation; 2) wages paid by employers for similar skills and 3) where we live. Other pricing factors include image, inflation, supply and demand, and competition.
Profit is a desired percentage added to our total costs. We will need to determine the percentage of profit added to each service. It will be important to cover all our costs to stay in business. We will investigate available computer software programs to help us price our services and keep financial data for decision-making purposes. Close contact with patients will allow our company to react quickly to changes in demand.

We will develop a pricing strategy that will reinforce the perception of value to the patient and manage profitability, especially in the face of rising inflation. To ensure our success, we will use periodic competitor and patient research to continuously evaluate our pricing strategy. We intend to review our profit margins every six months.

6.8   Differentiation Strategies

We will use differentiation strategies to develop and market unique products for different patient segments. To differentiate ourselves from the competition, we will focus on the assets, creative ideas and competencies that we have that none of our competitors has. The goal of our differentiation strategies is to be able to charge a premium price for our unique Medical Marijuana Dispensary products and services and/or to promote loyalty and assist in retaining our patients.

Differentiating will mean defining who our perfect target market is and then catering to their needs, wants and interests better than everyone else. It will be about using surveys to determine what's most important to our targeted market and giving it to them consistently. It will not be about being "everything to everybody"; but rather, "the absolute best to our chosen targeted group".

Specific Differentiators will include the following:
1. Being a Certified Specialist in one strain
2. Utilizing state-of-the-art technology to develop a photo ID system.
3. Possessing extensive retailing experience
4. Building an exceptional facility
5. Consistently achieving superior results
6. Having a caring and empathetic personality
7. Giving patient s WOW experience, including a professional patient welcome package.
8. Enabling mobile service convenience and 24/7 online accessibility
9. Calling patients the night of a treatment/procedure to express interest
10. Keeping to the appointment schedule.
11. Remembering patient names and details like they were family
12. Assuring patient fears.
13. Building a visible reputation and recognition around our community
14. Acquiring special credentials or professional memberships
15. Providing added value services, such as taxi service, longer hours, financing plans, and post-op services.

Other Differentiation Strategies
1. Our mobile service is provided out of an eco-friendly transportable dispensary vehicle that was built using natural, green products, methods and materials.
2. We provide patient with selected beverages and a comfortable setting in which to chat with friends, between dispensary treatments.
3. We enrich the dispensary stress reducing experience with the fragrance of aromatherapy candles and the playing of mood-setting music.
4. We will develop a referral program that turns our patients into referral agents.
6. We will use regular patient satisfaction surveys to collect feedback, improvement ideas, referrals and testimonials.
7. We will promote our eco-friendly "green" practices.
8. We will customize our offerings according to the cultural influences, customs, interests and tastes of our local market to create loyalty and increase sales.
9. Low staff turnover rate translates to service consistency.

10. We will develop the expertise to satisfy the needs of targeted market segments with customized and exceptional support services.
11. We will develop a Needs Analysis Worksheet to precisely understand the preferred communications methods and progress reporting mechanisms of the referring professionals and our patients.
12. We will sell a basic line of health related products to become a one-stop resource.
13. We will become a specialty Medical Marijuana Dispensary or dispensary that focuses on a niche or specialty service.
14. We will develop the systems and reputation for delivering consistent patient service.

6.9 Milestones

The Milestones Chart is a timeline that will guide our company in developing and growing our business. It will list chronologically the various critical actions and events that must occur to bring our business to life. We will make certain to assign real, attainable dates to each planned action or event.

_____ (company name) has identified several specific milestones which will function as goals for the company. The milestones will provide a target for achievement as well as a mechanism for tracking progress. The dates were chosen based on realistic delivery times and necessary construction times. All critical path milestones will be completed within their allotted time frames to ensure the success of contingent milestones. The following table will provide a timeframe for each milestone.

Table: Milestones

Milestones	Start Date	End Date	Budget	Responsibility
Business Plan Completion				
Secure Permits/Licenses				
Locate & Secure Space				
Obtain Insurance				
Secure Additional Financing				
Get Start-up Supplies Quotes				
Obtain County Certification				
Purchase Office Equipment				
Renovate Facilities/Vehicles				
Define Marketing Programs				
Install Equipment/Displays				
Technology Systems				
Set-up Accounting System				
Apply for Provider Numbers				
Finalize Media Plan				
Create Facebook Brand Page				

Set up Twitter Account _____

Conduct Blogger Outreach _____

Develop Personnel Plan _____

Develop Staff Training Programs _____

Hire Staff _____

Train Staff _____

Implement Marketing Plan _____

Get Website Live _____

Conduct SEO _____

Form Strategic Alliances _____

Purchase Inventory/Supplies _____

Press Release Announcements _____

Advertise Grand Opening _____

Kickoff Advertising Program _____

Join Community Orgs./Network _____

Conduct Satisfaction Surveys _____

Monitor Social Media Networks _____

Respond to reviews _____

Measure Return on Marketing $$$ _____

Devise Growth Strategy _____

Revenues Exceed $_____ _____

Profitability _____

_____ _____

Totals: _____

7.0 Website Plan Summary

_____ (company name) is currently developing a website at the URL address www. (company name).com. We will primarily use the website to advertise services offered, community activity calendar, present testimonials and helpful articles. We will use email to communicate with patients wishing to sign-up for email specials and our newsletter.

In order to convey a professional image for our medical marijuana dispensary, we will incorporate the following items into our website:

1.   Pictures of our retail dispensary storefront.
2.   Pictures of our friendly and knowledgeable staff.
3.   A contact phone number, directions to our store, store hours and a map.
4.   A complete collection of our medicine and edibles, along with high-end graphics, descriptions of the effects and prices.
5.   Patient testimonials.
6.   Any coupons or current running specials.
7.   An updated blog to dialogue with our community.
8   A Facebook and Twitter page to foster online contact.
9.   A newsletter sign-up request to present patient questions and answers, legislative news alerts, case studies, testimonials and survey results.

The website will be developed eventually to offer customers a product catalog for online orders. The overriding design philosophy of the site will be ease of use. We want to make the process of placing an order as easy and fast as possible thereby encouraging increased sales. We will incorporate special features such as a section that is specific to each customer so the customer can easily make purchases of repeat items. Instead of going through the website every month and locating their monthly needs, the site will capture regularly ordered items for that specific customer, significantly speeding up the ordering process. This ease-of-use feature will help increase sales as customers become more and more familiar with the site and appreciate how easy it is to place an order.

We will also provide multiple incentives to sign-up for various benefits, such as our newsletters and promotional sale notices. This will help us to build an email database, which will supply our automated customer follow-up system. We will create a personalized drip marketing campaign to stay in touch with our customers and prospects.

We will develop our website to be a resource for web visitors who are seeking knowledge and information about the medical uses for cannabis, with a goal to service the knowledge needs of our customers and generate leads. Our home page will be designed to be a "welcome mat" that clearly presents our service offerings and provides links through which visitors can gain easy access to the information they seek. We will use our website to match the problems our customers face with the solutions we offer.

We will use the free tool, Google Analytics (http://www.google.com/analytics), to generate a history and measure our return on investment. Google Analytics is a free tool that can offer insight by allowing the user to monitor traffic to a single website. We will just add the Google Analytics code to our website and Google will give our firm a dashboard providing the number of unique visitors, repeat traffic, page views, etc.

To improve the readability of our website we will organize content in the following ways.

1.	Headlines	2.	Bullet points
3.	Callout text	4.	Top of page summaries

To improve search engine optimization we will maximize the utilization of the following;

1.	Links	2.	Headers
3.	Bold text	4.	Bullets
5.	Keywords	6.	Meta tags

This website will serve the following purposes:

About Us	How We Work/Our Philosophy
State Laws and Regulations	
Contact Us	Patient service contact info
Our Medical Marijuana Dispensary Services	
Pre and Post Treatment Instructions	By specific procedure.
Promotions	Specials
Schedule an Appointment	Medical Marijuana Dispensary
Booking Form	
Make a Payment	PayPal
Online Product Catalog	
Frequently Asked Questions	FAQs
Ask Dr. _____ a Question	Form
Management Team	Resumes
Newsletter Sign-up	Mailing List
Newsletter Archives	
Article Archive	Dispensary Treatment Benefits
Are You Ready?	Motivation Checklist
Purchase Gift Certificate	Form
Our Competitive Advantages	
Upcoming Events	Seminar/Community Schedule
Testimonials	With Patient Photos
Facilities Photo Gallery	Photos/Video Tour
Referral Program	Details
Get Directions	Location directions.
Patient Satisfaction Survey	Feedback
Hours of Operation	
Our Policies	
Press Releases	Community Involvement
Strategic Alliance Partners	Links
Our Blog	Center diary/Accept comments

Refer-a-Friend
YouTube Video Clips
Patient Forms
Code of Ethics
Terms and Conditions
Glossary of Terms
Privacy Policy
Mission Statement
Career Opportunities
Classified Ads

Viral marketing
Seminar Presentation/Testimonials
Treatment Consent/Medical History

Classified Ads

By joining and incorporating a classified ad affiliate program into our website, we will create the ultimate win-win-win. We will provide our guests with a free benefit, increase our rankings with the search engines by incorporating keyword hyperlinks into our site, attract additional markets to expose to our product, create an additional income source as they upgrade their ads, and provide our prospects a reason to return to our web site again and again

Resources:

App Themes	www.appthemes.com/themes/classipress/
e-Classifieds	http://www.e-classifieds.net/
Noah's Classifieds	http://www.noahsclassifieds.org/
Joom Prod	http://www.joomprod.com/
Flynax	http://www.flynax.com/
Market Grabber	http://www.marketgrabber.com/

7.1 Website Marketing Strategy

Our online marketing strategy will employ the following distinct mechanisms:

1. Search Engine Submission

    This will be most useful to people who are unfamiliar with _____ (company name), but are looking for a local Medical Marijuana Dispensary. There will also be searches from patients who may know about us, but who are seeking additional information.

2. Website Address (URL) on Marketing Materials

    Our URL will be printed on all marketing communications, business cards, letterheads, faxes, and invoices and product labels. This will encourage a visit to our website for additional information

3. Online Directories Listings

    We will make an effort to list our website on relevant, free and paid online directories and manufacturer website product locators.

    The good online directories possess the following features:

    Free or paid listings that do not expire and do not require monthly renewal.

Ample space to get your advertising message across.

Navigation buttons that are easy for visitors to use.

Optimization for top placement in the search engines based on keywords that people typically use to find Medical Marijuana Dispensary.

Direct links to your website, if available.

An ongoing directory promotion campaign to maintain high traffic volumes to the directory site.

4. Strategic Business Partners

We will use a Business Partners page to cross-link to prominent _____ (city) area dance web sites as well as the city Web sites and local recreational sites. We will also cross-link with brand name suppliers.

5. YouTube Posting

We will produce a video of testimonials from several of our satisfied patients and educate viewers as to the range of our services and products. Our research indicates that the YouTube video will also serve to significantly improve our ranking with the Google Search Engine.

6. Exchange of links with strategic marketing partners.

We will cross-link to non-profit businesses that accept our gift certificate donations as in-house run contest prize awards.

7. E-Newsletter

Use the newsletter sign-up as a reason to collect email addresses and limited profiles, and use embedded links in the newsletter to return readers to website.

8. Create an account for your photos on flickr.com

We will use the name of our site on flickr so we have the same keywords. To take full advantage of Flickr, we will use a JavaScript-enabled browser and install the latest version of the Macromedia Flash Player.

9. Geo Target Pay Per Click (PPC) Campaign

Available through Google Adwords program. Example keywords include health, marijuana, medical marijuana, cooperative, dispensary, pot, legal weed, alternative medicine and _____ (city).

10. Post messages on Internet user groups and forums.

Get involved with Medical Marijuana Dispensary related discussion groups and forums and develop a descriptive signature paragraph.

Ex: http://www.marijuana.com/forums/

11. Write up your own LinkedIn.com and Facebook.com profiles.

Highlight your background and professional interests.

12. Facebook.com Brand-Building Applications:

As a Facebook member, we will create a specific Facebook page for our business through its "Facebook Pages" application. This page will be used to promote who we are and what we do. We will use this page to post alerts when we have new articles to distribute, news to announce, etc. Facebook members can then become fans of our page and receive these updates on their newsfeed as we post them. We will create our business page by going to the "Advertising" link on the bottom of our personal Facebook page. We will choose the "Pages" tab at the top of that page, and then choose "Create a Page." We will upload our logo, enter our company profile details, and establish our settings. Once completed, we will click the "publish your site" button to go live. We will also promote our Page everywhere we can. We will add a Facebook link to our website, our email signatures, and email newsletters. We will also add Facebook to the marketing mix by deploying pay-per-click ads through their advertising application. With Facebook advertising, we will target by specifying sex, age, relationship, location, education, as well as specific keywords. Once we specify our target criteria, the tool will tell us how many members in the network meet our target needs.

13. Blog to share our success stories and solicit comments.

Blogging will be a great way for us to share information, expertise, and news, and start a conversation with our patients, the media, potential partners, suppliers, and any other target audiences. Blogging will be a great online marketing strategy because it keeps our content fresh, engages our audience to leave comments on specific posts, improves search engine rankings and attracts links.

Resource: www.blogger.com

7.2 Development Requirements

A full development plan will be generated as documented in the milestones. Costs that _____ (company name) will expect to incur with development of its new website include:

Development Costs

User interface design	$_____ .
Site development and testing	$_____
Site Implementation	$._____

Ongoing Costs

Website name registration	$_____ per year.
Site Hosting	$_____ or less per month.

Site design changes, updates and maintenance are considered part of Marketing.

The site will be developed by _____ (company name), a local start-up company. The user interface designer will use our existing graphic art to come up with the website logo and graphics. We have already secured hosting with a local provider, _____ (business name). Additionally, they will prepare a monthly statistical usage report to analyze and improve web usage and return on investment.

The plan is for the website to be live by _____ (date). Basic website maintenance, including update and data entry will be handled by our staff. Site content, such as images and text will be maintained by _____ (owner name).

In the future, we may need to contract with a technical resource to build the trackable article download and newsletter capabilities.

Resources:
  www.ProResultsInternetMarketing.com
  http://420webpros.com/marijuana-marketing-from-a-to-z-at-420-web-pros/
  http://customadesign.com/discover/
  http://cannadvertising.com/what-we-do/
Model Websites:
http://thefarmco.com/

7.3   Frequently Asked Questions

We will use the following guidelines when developing the frequently asked questions for our the ecommerce section of the website:
1.   Use a Table of Contents: Offer subject headers at the top of the FAQ page with a hyperlink to that related section further down on the page for quick access.
2.   Group Questions in a Logical Way and group separate specific questions related to a subject together.
3.   Be Precise With the Question: Don't use open-ended questions.
4.   Avoid Too Many Questions: Publish only the popular questions and answers.
5.   Answer the Question with a direct answer.
6.   Link to Resources When Available: via hyperlinks so the patient can continue with self-service support.
7.   Use Bullet Points to list step-by-step instructions.
8.   Focus on Patient Support and Not Marketing.
9.   Use Real and Relevant Frequently Asked Questions from actual patients.
10.   Update Your FAQ Page as patients continue to communicate questions.

The following frequently asked questions will enable us to convey a lot of important information to our patients in a condensed format. We will post these questions and answers on our website and create a hardcopy version to be included on our sales presentation folder.

How do I obtain the application to register to use medical marijuana?
First download the Physician Recommendation Form and give this to your physician. Second, download the Patient Application form. Attach this to the physician recommendation form and mail to the state's Department of Health.

What are the qualifying medical conditions?

At this time, legislation and regulations allow for the recommendation of medical marijuana for the following:

1.   Human Immunodeficiency Virus (HIV)
2.   Acquired Immune Deficiency Syndrome (AIDS)
3.   Cancer
4.   Glaucoma
5.   Conditions characterized by severe and persistent muscle spasms, such as multiple sclerosis

What are the qualifying medical treatment?

Qualifying medical treatments include any of the following:

1.   Chemotherapy
2.   Use of azidothymidine or protease inhibitors
3.   Radiotherapy

Who may recommend medical marijuana?

A licensed physician in good standing to practice medicine or osteopathy in the state of _____ may recommend the use of medical marijuana to a qualifying patient if the physician:

1.   Is in a bona fide physician-patient relationship with the qualifying patient.
2.   The physician has completed a full assessment of the patient's medical history and current medical condition, including an in-person physical examination, performed not more than ninety (90) days prior to making the recommendation.
3.   Has responsibility for the ongoing care and treatment of the patient, provided that such ongoing treatment shall not be limited to or for the primary purpose of the provision of medical marijuana use or consultation.
4.   Makes the recommendation based upon the physician's assessment of the qualifying patient's.
5.   Medical history and Current medical condition
     Completed a review of other approved medications and treatments that might provide the qualifying patient with relief from a qualifying medical condition or the side effects of a qualifying medical treatment.

How much medical marijuana can I purchase?

Members are permitted to purchase up to two (2) ounces of medical cannabis per month in raw or edible form. They are not permitted to grow it themselves.

What are your business hours?

We will have the capacity to operate 7 days a week during normal business hours (9AM to 6PM) pending available supply. Please contact us to schedule an appointment.
Examples:
https://essencevegas.com/faqs/

7.4   Website Performance Summary

We will use web analysis tools to monitor web traffic, such as identifying the number of site visits. We will analyze patient transactions and take actions to minimize problems, such as incomplete sales and abandoned shopping carts. We will use the following table to track the performance of our website:

Category	2017		2018		2019	
	Fcst	Act	Fcst	Act	Fcst	Act
No. of Patients						
New Subscribers						
Unique Visitors						
Total Page Views						
Bounce Rate						
Avg. Time on Site						
Page Views/Visit						
No. of Products						
Product Categories						
Number of Incomplete Sales						
Conversion Rate						
Affiliate Sales						
Patient Satisfaction Score						

7.5 Website Retargeting/Remarketing

Research indicates that for most websites, only 2% of web traffic converts readers on the first visit. Retargeting will keep track of people who have visited our website and displays our ads to them as they browse online. This will bring back 98% of users who don't convert right away by keeping our brand at the top of their mind. Setting up a remarketing tracking code on our website will allow us to target past visitors who did not convert or take the desired action on our site. After people have been to our website and are familiar with our brand, we will 'market more aggressively to this 'warm traffic.'

Resource:
www.marketing360.com/remarketing-software-retargeting-ads/

8.0 Operations Plan

Operations include the business aspects of running our business, such as conducting quality assessment and improvement activities, auditing functions, cost-management analysis, and patient service.

Our operations plan will present an overview of the flow of the daily activities of the business and the strategies that support them. It will focus on the following critical operating factors that will make the business a success:

1.   We will enjoy the following advantages in the sourcing of our inventory:

     _____

2.   We will utilize the following technological innovations in the patient relationship management (CRM) process:

     _____

3.   We will make use of the following advantages in our distribution process:

     _____

4.   We will develop the following in-house training program to improve staff productivity: _____

5.   We will utilize the following system to better control inventory shrinkage and carrying costs.

     _____

6.   We will implement the following quality control plan:

     _____

Quality Control Plan
Our Quality Control Plan will include a review process that checks all factors involved in our operations. The main objectives of our quality control plan will be to uncover defects and bottlenecks, and reporting to management level to make the decisions on the improvement of the whole production process. Our review process will include the following activities:

Quality control checklist	Finished service review
Structured walkthroughs	Statistical sampling
Testing process	

Operations Planning
We will use Microsoft Visio to develop visual maps, which will piece together the different activities in our organization and show how they contribute to the overall "value stream" of our business. We will rightfully treat operations as the lifeblood of our business. We will develop a combined sales and operations planning process where sales and operations managers will sit down every month to review sales, at the same time creating a forward-looking 12-month rolling plan to help guide the product development and manufacturing processes, which can become disconnected from sales. We will approach our operations planning using a three-step process that analyzes the company's current state, future state and the initiatives it will tackle next. For each initiative, such as launching a new product or service, the company will examine the related financials, talent and operations needs, as well as target customer profiles. Our management team

will map out the cost of development and then calculate forecasted return on investment and revenue predictions.

Our dispensary operations plan will include the following:

1. Patient ID Verification and Care Procedures
2. Cultivation Production safeguards
3. Controls on Edibles, Concentrates & Tinctures
4. Non-Diversion and Inventory Controls
5. Product Labeling standards, including amount of CBD in products.
6. Patient Recordkeeping formats and sign-offs
7. Business Reporting and Recordkeeping Guidelines
8. Safety and Security Documented Procedures
9. End-of-day register reconcilement procedures
10. Use of approved scales.
11. Us of child-resistant containers
12. Marijuana testing procedures
13. Entranceway Video Surveillance with 30 day retention file
14. Display of Registration Certificate

Other Operating Basics

1. Comply with the state regulations on the product.
2. Pay your taxes.
3. Acquire a reliable team of investors.
4. Have enough capital to make and maintain an active supply of marijuana.
5. Don't put out an inferior product.
6. Don't put your dispensary in a location where it won't be wanted (i.e. near schools, community centers, parks or day care facilities).
7. Have a good, strong security system to protect your product from thieves.
8. Hire someone with the experience to handle the purchasing.
   Note: Knowing how to identify good marijuana is crucial because testing it requires skills. Making sure marijuana is good for customers involves touch, odor and a visual examination via microscope.

Inventory Grow Controls

Every single leaf will be accounted for in our Clinic's operation under the seed- to-sale law. To track each plant, we will use a tag that includes patient ID, dispensary ID, strain information and the date it was planted. The tag will stay with the plant from harvest to drying, packaging and delivery. Keeping daily, weekly and quarterly records that analyze the grow locations, strains and yields will be useful in helping our business to determine best practices and how to successfully run the business. We will use grow software called MJ Freeway that organizes and tracks all of the information once a plant is harvested. Resource:

MJ Freeway Software   **www.mjfreeway.com**
Custom POS, patent-pending Inventory, Sales and Grow tools: GramTracker®, MixTracker™ & GrowTracker®.

Patient Education Plan

As a dispensary owner, we will be committed to providing patients accurate information regarding the health effects of medical marijuana. Patient education and support will be essential to achieving overall patient wellness. With our well-designed and well-delivered education and support program, each patient will learn about important legal and medical aspects of medical cannabis.

Topics will include the following:
1. Patient Education Overview
2. Research and medicinal Effects Tracking
3. Substance Abuse and Misuse
4. Patient Handbook
5. Patient Welcome
6. Patient Guidelines to Stay Safe and Healthy
7. Patient's Rights
8. Medical Marijuana Law Overview
9. Patient Services
10. Guide to Using Marijuana
11. Dosage, Potency and Tolerance
12. Side Effects of Using Marijuana
13. Sativa vs. Indica
14. Understanding Edibles

Patient Recordkeeping Plan

To protect patient confidentiality, many medical marijuana states require performance standards and guidelines to be met. Concerns of patient privacy require medical marijuana dispensary and cultivation owners to be more careful than ever before. For instance, records should not be kept under patients' names, but under their state or city medical cannabis ID number or an assigned dispensary membership number if they do not have a state or city ID. The dispensary should track when members' recommendations or IDs expire to avoid providing cannabis to ineligible patients. Records should be kept on all patient consultations in which the patient's health and cannabis use are discussed.

There are many other requirements this plan discusses, including:
1. Patient Recordkeeping Handbook
2. Privacy, Confidentiality and Information Security
3. Record Retention Policies
4. Record Review and Quality Assurance
5. Documentation Handling
6. Staff Training
7. HIPAA Compliance

Source: http://dispensarypermits.com/dispensary-plans/qualifying-patient-record-keeping-plan

To keep our dispensary license in good standing, we will adhere to the following legal guidelines for operating a legitimate medical marijuana dispensary:

1. Operate as a non-profit organization
2. Collect sales tax from all patients.
3. Only dispense to qualified patients and caregivers.
4. Don't sell other prescription drugs, unless licensed to do so.
5. Obtain cannabis stock from qualified growers and distributors only.
6. Follow the attorney general guidelines for our State.
7. Keep complete and accurate records of our marijuana dispensary's compliance with all laws and regulations.
8. Set up an automated dispensing machine for patients, to insure our facility is following all of the above rules and regulations.

Inventory Control Plan

The tracking and control of inventory will be essential to all aspects of our medical marijuana cultivation and dispensing, from keeping products and the facility secure to fulfilling our compassionate mission. While preventing opportunities for diversion, this plan will detail ways to provide a steady supply of high-quality marijuana to meet the medical needs of patients. The goal of inventory control will be to create a wholly transparent process of production and distribution so that at any time the condition and quantity of every product, regardless of its production stage, will be documented. This will allow exceptional quality of cannabis while avoiding over- or underproduction, and allowing detection and prevention of any misallocation or theft.

The goals of our inventory policies and procedures will be as follows:

1. Ensuring product integrity for patients
2. Preventing internal or external product diversion
3. Complying with Department regulations
4. Tracking key statistics related to patients, products, and business

There will four components to our comprehensive inventory control system:

1. Well-trained and well-supervised staff
2. State-of-the-art electronic inventory tracking
3. Information security
4. Rigorous operational protocols of management, oversight, and accountability

Cultivation Plan

The cultivation plan covers a comprehensive hydroponic growing process. The entire plant growth process will be illustrated in diagrams that cover the various stages of a cannabis plant's development as it travels down the supply chain from seed to sale.

The cultivation overview includes a detailed explanation of each stage of the plant production and supply chain process, including:

1. Breeding (if applicable)
2. Cloning
3. Vegetation

4. Flowering
5. Harvesting & Drying
6. Trimming
7. Curing
8. Packaging
9. Distribution

The Cultivation Plan describes the technology and facility designs to simplify and streamline the hydroponic growing process. The hydroponic design content will describe today's advanced indoor growing systems for sustainable plant production. While there are many different ways to grow, the primary cultivation method our Cultivation Plan describes is a hydroponic drip system. This method gives a plant exactly what it needs, when it needs it, in the amount that it needs, allowing the plant to be as healthy as is genetically possible while also meeting sustainability objectives.

The hydroponic design section will include topics on:
1. Hydroponic Facility Setup
2. Innovative Growing Systems
3. Advanced Lighting Setups
4. Organic Nutrients & Additives
5. Organic Growing Medium
6. Non-Harmful Pest & Disease Control
7. Environmental Controls
8. Irrigation Systems & Controls
9. Propagation & Cloning
10. Post Harvest

Automation Grow Insights
Includes everything from the biologicals used in the living soil to AutoPot watering and LED lighting systems.
Resource:
www.cannabisbusinesstimes.com/article/10-questions-with-demetri-kouretas--kevin-
    biernacki-august-2017/

Security Plan

We will develop a comprehensive cultivation and dispensary Security Plan for protecting our equipment, inventory, products, and more importantly, your people. There are added security challenges that medical marijuana dispensaries face, so our Security Plan considers many policies, procedures, and systems that provide sufficient protection. The Security Plan will be divided into two main sections: Facility Security and Operational Security. Both categories are designed to minimize security exposure and prevent breaches before they even occur. However, in the event that preventative measures fail, the Operational Security Plan is designed to quickly observe, monitor, protect, counter and report any situations that do occur.

Our Facility Security Plan will include the following:

1. Location and Site Security Characteristics
2. Secured Employee Parking
3. Around the Clock Coverage
4. Security Systems
5. Maintenance of Security Systems
6. Access Control / Ingress & Egress
7. Perimeter Security
8. Product Security

Our Operational Security Plan will include the following:
1. Security Threats & Contingency Planning
2. Transactional Security
3. Delivery Security
4. Human Resource Policies
5. Employee Security Training
6. Inventory Control
7. Guest, Media & Visitor Procedures
8. Neighborhood Involvement
9. Emergency Response

Fire Safety Plan

We will develop a comprehensive cultivation and dispensary Fire Plan for protecting our equipment, inventory, products, and more importantly, our people. There are added security challenges that medical marijuana dispensaries face, so our Fire Plan considers many policies, procedures, and systems that provide sufficient protection. The Security Plan will be divided into two main sections: Preventive Safety Measures and Fire Suppression. Both categories are designed to minimize fire exposure and prevent breaches before they even occur.

Our Dispensary Fire Plan will include the following:
1. Going Beyond Code Requirements
2. Ensuring Electrical Safety
3. Good Housekeeping and Site Maintenance
4. Adequate Complying with State and Local Fire Codes
5. Signs and Notification for Hazardous Materials
6. Fire Safety Training and Drills
7. Effective Emergency Response Plans

Our Fire Suppression Plan will include the following:
1. Fire Risk Survey
2. Fire Protection Checklist
3. Exits Checklist
4. Flammable and Combustable Material Checklist
5. Evaluation of Independent Fire Consultant

The marijuana will be grown under 600-watt sodium lights inside a _____ (#)-square-foot facility in _____ (city) by a team led by a University of _____ biology graduate with _____ (#) years of cultivation experience at a similar site in _____ State). Each plant's growth will be tracked by computer software.

After it has been grown and cut, the marijuana will be tested for bacteria, mold and heavy metals, in addition to its potential medicinal benefits. Any plant that doesn't make the grade will be ground down and mixed with a material like paper, plastic or cardboard, then sent to a solid waste facility.

Much of the marijuana will be sold as is, but some of it will be converted into products such as tinctures or baked goods like cookies, chocolates or granola bars, all made with marijuana-infused butter. The goods will be packaged in child-proof, opaque containers devoid of any images except the dispensary's logo, which does not resemble marijuana or related paraphernalia.

From _____ (city), the products will be brought to the dispensary in _____ (city) by professional guards in an unmarked van with a security compartment, or directly to the patient via a home-delivery program.

Control Costs

We will implement the following cost of goods profit controls and manage them consistently to have a profound impact on the profitability of the business.

1. **Systematize Ordering** This means that the operation has an organized practice of procuring products each day. Components of that system include order guides, par levels, count sheets, inventory counts, a manager in charge of all procurement and a prime vendor relationship to reduce price and product fluctuations.
2. **Check It In.** We will assign a teammate to check in every product that comes through the door using an organized process of time and date specific delivery windows. We will not only check product count but also vigorously demand and inspect the consistency of product quality and product price.
3. **Store it well.** We will manage against profit erosion through theft, spoilage and other mishandling issues. We will ensure that each product has a specific home, that each product is labeled, that products are stored using the first-in, first-out storage method to ensure quality rotation and that products are locked and put away until they are needed.
4. **Standardize.** We will create process standards that can be duplicated through consistent training and management of staff members.
5. **Manage the Cash Flow.** We will follow a strict process whereby every item that is sold is accounted for and paid for by the end-user. We will carefully manage voided checks.

Inventory Controls

We will develop a consistent and proper inventory control method. To simplify the process of taking inventory, inventory controls will be instituted. Storage space will be locked and the keys kept in only the hands of the owner or manager. Whenever product must be removed from this storage to be put in display, a register of this transaction will be kept. In this way, the periodic inventory process will not require a recount of items in the secure storage area. To reduce counting errors when taking inventory, we will count items in the same order each time and use a standard form or worksheet to note items. To make the process faster, the worksheet will be organized in the same order as items on display, or even in a visual representation of the display shelves. Taking care to have a standard inventory method, carried out by the same person each time, will reduce errors and the waste of time associated with double-checking inventory.

We will conduct a quality improvement plan, which consists of an ongoing process of improvement activities and includes periodic samplings of activities not initiated solely in response to an identified problem. Our plan will be evaluated annually and revised as necessary. Our patient satisfaction survey goal is a 98.0% satisfaction rating.

We will use the Patient Needs Analysis Worksheet, as provided in the appendix, to precisely document patient needs and specifications, preferences, and time and budget constraints.

We also plan to develop a list of specific interview questions and a worksheet to evaluate, compare and pre-screen potential suppliers. We will also check vendor references and their rating with the Hoovers.com.

Before opening our medical marijuana dispensary, we will assemble the following plans to ensure the consistent management of our business: (select)
1.   Business Plan
2.   Patient Education Plan
3.   Patient Evaluation Plan
4.   Cultivation Plan
5.   Supply Sourcing Plan
6.   Product Safety Plan
7.   Security Plan
8.   Inventory Control Plan
9.   Financial Plan
10.   Staffing Plan
11.   Operations Plan
12.   Environmental Plan

We plan to write and maintain an operations manual and a personnel policies handbook. The Operating Manual will be a comprehensive document outlining virtually every aspect of the business. The operating manual will include management and accounting procedures, hiring and personnel policies, and daily operations procedures, such as opening and closing the store, and how to __. The manual will cover the following topics:

- Community Relations   - Patient Relations
- Media Relations   - Employee Relations
- Vendor Relations   - Government Relations

- Competition Relations
- Environmental Concerns
- Intra Company Procedures
- Banking and Credit Cards
- Computer Procedures
- Quality Controls
- Open/Close Procedures
- Software Documentation
- Clinical Policies and Procedures
- Intake Questionnaire
- Job descriptions
- Employee Regulations
- Non-Compete Agreements
- Equipment Maintenance Checklist
- Inventory Controls
- Accounting and Billing
- Financing
- Scheduling Tips
- Safety Procedures
- Security Procedures
- HIPAA manuals and staff training,
- Treatment Instructions
- Consent Forms.
- Employee Manual
- Ind. Contractor Agreements
- Employee Appraisal Program

We plan to create the following business manuals:

Manual Type		Key Elements
1.	Operations Manual	Process flowcharts
2.	Employee Manual	Benefits/Appraisals/Practices
3.	Managers Manual	Job Descriptions
4.	Customer Service Policies	Inquiry Handling Procedures

Our plan is to automate our sales process, by developing an online registration calculator. We plan to adapt Quickbooks to track product inventory and sales. The plan is to place special emphasis on using technology to make the transaction with patients more efficient and to accept a wide range of automatic credit and debit card options. All systems are computer based and allow for accurate off-premises control of all aspects of our service business.

We plan to purchase a P.O.S. Software Package that will help us to accomplish the following objectives:
1. Speed our order entry and database build processes.
2. Assist in sales forecasting
3. Allow us to provide a higher level of patient service.
4. Lower our inventory costs.
5. Improve overall operational efficiency.

Software Options

Quickbooks	//quickbooks.intuit.com/product/accounting-software/
Scheduling Software	www.netwaveonlinescheduling.com/
Dispensary Finder Management Software	www.dispensary-booker.com/
Orchid Medical Marijuana Dispensary Software	www.medicaldispensarysoftware.com/

8.1 Operational Security Measures

Note: Several states require that every licensed medical marijuana facility must have a closed-circuit security alarm system on all perimeter entry points and perimeter windows installed by an alarm installation company approved by the enforcement division. The surveillance has to be done by a security company that must also be authorized by state regulators. Medical marijuana businesses also have to put in motion detectors, pressure switches, and panic alarms.

Our dispensary will abide by strict state guidelines governing both the security of the facility and how the marijuana is distributed. We will provide adequate security on the premises of a medical marijuana dispensary including, but not limited to, the following:

1. Security surveillance cameras installed to monitor the main entrance along with the interior and exterior of the premises to discourage and to facilitate the reporting and investigation of criminal acts and nuisance activities occurring at the premises.

2. Security video will be preserved for at least seventy-two (72) hours and be made available to law enforcement officers upon demand.

3. A locking safe or secure vault permanently affixed to or built into the premises that is suitable for storage of all of the saleable inventory of marijuana.

4. Exterior windows (without shades) of sufficient size to permit observation of the inside of the dispensary premises by a law enforcement officer standing outside of the dispensary; and

5. Exterior lighting that illuminates the exterior walls of the business.
6. There will be 24-hour-a-day guards every day of the year.
7. An additional a boundary fence around the dispensary for added security.
8. We will verify that all patients must be residents of our state and have a state-issued card issued indicating they are in the state's medical marijuana program.

Resources:
Amcrest Technologies, Inc.   https://amcrest.com/
Offers high-end video surveillance systems.

9.0 Management Summary

The Management Plan will reveal who will be responsible for the various management functions to keep the business running efficiently. It will further demonstrate how that individual has the experience and/or training to accomplish each function. It will address who will do the planning function, the organizing function, the directing function, and the controlling function. We will also develop an employee retention plan because there are distinct cost advantages to retaining employees. It costs a lot to recruit and train a new employee, and in the early days, new employees are a lot less productive. We will need to make sure that our employees are satisfied in order to retain them and, in turn, create satisfied patients.

At the present time _____ (owner name) will run all operations and manage the performance of the dispensary treatments for the _____ (company name) patients.
However, in the future, _____ (company name) plans to outsource support personnel who will aid in the running of the growing number of dispensary parties.

_____ (His/Her) background in _____ (business management?) indicates an understanding of the importance of financial control systems. There is not expected to be any shortage of qualified staff from local labor pools in the market area.

_____ (owner name) will be the owner and operations manager of _____ (company name). His/her general duties will include the following:
1.   Oversee the daily operations
2.   Ordering inventory and supplies.
3.   Develop and implementing the marketing strategy
4.   Purchasing equipment.
5.   Arranging for the routine maintenance and upkeep of the facility.
6.   Teaching therapists and technicians .
7.   Hiring, training and supervision of new instructors.
8.   Scheduling and planning lessons and special events.
9.   Creating and pricing programs and packages.
10.   Managing the accounting/financial aspect of the business.
11.   Contract negotiation/vendor relations.

9.1 Organizational Structure
I.   Owner/President/Executive Director/General Manager
II.   Human Resources Manager
III.   Business Operations Manager/Director
IV.   Sales & Marketing Manager

9.2 Owner Personal History
The owner has been working in the _____ () industry for over ____ (#)

years, gaining personal knowledge and experience in all phases of the industry. _____ (owner name) is the founder and operations manager of _____ (company name). He/she began his/her career as a _____ . Over the last _____ (#) years, _____ (owner name) became quite proficient in a wide range of management activities and responsibilities, becoming an operations manager for _____ (former employer name) from _____ to _____ (dates). There he/she was able to achieve _____.
_____ , owner of _____ (company name), has a ____ degree in _____ . For ____ years he/she has managed a business similar to _____ (company name). _____ (His/her) duties included _____.
Specifically, the owner brings _____ (#) years of experience as a _____ , as well as certification as a _____ from the _____ (National _____ Association). He/she is an experienced entrepreneur with ____ years of small business accounting, finance, marketing and management experience. Education includes college course work in business administration, banking and finance, investments, and commercial credit management.

The owner will draw an annual salary of $_____ from the business although most of this goes to repay loans to finance business start-up costs. These loans will be paid-in-full by _____ (month) of _____ (year).

9.3 Management Team Gaps

Despite the owner's and manager's experience in the _____ (?) industry, the company will also retain the consulting services of _____ (consultant company name). This company has over _____ (#) years of experience in the _____ industry, and has successfully opened dozens of Medical Marijuana Dispensary businesses across the country. The Consultants will be primarily used for certification approval, market research, patient satisfaction surveys and to provide additional input in the evaluation of new business opportunities. The company also expects to retain the services of a local CPA to help the owner manage cash flow. Additionally the business will make use of the following advisory board to provide support for strategic planning and human resource related issues.

The Board of Advisors will provide continuous mentoring support on business matters. Expertise gaps in legal, tax, marketing and personnel will be covered by the Board of Advisors. The owner will actively seek free business advice from SCORE, a national non-profit organization with a local office. This is a group of retired executives and business owners who donate their time to serve as business counselors to new business owners.

_____(company name) will be forming a Community Advisory Board that will include former State Senator _____ and former City Councilor _____ . The board will determine how to disburse extra money earned by the nonprofit, and will also work to curb youth marijuana use and study whether medical marijuana is making its way to people who are not patients.

Advisory Resources Available to the Business Include:

	Name	Address	Phone
CPA/Accountant			
Attorney			
Insurance Broker			
Banker			
Business Consultant			
Wholesale Suppliers			
Trade Association			
Realtor			
SCORE.org			

9.4   Management Matrix

Note: See appendix for attached management resumes.

Name	Title	Credentials Functions	Responsibilities

9.5   Outsourcing Matrix

Company Name	Functions	Responsibilities	Cost

Note: Marketing and public relations will be handled mainly by the owner. If there is a greater need, a marketing consultant will be hired to help issue press releases and generate seminar and website content.

9.6.0   Personnel Plan

Employee Requirements:

1.   Skills and Abilities
Staff must have a high school education, be self-motivating, and have strong patient service skills. All aestheticians that are outsourced will be supervised by company managers and must be licensed by the state.

2.   Recruitment
Experience suggests that postings to our own website and networking via industry contacts are excellent sources for experienced staffers. We will also make effective use of our Newsletter to post positions available. The website www.420careers.com is a marijuana jobs board where employers can post marijuana industry jobs for free, as well is the marijuana classifieds section on this site.

Other resources include:

Hemp Temps	www.hemptemps.com
Craigslist	www.craigslist.org
Canna Jobs	www.cannjobs.com
420 Careers	www.420careers.com

Example:
https://sfbay.craigslist.org/eby/ret/d/medical-marijuana-dispensary/6285044599.html

3.   **Training and Supervision**

We will test our employees, who are not allowed to take drugs other than marijuana, and regularly quiz them on the latest studies and literature about medical marijuana, different strains and their effects.

Training is largely accomplished through hands-on experience with supplemental instruction. Additional knowledge is gained through our policy and operations manuals, and promotional materials. We will foster professional development and independence in all phases of our business. Supervision is task-oriented and the quantity is dependent on the complexity of the job assignment. Employees are called team members because they are part of Team _____ (company name). To help them succeed, employees will receive assistance with certification. They will participate in our written training modules and we will cross-train our staff so they become multi-skilled technicians, able to perform several functions. We will schedule five days of onsite management training and support. During this time the following functional areas of the business will be reviewed with management and the operating team:

- Front Desk Operations
- Sales & Marketing
- Management Training
- Reservations and Appointment Book Management
- Facility Management
- Patient Service

Resource:

Cannabis Career Institute   https://cannabiscareerinstitute.com/

4.   **Salaries and Benefits**

Employees will be basically paid a wage plus commission. Message therapists will receive a starting base rate of $_____ (20.00) per hour. Nail technicians will receive a starting base rate of $ _____ (12.00) per hour. All employees will also be able to keep gratuity earned at each session. Good training and incentives, such as cash bonuses handed out monthly to everyone for reaching goals, will serve to retain good employees. An employee discount of __ percent on personal sales is offered. As business warrants, we hope to put together a benefit package that includes insurance, and paid vacations. The personnel plan also assumes a 5% annual increase in salaries.

9.6.1   Job Description Format

Our job descriptions will adhere to the following format guidelines:

1.	Job Title	2.	Reports to:
3.	Pay Rate	4.	Job Responsibilities
5.	Travel Requirements	5.	Supervisory Responsibilities
6.	Qualifications	7.	Work Experience
8.	Required Skills	10.	Salary Range
11.	Benefits	12.	Opportunities

9.6.2   Job Descriptions

1.   Administrative Director

This position will be held by the owner.

2.   Director of Operations

A leadership position responsible for overall organization and direction of operations and functions according to approved policies, procedures, and standards. Ensures delivery of quality dispensary services to patients, enhancement of business development, and continuous improvement of business efficiency and fiscal success. Must demonstrate strong fiscal planning and management skills.

3.   Administrative Assistant

This position is based on ____ (#) hours per week, reimbursed at $___ per hour.

4.   Receptionist

Provides excellent service to members/guests by answering phone calls, setting appointments, greeting members/guests upon arrival and selling memberships. Assists in administrative tasks including filing, medical patient maintenance, and data entry of patient records as well as various duties as assigned by Dispensary Manager.

Ability to effectively communicate with members/guests on membership benefits, and the dispensary's policies and procedures.

Ability to work cohesively with others in a fun and very fast paced environment.

Must be patient service oriented and able to communicate effectively with patients, dispensary manager and staff.

Handles all phone system, scheduling services, checking in and checking out patients.

Assists patients with gift certificate purchases, product sales and inquiries.

Thoroughly opening and closing of the dispensary.

Maintaining/Restocking/cleaning facility.

6.   Dispensary Manager

The manager must interface with the ownership, staff, law enforcement, vendors and landlords. The main responsibility of the dispensary manager is to coordinate and facilitate the transactions of the dispensary. He must maintain records, maintain contact with the dispensary grow site as well as other grow site, embrace patient education and understand marketing. He/she must train employees and decide which products to carry and determine the best pricing based on market conditions. He/she is responsible for keeping up with all the changes in local and state law regarding operation of the facility. Often, if a dispensary is raided or if an unexpected visit is made the ADHS, the manager will be the one that will have to answer questions during an investigation. The most important job of the dispensary manager is to ensure that only the best and safest quality medicine is available at the dispensary.

Key Duties and Responsibilities:
A. Managing all dispensary staff members including rotas, payroll and staff cover when required
B. Assuming responsibility for recruitment and training of both new and existing staff, organizing participation in external courses and encouraging further qualifications
C. Review salaries, write appraisals and discipline dispensary staff when required
D. Attending and contributing to regular Ownership meetings
E. Regularly checking the market for fluctuations in price, as well as the research for new or discontinued strains, products, etc.
F. Following up changes to product prices, categories and availability with supplier representatives
G. Maintaining a computerized directory for all new strains and for monitoring repeat prescriptions
F. Regular communication with medical doctors and medical director
G. Maintaining stock levels within the dispensary and reordering when necessary
H. Checking inventory for expiry dates, as well maintaining adequate stock control and rotation with suppliers and/or internal grow facility
I. Taking responsibility for invoices, payment and statements
J. Following up outstanding credits and credit notes from returns
K. Performing monthly, quarterly and annual sales reviews and provide suggestions for improvement to Ownership.
L. Prepare value report for end of year accounts
M. Organize regular meetings with suppliers to optimize discounts and achieve the best pricing in the market
N. Overseeing accuracy and efficiency of dispensing staff
O. Taking prescription requests and issuing repeat prescriptions to patients according to agreed time-scale and directions of authorizing Doctor
P. Work with receptionist or administrative staff to ensure that all relevant paperwork, including the declarations are signed by the patient
Q. Ensuring ongoing compliance with ADHS Medical Marijuana Program.
R. Preparation and submission of all required documents annually.
S. Handling returned medication from patients
T. Adhering to practice policies for controlled drugs
U. Disposing of returned or expired controlled drugs according of ADHS

guidelines and Health Authority protocol

V. Taking informed and appropriate action should any drug alert bulletins be received

W. Communicating effectively using email, telephone, fax and face-to-face regarding all enquiries from patients, doctors, hospitals, hospices and suppliers

X. Liaising with members of clinical staff regarding the medication of individual patients

Y. Maintaining safe and hygienic work surfaces within the dispensing with regular cleaning and ensuring all equipment is in a good state of repair

Z. Running a safe working environment free from hazards, maintaining familiarity with ADHS Rules & Regulations

7. Bud Tender

Budtenders are the faces of Medical Marijuana Industry receiving more one on one face time with Patients than recommending physicians. Budtenders assist Medical Marijuana Patients to find the best Cannabinoid Therapy for their ailments. Budtenders have a working knowledge of plant genetics as they have to know the Cannabinoid structure of the medicine and how it best serves the patient to be able to exceed at their job.

Many in the industry are moving away from the traditional title "Bud Tender" onto more service oriented titles such as "Patient Service Representative" or "Patient Consultants". Budtenders are required to have superior patient service skills and the patience to work with people who are in pain and oftentimes short tempered. Budtenders oftentimes assume the role of caregiver as they have extensive conversations with their patients regarding symptoms. Exemplary listening and recording skills are a must.

Budtenders are on the front lines with regards to law enforcement and must have current knowledge of all local policy and state laws to ensure the business is staying in compliance. Budtenders work very closely with Company Compliance Officers to adjust front end policies and procedures in order to work within the letter of the law. Should there be a raid by Federal Officers during business hours, Budtenders must know their rights and that of the business and according to business instruction when speaking with law enforcement.

Budtender Duties may include weighing and packaging, patient consultation, medical recommendation verifications, cash register management, front end office administrative duties and patient record keeping. It is of the utmost importance Budtenders maintain a running knowledge of all new smoking accessories, reasons for using each one and technical knowledge of each product for demonstration purposes.

9.6.3   Personnel Plan

1. We will develop a system for recruiting, screening and interviewing employees.

2. Background checks will be performed as well as reference checks and drug tests.
3. We will develop an technician certification training course.
4. We will keep track of staff scheduling.
5. We will develop patient satisfaction surveys to provide feedback and ideas.
6. We will develop and perform semi-annual employee evaluations.
7. We will "coach" all of our employees to improve their abilities and range of skills.
8. We will employ temporary employees via a local staffing agency to assist with one-time special projects.
9. Each employee will be provided a detailed job description and list of business policies, and be asked to sign these documents as a form of employment contract.
10. Incentives will be offered for reaching quarterly financial and enrollment goals, completing the probationary period, and passing county inspections.
11. Patient service awards will be presented to those employees who best exemplify our stated mission and exceed patient expectations.
12. We will arrange for a pool of substitute therapists to be called upon to fill vacancies.

Our Employee Handbook will include the following sections:
1. Overview
2. Introduction to the Company
3. Organizational Structure
4. Employment and Hiring Policies
5. Performance Evaluation and Promotion Policies
6. Compensation Policies
7. Time Off Policies
8. Training Programs and Reimbursement Policies
9. General Rules and Policies
10. Termination Policies.

The following table summarizes our personnel expenditures for the first three years, with compensation costs increasing from $_____ in the first year to about $_____ in the third year, based on ____ (5?) % payroll increases each year and 100% enrollment. The payroll includes tuition reimbursement, pay increases, vacation pay, bonuses and state required certifications.

9.6.4   Staffing Plan

The personnel plan is included in the following table. It shows the owner's salary and ____ full-time salaries for other key positions. There will be no benefits offered at this time. Everyone but the receptionist will be contract workers, and will be paid a sliding commission scale based on the amount of revenue created.

Table: Personnel

	Number of Employees	Hourly Rate	Annual Salaries		
			2017	2018	2019

Owner/Admin Director _____

Dispensary Manager _____

Chief Medical Officer _____

Nurse Practitioner _____

Compliance & General Counsel _____

Director of Security _____

Addiction Prevention Director _____

Community Outreach Director _____

Head of Cultivating/Dispensing _____

Supervising Physician _____

Horticulturist _____

Bud Tenders/Growers _____

Trimmers _____

MIP Processors _____

Patient education specialist _____

Product dispensers _____

Product control specialist _____

Cashier. _____

Couriers _____

Security guard _____

Inventory control _____

Administrative Assistant _____

Appointment Scheduler _____

Front Desk/Receptionist _____

Patient Service _____

Event Coordinator _____

Marketing Coordinator _____

Bookkeeper _____

Facilities Manager _____

Janitor _____

Total People: Headcount _____

Total Annual Payroll _____

Payroll Burden (Fringe Benefits) (+) _____

Total Payroll Expense (=) _____

Salary Notes:
Starting salaries for management will range from $80,000 to $100,000. Workers on the lower end of the hierarchy will make $40,000 to $45,000. The group's board of directors will determine exact amounts.

10.0   Risk Factors

Risk management is the identification, assessment, and prioritization of risks, followed by the coordinated and economical application of resources to minimize, monitor, and control the probability and/or impact of unfortunate events or to maximize the realization of opportunities. For the most part, our risk management methods will consist of the following elements, performed, more or less, in the following order.

1. Identify, characterize, and assess threats
2. Assess the vulnerability of critical assets to specific threats
3. Determine the risk (i.e. the expected consequences of specific types of attacks on specific assets)
4. Identify ways to reduce those risks
5. Prioritize risk reduction measures based on a strategy

Types of Risks:

_____ (company name) faces certain risks inherent to service business in general and Health care in particular.

1. **Financial Risks**

   Our quarterly revenues and operating results are difficult to predict and may fluctuate significantly from quarter to quarter as a result of a variety of factors. Among these factors are:

   -Changes in our own or competitors' pricing policies.

   - Recession pressures.

   - Fluctuations in expected revenues from advertisers, sponsors and strategic relationships.

   - Timing of costs related to acquisitions or payments.

2. **Legislative / Legal Landscape.**

   Our participation in the medical marijuana arena presents unique risks:

   - Malpractice and other related liability.

   - Federal and State regulations on controls, licensing and insurance.

3. **Operational Risks**

   For the past ___ (#) years the owner has been dealing with computers so he is comfortable with technology and understands a wide array of software applications. However, the biggest potential problem will be equipment malfunction. To minimize the potential for problems, the owner will be taking equipment repair training from the manufacturer and will deal with basic troubleshooting and minor repairs. Beyond that, we have identified a service technician who is located close-by.

   To attract and retain patient to the _____ (company name) community, we must continue to provide differentiated and quality services . This confers certain risks including the failure to:

   - Anticipate and respond to consumer preferences for partnerships and service.

   - Attract, excite and retain a large audience of users to our community.

- Create and maintain successful strategic alliances with quality partners.
- Deliver high quality, "24/7" patient service.
- Build our brand rapidly and cost-effectively.
- Compete effectively against better-established Medical Marijuana Dispensary companies.

4. **Human Resource Risks**

The most serious human resource risk to our business, at least in the initial stages, would be my inability to operate the business due to illness or disability. The owner is currently in exceptional health and would eventually seek to replace himself on a day-to-day level by developing systems to support the growth of the business.

5. **Marketing Risks**

Advertising is our most expensive form of promotion and there will be a period of testing headlines and offers to find the one that works the best. The risk, of course, is that we will exhaust our advertising budget before we find an ad that works. Placing greater emphases on sunk-cost marketing, such as our storefront and on existing relationships through direct selling will minimize our initial reliance on advertising to bring in a large percentage of business in the first year.

6. **Business Risks**

A major risk to retail service businesses is the performance of the economy and the small business sector. Since economists are predicting this as the fastest growing sector of the economy, our risk of a downturn in the short-term is minimized. The entrance of one of the three major chains into our marketplace is a risk. They offer more of the latest equipment, provide a wider array of products and services, competitive prices and 24-hour service. This situation would force us to lower our prices in the short-term until we could develop an offering of higher margin, value-added services not provided by the large spays. It does not seem likely that the relative size of our market today could support the overhead of one of those operations. Projections indicate that this will not be the case in the future and that leaves a window of opportunity for ___ (company name) to aggressively build a loyal patient base.

To combat the usual start-up risks we will do the following:

1. Utilize our industry experience to quickly establish desired strategic relationships.
2. Pursue business outside of our immediate market area.
3. Diversify our range of product and service offerings.
4. Develop multiple distribution channels.
5. Monitor our competitor actions.
6. Stay in touch with our patients and suppliers.
7. Watch for trends which could potentially impact our business.
8. Continuously optimize and scrutinize all business processes.
9. Institute daily financial controls using Business Ratio Analysis.
10. Create pay-for-performance compensation and training programs to reduce

employee turnover.

Further, to attract and retain patients the Company will need to continue to expand its market offerings, utilizing third party strategic relationships. This could lead to difficulties in the management of relationships, competition for specific services and products, and/or adverse market conditions affecting a particular partner.

The Company will take active steps to mitigate risks. In preparation of the Company's pricing, many factors will be considered. The Company will closely track the activities of all third parties, and will hold monthly review meetings to resolve issues and review and update the terms associated with strategic alliances.

Additionally, we will develop the following kinds of contingency plans:
Disaster Recovery Plan
Business Continuity Plan
Business Impact and Gap Analysis
Testing & Maintenance

The Company will utilize marketing and advertising campaigns to promote brand identity and will coordinate all expectations with internal and third party resources prior to release. This strategy should maximize patient satisfaction while minimizing potential costs associated with unplanned expenditures and quality control issues.

10.1 Risk Management

We will develop plans to mitigate the following risk management issues:
1. We will have a patient waiver written or reviewed by an attorney that releases us from liability when patients are participating in our dispensary treatments. Patients should review and sign dispensary policies prior to receiving treatment.
2. In addition to the waiver, we will have patients fill out a pre-treatment questionnaire that is reviewed by the therapist to look for contraindications.
3. We will perform an annual safety audit to look for vehicle potential hazards and fix them before they become a problem. We will look at flooring, equipment, air quality and humidity levels.
4. We will put safety policies in writing and give copies to our employees for their review and sign-off.
5. We will make sure parking facilities and walkways are free or debris and well lit to reduce accidents, and install slip-resistant flooring and placing nonskid floor coverings in locker rooms and wet areas.
6. We will make certain that we have the proper general liability insurance, and that we are covered for any new service we add to our list of offerings.
7. We will regularly remind staff of the proper methods of performing treatments to reduce repetitive strain injuries and workman's compensation claims.
8. We will practice internal control and prevent employee theft by limiting the amount of cash on hand and changing deposit schedules regularly.

9. We will keep vehicles and storage facilities spotlessly clean, and make sure equipment such as pedicure thrones have the capability to be completely free of bacteria through daily disinfectant cleaning.
10. To help guard against potential fire hazards, we will avoid overloading electrical circuits, keep properly maintaining fire extinguishers and test the use fire alarms.

10.2   Reduce New Business Risk Tactics

We plan to use the following tactics to reduce our new business start-up risk:
1. Implement your business plan based on go, no-go stage criteria.
2. Develop employee cross-training programs.
3. Regularly back-up all computer files/Install ant-virus software.
4. Arrange adequate insurance coverage with higher deductibles.
5. Develop a limited number of prototype samples.
6. Test market offerings to determine level of market demand and appropriate pricing strategy.
7. Thoroughly investigate and benchmark to competitor offerings.
8. Research similar franchised businesses for insights into successful prototype business/operations models.
9. Reduce operation risks and costs by flowcharting all structured systems & standardized manual processes.
10. Use market surveys to listen to patient needs and priorities.
11. Purchase used equipment to reduce capital outlays.
12. Use leasing to reduce financial risk.
13. Outsource manufacturing to job shops to reduce capital at risk.
14. Use subcontractors to limit fixed overhead salary expenses.
15. Ask manufacturer about profit sharing arrangement.
16. Pay advertisers with a percent of revenues generated.
17. Develop contingency plans for identified risks.
18. Set-up procedures to control employee theft.
19. Do criminal background checks on potential employees.
20. Take immediate action on delinquent accounts.
21. Only extend credit to established account with D&B rating
22. Get regular competitive bids from alternative suppliers.
23. Check that operating costs as a percent of rising sales are lower as a result of productivity improvements.
24. Request bulk rate pricing on fast moving supplies.
25. Don't be tempted to tie up cash in slow moving inventory to qualify for bigger discounts.
26. Reduce financial risk by practicing cash flow policies.
27. Reduce hazard risk by installing safety procedures.
28. Use financial management ratios to monitor business vitals.
29. Make business decisions after brainstorming sessions.
30. Focus on the products/services with biggest return on investment.
31. Where possible, purchase off-the-shelf components.

32. Request manufacturer samples to build your prototype.
33. Design your production facilities to be flexible and easy to change.
34. Develop a network of suppliers with outsourcing capabilities.
35. Analyze and shorten every cycle time, including product development.
36. Develop multiple sources for every important input.

10.3   Reduce Patient Perceived Risk Tactics

We will utilize the following tactics to help reduce the new patient's perceived risk of starting to do business with our company.

Status

1. Publish a page of testimonials.
2. Secure Opinion Leader written endorsements.
3. Offer an Unconditional Satisfaction Money Back Guarantee.
4. Long-term Performance Guarantee (Financial Risk).
5. Guaranteed Buy Back (Obsolete time risk)
6. Offer free trials and samples.
7. Brand Image (consistent marketing image and performance)
8. Patents/Trademarks/Copyrights
9. Publish case studies
10. Share your expertise (Articles, Seminars, etc.)
11. Get recognized Certification
12. Conduct responsive patient service
13. Accept Installment Payments
14. Display product materials composition or ingredients.
15. Publish product test results.
16. Publish sales record milestones.
17. Foster word-of-mouth by offering an unexpected extra.
18. Distribute factual, pre-purchase info.
19. Reduce consumer search costs with online directories.
20. Reduce patient transaction costs.
21. Facilitate in-depth comparisons to alternative services.
22. Make available prior patient ratings and comments.
23. Provide customized info based on prior transactions.
24. Become a Better Business Bureau member.
25. Publish overall patient satisfaction survey results.
26. Offer plan options that match niche segment needs.
27. Require patient sign-off before proceeding to next phase.
28. Document procedures for dispute resolution.
29. Offer the equivalent of open source code.
30. Stress your compatibility features (avoid lock-in fear).
31. Create detailed checklists & flowcharts to show processes
32. Publish a list of frequently asked questions/answers.
33. Create a community that enables patients to connect with each other and share common interests.
34. Inform patients as to your stay-in-touch methods.

35. Conduct and handover a detailed needs analysis worksheet.   _____
36. Offer to pay all return shipping charges and/or refund all
    original shipping and handling fees.   _____
37. Describe your product testing procedures prior to shipping.   _____
38. Highlight your competitive advantages in all marketing materials.   _____

11.0   Financial Plan

The most important factor in our plan is dispensary party bookings. Therefore, we must remain focused on the execution of our booking plan and maintain budgeted sign-up levels.

The over-all financial plan for growth allows for use of the significant cash flow generated by operations. We are basing projected sales on the market research, industry analysis and competitive environment.

_____ (company name) expects a profit margin of over _____ % starting with year one. By year two, that number should slowly increase as the law of diminishing costs takes hold, and the day-to-day activities of the business become less expensive.

Sales are expected to grow at _____ % per year, and level off by year _____.

The initial investment in _____ (company name) will be provided by _____ (owner name) in the amount of $ _____. The owner will also seek a ____ (#) year bank loan in the amount of $ _____ to provide the remainder of the required initial funding.

The funds will be used to customize additional vehicles and to cover initial operating expenses. The owner financing will become a return on equity, paid in the form of dividends to the owner. We expect to finance slow and steady growth through cash flow. Salaries and vehicle expenses are the two major expenses.

The owners do not intend to take any profits out of the business until the long-term debt has been satisfied.

Our financial plan includes:
    Moderate growth rate with a steady cash flow.
    Investing residual profits into company expansion.
    Company expansion will be an option if sales projections are met and/or exceeded.
    Marketing costs will remain below ____ (5?) % of sales.
    Repayment of our loan calculated at a high A.P.R. of ____ (10?) percent and at a 10-year-payback on our $_____ loan.

11.1   Important Assumptions

The financial plan depends on important assumptions, most of which are shown in the following table. The Personnel Burden is low because benefits are not paid to our staff.

The following basic assumptions need to be considered:
1.   The economy will grow at a steady slow pace, without another major recession.

2. There will be no major changes in the industry, other than those discussed in the trends section of this document.
3. The State will not enact 'impact' legislation on our industry.
4. Sales are estimated at minimum to average values, while expenses are estimated at above average to maximum values..
5. Staffing and payroll expansions will be driven by increased sales.
6. Rent expenses will grow at a slow, predictable rate.
7. Materials expenses will not increase dramatically over the next several years, but will grow at a rate that matches increasing consumption.
8. We assume access to equity capital and financing sufficient to maintain our financial plan as shown in the tables.
9. The amount of the financing needed from the bank will be approximately $_____ and this will be repaid over the next 10 years at $_____ per month.
10. We assume that people in _____ (city) will be interested in learning how to best use medical marijuana and will give us the opportunity to provide such lessons.
11. We assume that the area will continue to grow at present rate of __ % per year.
12. Interest rates and tax rates are based on conservative assumptions.
13. We will not offer consumer credit, but will extend 30 days credit terms to our qualified commercial accounts.
14. Total dispensary bookings is a critical factor that must be immediately influenced.

Revenue Assumptions:

	Year	Sales/Month	Growth Rate
1.			
2.			
3.			

Assumptions	FY2017	FY2018	FY2019
Short-term Interest Rate %	10.00%	10.00%	10.00%
Long-term Interest Rate %	10.00%	10.00%	10.00%
Payment Days Estimator	30	30	30
Collection Days Estimator	45	45	45
Tax Rate %	25.00%	25.00%	25.00%
Expenses in Cash %	10.00%	10.00%	10.00%
Sales on Credit %	15.00%	15.00%	15.00%
Personnel Burden %	15.00%	15.00%	15.00%

Resource:
www.score.org/resources/business-plans-financial-statements-template-gallery

11.2   Break-even Analysis

Break-Even Analysis will be performed to determine the point at which revenue received equals the costs associated with generating the revenue. Break-even analysis calculates what is known as a margin of safety, the amount that revenues exceed the break-even point. This is the amount that revenues can fall while still staying above the break-even point. The two main purposes of using the break-even analysis for marketing is to (1) determine the minimum number of sales that is required to avoid a loss at a designated sales price and (2) it is an exercise tool so that we can tweak the sales price to determine the minimum volume of sales we can reasonably expect to sell in order to avoid a loss.

Fixed costs are based on running costs estimated by the owner(s) of the company and include payroll for all employees. Variable costs are based on a _____% estimate of the average sales per unit. The average revenue estimate is based on the judgment of the owner(s) who have had many years of experience in the industry and on the realistic assumption of the types of contracts the company will get in the beginning and the requirements needed to complete such commitments.

Definition: Break-Even Is the Volume Where All Fixed Expenses Are Covered.

Based on projections, we will need an average of __ students each month to breakeven.

Three important definitions used in break-even analysis are:
·   **Variable Costs** (Expenses) are costs that change directly in proportion to changes in activity (volume), such as raw materials, labor and packaging.

·   **Fixed Costs** (Expenses) are costs that remain constant (fixed) for a given time period despite wide fluctuations in activity (volume), such as rent, loan payments, insurance, payroll and utilities.

·   **Unit Contribution Margin** is the difference between your product's unit selling price and its unit variable cost.
Unit Contribution Margin = Unit Sales Price - Unit Variable Cost

For the purposes of this breakeven analysis, the assumed fixed operating costs will be approximately $ _____ per month, as shown in the following table.

Averaged Monthly Fixed Costs:		**Variable Costs:**	
Payroll	_____	Cost of Inventory Sold	_____
Rent	_____	Labor	_____
Insurance	_____	Supplies	_____
Utilities	_____	Direct Costs per Patient	_____
Security.	_____	Other	_____
Legal/Technical Help	_____		
Other	_____		

Total: _____   Total   _____

A break-even analysis table has been completed on the basis of average costs/prices. With monthly fixed costs averaging $_____ , $____ in average sales and $_____ in average variable costs, we need approximately $_____ in sales per month to break-even.

Based on our assumed ___ % variable cost, we estimate our breakeven sales volume at around $_____ per month. We expect to reach that sales volume by our _____ month of operations. Our break-even analysis is shown in further detail in the following table.

Breakeven Formulas:

Break Even Units = Total Fixed Costs / (Unit Selling Price - Variable Unit Cost)

. _____ = _____ / (_____ - _____)

·BE Dollars = (Total Fixed Costs / (Unit Price – Variable Unit Costs))/ Unit Price

_____ = (_____ / (_____ - _____)) / _____

·BE Sales = Annual Fixed Costs / (1- Unit Variable costs / Unit Sales Price)

_____ = _____ / (1 - _____ / _____)

Table: Break-even Analysis

Monthly Units Break-even   _____
Monthly Revenue Break-even $ _____
Assumptions:
Average Per-Unit Revenue $ _____
Average Per-Unit Variable Cost $ _____
Estimated monthly Fixed Cost $ _____

Ways to Improve Breakeven Point:
1. Reduce Fixed Costs via Cost Controls
2. Raise unit sales prices.
3. Lower Variable Costs by improving employee productivity or getting lower competitive bids from suppliers.
4. Broaden product/service line to generate multiple revenue streams.

11.3   Projected Profit and Loss

Pro forma income statements are an important tool for planning our future business operations. If the projections predict a downturn in profitability, we can make operational changes such as increasing prices or decreasing costs before these projections become reality.

Our monthly profit for the first year varies significantly, as we aggressively seek improvements and begin to implement our marketing plan. However, after the first ___ months, profitability should be established.

We predict advertising costs will go down in the next three years as word-of-mouth about our Medical Marijuana Dispensary gets out to the public and we are able to find what has worked well for us and concentrate on those advertising methods, and corporate affiliations generate sales without the need for extra advertising.

Our net profit/sales ratio will be low the first year. We expect this ratio to rise at least _____ (15?) percent the second year. Normally, a startup concern will operate with negative profits through the first two years. We will avoid that kind of operating loss on our second year by knowing our competitors and having a full understanding of our target markets.

Our projected profit and loss is indicated in the following table. From our research of the Medical Marijuana Dispensary industry, our annual projections are quite realistic and conservative, and we prefer this approach so that we can ensure an adequate cash flow.

Key P & L Formulas:

Gross Margin = Total Sales Revenue - Cost of Goods Sold

Gross Margin % = (Total Sales Revenue - Cost of Goods Sold) / Total Sales Revenue
This number represents the proportion of each dollar of revenue that the company retains as gross profit.

EBITDA =Revenue - Expenses (exclude interest, taxes, depreciation & amortization)

PBIT = Profit (Earnings) Before Interest and Taxes = EBIT
A profitability measure that looks at a company's profits before the company has to pay corporate income tax and interest expenses. This measure deducts all operating expenses from revenue, but it leaves out the payment of interest and tax. Also referred to as "earnings before interest and tax ".

Net Profit = Total Sales Revenues - Total Expenses

Pro Forma Profit and Loss

	Formula	2017	2018	2019
Revenue:				
Cannabis Sales				
Edibles				
Health & Wellness Counseling				
Product Sales				
Other				
Total Sales Revenue	**A**			
Direct Cost of Sales	B			
Other Costs of Goods	C			
Total Costs of Goods Sold	B+C=D			
Gross Margin	A-D=E			
Gross Margin %	E / A			
Expenses				
Payroll				
Payroll Taxes				
Sales & Marketing				
Conventions/Trade Shows				
Depreciation				
License/Permit Fees				
Dues and Subscriptions				
Rent				
Utilities				
Deposits				
Repairs and Maintenance				
Janitorial Supplies				
Dispensary Supplies				
Leased Equipment				
Buildout Costs				
Insurance				
Location Rental				
Van Expenses				
Contracted Therapists				
Professional Development				
Office Supplies				
Merchant Fees				
Bad Debts				
Miscellaneous				
Total Operating Expenses	**F**			
Profit Before Int. & Taxes	**E - F = G**			
Interest Expenses	H			
Taxes Incurred	I			
Net Profit	**G - H - I = J**			
Net Profit / Sales	**J / A = K**			

11.5   Projected Cash Flow

The Cash Flow Statement shows how the company is paying for its operations and future growth, by detailing the "flow" of cash between the company and the outside world. Positive numbers represent cash flowing in, negative numbers represent cash flowing out.

The first year's monthly cash flows are will vary significantly, but we do expect a solid cash balance from day one. We expect that the majority of our sales will be done in cash or by credit card and that will be good for our cash flow position. Additionally, we will stock only slightly more than one month's inventory at any time. Consequently, we do not anticipate any problems with cash flow, once we have obtained sufficient start-up funds.

A __ year commercial loan in the amount of $_____, sought by the owner will be used to cover our working capital requirement.   Our projected cash flow is summarized in the following table, and is expected to meet our needs. In the following years, excess cash will be used to finance our growth plans.

Cash Flow Management:
We will use the following practices to improve our cash flow position:
1.   Become more selective when granting credit.
2.   Seek deposits or multiple stage payments.
3.   Reduce the amount/time of credit given to patients.
4.   Reduce direct and indirect costs and overhead expenses.
5.   Use the 80/20 rule to manage inventories, receivables and payables.
6.   Invoice as soon as the service has been performed.
7.   Generate regular reports on receivable ratios and aging.
8.   Establish and adhere to sound credit practices.
9.   Use more pro-active collection techniques.
10.   Add late payment fees where possible.
11.   Increase the credit taken from suppliers.
12.   Negotiate extended credit terms from vendors.
13.   Use some barter arrangements to acquire goods and service.
14.   Use leasing to gain access to the use of productive assets.
15.   Covert debt into equity.
16.   Regularly update cash flow forecasts.
17.   Defer projects which cannot achieve acceptable cash paybacks.
18.   Require a 50% deposit upon the signing of the contract and the balance in full, due five days before the event.

Cash Flow Formulas:
Net Cash Flow = Incoming Cash Receipts - Outgoing Cash Payments
Equivalently, net profit plus amounts charged off for depreciation, depletion, and amortization. (also called cash flow).
Cash Balance = Opening Cash Balance + Net Cash Flow
We are positioning ourselves in the market as a medium risk concern with steady cash flows. Accounts payable is paid at the end of each month, while sales are in cash, giving our company an excellent cash structure.

Pro Forma Cash Flow

	Formula	2017	2018	2019

Cash Received
Cash from Operations

	Formula			
Cash Sales	A			
Cash from Receivables	B			
Subtotal Cash from Operations	A + B = C			
Additional Cash Received				
Non Operating (Other) Income				
Sales Tax, VAT, HST/GST Received				
New Current Borrowing				
New Other Liabilities (interest fee)				
New Long-term Liabilities				
Sales of Other Current Assets				
Sales of Long-term Assets				
New Investment Received				
Total Additional Cash Received	D			
Subtotal Cash Received	C + D = E			

Expenditures
Expenditures from Operations

	Formula			
Cash Spending	F			
Payment of Accounts Payable	G			
Subtotal Spent on Operations	F+G = H			
Additional Cash Spent				
Non Operating (Other) Expenses				
Sales Tax, VAT, HST/GST Paid Out				
Principal Repayment Current Borrowing				
Other Liabilities Principal Repayment				
Long-term Liabilities Principal Repayment				
Purchase Other Current Assets				
Dividends				
Total Additional Cash Spent	I			
Subtotal Cash Spent	H + I = J			
Net Cash Flow	**E - J = K**			
Cash Balance				

11.6   Projected Balance Sheet

Pro forma Balance Sheets are used to project how the business will be managing its assets in the future. As a pure start-up business, the opening balance sheet may contain no values.

Note: The projected balance sheets must link back into the projected income statements and cash flow projections.

_____ (company name) does not project any real trouble meeting its debt obligations, provided the revenue predictions are met. We are very confident that we will meet or exceed all of our objectives in the Business Plan and produce a slow but steady increase in net worth.

All of our tables will be updated monthly to reflect past performance and future assumptions. Future assumptions will not be based on past performance but rather on economic cycle activity, regional industry strength, and future cash flow possibilities. We expect a solid growth in net worth by the year _____.

The Balance Sheet table for fiscal years 2017, 2018, and 2019 follows. It shows managed but sufficient growth of net worth, and a sufficiently healthy financial position.

Key Formulas:

Paid-in Capital = Capital contributed to the corporation by investors on top of the par value of the capital stock.

Retained Earnings = The portion of net income which is retained by the corporation rather than distributed to the owners as dividends.

Earnings = Revenues - (Cost of Sales + Operating Expenses + Taxes)

Net Worth = Total Assets - Total Liabilities
          Also known as 'Owner's Equity'.

Pro Forma Balance Sheet

	Formulas	2017	2018	2019
Assets				
Current Assets				
Cash				
Accounts Receivable				
Inventory				
Other Current Assets				
Total Current Assets	A			
Long-term Assets				
Long-term Assets	B			
Accumulated Depreciation	C			
Total Long-term Assets	B - C = D			
Total Assets	**A + D = E**			

Liabilities and Capital

	Formulas	2017	2018	2019
Current Liabilities				
Accounts Payable				
Current Borrowing				
Other Current Liabilities				
Subtotal Current Liabilities	**F**			
Long-term Liabilities				
Notes Payable				
Other Long-term Liabilities				
Subtotal Long-term Liabilities	**G**			
Total Liabilities	**F + G = H**			
Capital				
Paid-in Capital	I			
Retained Earnings	J			
Earnings	K			
Total Capital	I - J + K = L			
Total Liabilities and Capital	**H + L = M**			
Net Worth	**E - H = N**			

11.7   Business Ratios

The following table provides significant ratios for the personal services industry. The final column, Industry Profile, shows ratios for this industry as it is determined by the Standard Industrial Classification SIC 7991 (Dispensary Services), for comparison purposes.

Our comparisons to the SIC Industry profile are very favorable and we expect to maintain healthy ratios for profitability , risk and return.   Use Business Ratio Formulas provided to assist in calculations.

Key Business Ratio Formulas:

EBIT = Earnings Before Interest and Taxes
EBITA = Earnings Before Interest, Taxes & Amortization. (Operating Profit Margin)

Sales Growth Rate =((Current Year Sales - Last Year Sales)/(Last Year Sales)) x 100
Ex: Percent of Sales = (Advertising Expense / Sales) x 100

Net Worth = Total Assets - Total Liabilities

Acid Test Ratio = Liquid Assets / Current Liabilities
Measures how much money business has immediately available. A ratio of 2:1 is good.

Net Profit Margin = Net Profit / Net Revenues
The higher the net profit margin is, the more effective the company is at converting revenue into actual profit.

Return on Equity (ROE) = Net Income / Shareholder's Equity
The ROE is useful for comparing the profitability of a company to that of other firms in the same industry. Also known as "return on net worth" (RONW).

Current Ratio = Current Assets / Current Liabilities
The higher the current ratio, the more capable the company is of paying its obligations. A ratio under 1 suggests that the company would be unable to pay off its obligations if they came due at that point.

Quick Ratio = Current Assets - Inventories / Current Liabilities
The quick ratio is more conservative than the current ratio, because it excludes inventory from current assets.

Pre-Tax Return on Net Worth = Pre-Tax Income / Net Worth
Indicates stockholders' earnings before taxes for each dollar of investment.

Pre-Tax Return on Assets = (EBIT / Assets) x 100

Indicates much profit the firm is generating from the use of its assets.

Accounts Receivable Turnover = Net Credit Sales / Average Accounts Receivable
A low ratio implies the company should re-assess its credit policies in order to ensure the timely collection of imparted credit that is not earning interest for the firm.

Net Working Capital = Current Assets - Current Liabilities
Positive working capital means that the company is able to pay off its short-term liabilities. Negative working capital means that a company currently is unable to meet its short-term liabilities with its current assets (cash, accounts receivable and inventory).

Interest Coverage Ratio = Earnings Before Interest & Taxes /Total Interest Expense
The lower the ratio, the more the company is burdened by debt expense. When a company's interest coverage ratio is 1.5 or lower, its ability to meet interest expenses may be questionable. An interest coverage ratio below 1 indicates the company is not generating sufficient revenues to satisfy interest expenses.

Collection Days = Accounts Receivables / (Revenues/365)
A high ratio indicates that the company is having problems getting paid for services.

Accounts Payable Turnover = Total Supplier Purchases/Average Accounts Payable
If the turnover ratio is falling from one period to another, this is a sign that the company is taking longer to pay off its suppliers than previously. The opposite is true when the turnover ratio is increasing, which means the firm is paying of suppliers at a faster rate.

Payment Days = (Accounts Payable Balance x 360) / (No. of Accounts Payable x 12)
The average number of days between receiving an invoice and paying it off.

Total Asset Turnover = Revenue / Assets
Asset turnover measures a firm's efficiency at using its assets in generating sales or revenue - the higher the number the better.

Sales / Net Worth = Total Sales / Net Worth

Dividend Payout = Dividends / Net Profit

Assets to Sales = Assets / Sales

Current Debt / Totals Assets = Current Liabilities / Total Assets

Current Liabilities to Liabilities = Current Liabilities / Total Liabilities

Business Ratio Analysis

	2017	2018	2019	Industry
Sales Growth				**4.0%**
Percent of Total Assets				
Accounts Receivable				
Inventory				
Other Current Assets				45.40%
Total Current Assets				69.40%
Long-term Assets				30.60%
Total Assets				100.00%
Current Liabilities				35.20%
Long-term Liabilities				21.50%
Total Liabilities				56.70%
Net Worth				43.30%
Percent of Sales				
Sales				100.00%
Gross Margin				97.00%
Selling G& A Expenses				85.60%
Advertising Expenses				0.78%
Profit Before Interest & Taxes				0.35%
Main Ratios				
Current				1.52
Quick				1.29
Total Debt to Total Assets				62.70%
Pre-tax Return on Net Worth				1.09%
Pre-tax Return on Assets				2.90%
Additional Ratios				
Net Profit Margin				
Return on Equity				
Activity Ratios				
Accounts Receivable Turnover				
Collection Days				
Inventory Turnover				
Accounts Payable Turnover				
Payment Days				
Total Asset Turnover				
Inventory Productivity				
Sales per sq/ft.				
Gross Margin Return on Inventory (GMROI)				
Debt Ratios				

Debt to Net Worth

Current Liabilities to Liabilities

Liquidity Ratios

Net Working Capital

Interest Coverage

Additional Ratios

Assets to Sales

Current Debt / Total Assets

Acid Test

Sales / Net Worth

Dividend Payout

Business Vitality Profile

Sales per Employee

Survival Rate

12.0 Summary

_____ (company name) will be successful. This business plan has documented that the establishment of _____ (company name) is feasible. All of the critical factors, such as industry trends, marketing analysis, competitive analysis, management expertise and financial analysis support this conclusion.

Project Description: (Give a brief summary of the product, service or program.)
_____

Description of Favorable Industry and Market Conditions.
(Summarize why this business is viable.)
_____

Summary of Earnings Projections and Potential Return to Investors:
_____

Summary of Capital Requirements:
_____

Security for Investors & Loaning Institutions:
_____

Summary of expected benefits for people in the community beyond the immediate business concern:
_____

Means of Financing:
A. Loan Requirements: $_____
B. Owner's Contribution: $ $_____
C. Other Sources of Income: $_____
Total Funds Available: $_____

13.0 Potential Exit Scenarios
Two potential exit strategies exist for the investor:

1. **Initial Public Offering. (IPO)**
   We seek to go public within ___ (#) years of operations. The funds used will both help create liquidity for investors as well as allow for additional capital to develop our _____ (international/national?) roll out strategy.

2. **Acquisition Merger with Private or Public Company.**
   Our most desirable option for exit is a merger or buyout by a large corporation. We believe with substantial cash flows and a loyal patient base our company will be attractive to potential corporate investors within five years. Real value has been created through the novel combination of Medical Marijuana Dispensary services as well as partnering with key referral groups.

Note:
In many instances, the real value of a medical dispensary is in the licenses, which can go from $800,000 to $1.2 million in Los Angeles due the limited number available.

APPENDIX

Purpose: Supporting documents used to enhance your business proposal.

Tax returns of principals for the last three years, if the plan is for new business

A personal financial statement, which should include life insurance and endowment policies, if applicable

A copy of the proposed lease or purchase agreement for building dispensaryce, or zoning information for in-home businesses, with layouts, maps, and blueprints

A copy of licenses and other legal documents including partnership, association, or shareholders' agreements and copyrights, trademarks, and patents applications

A copy of résumés of all principals in a consistent format, if possible

Copies of letters of intent from suppliers, contracts, orders, and miscellaneous.

In the case of a franchised business, a copy of the franchise contract and all supporting documents provided by the franchisor

Newdispensaryper clippings that support the business or the owner, including something about you, your achievements, business idea, or region

Promotional literature for your company or your competitors

Product brochures of your company or competitors

Photographs of your product. equipment, facilities, etc.

Market research to support the marketing section of the plan

Trade and industry publications when they support your intentions

Quotations or pro-forma invoices for capital items to be purchased, including a list of fixed assets, company vehicles, and proposed renovations

References

All insurance policies in place, both business and personal

Operation Schedules

Organizational Charts

Job Descriptions

Additional Financial Projections by Month

Patient Needs Analysis Worksheet

Personal Survival Budget

Business and Personal Credit Reports from suppliers, credit bureaus and banks

Letters of Reference

Copies of all business contracts both completed and currently in force.

Competition Analysis

Advertising Rate Sheets

Location Plans

Helpful Resources:

Associations:

American Association of Community of Care
American Association of Home Care   www.aahomecare.org
Center for Personal Assistance Services   www.pascenter.org
Association of Area Agencies on Aging.
National Association of Professional Geriatric Care Managers www.caremanager.org
National Association for Home Care   www.nahc.org

Publications

Home Care Magazine   www.homecaremag.com
Cosmetic Dermatology Magazine   http://www.cosderm.com/
Healthy Aging Magazine   http://healthy-aging.advanceweb.com/

Miscellaneous:

Vista Print Free Business Cards   www.vistaprint.com
Free Business Guides   www.smbtn.com/businessplanguides/
Open Office   http://download.openoffice.org/

US Census Bureau   www.census.gov
Federal Government   www.business.gov
US Patent & Trademark Office   www.uspto.gov
US Small Business Administration   www.sba.gov
National Association for the Self-Employed www.nase.org
International Franchise Association   www.franchise.org
Center for Women's Business Research   www.cfwbr.org

Advertising Plan Worksheet

Ad Campaign Title: _____

Ad Campaign Start Date: _____ End Date: _____

What are the features (what product has) and hidden benefits (what product does for consumer) of my products/services?

Who is the targeted audience?

What problems are faced by this targeted audience?

What solutions do you offer?

Who is the competition and how do they advertise?

What is your differentiation strategy?

What are your bullet point competitive advantages?

What are the objectives of this advertising campaign?

What are your general assumptions?

What positioning image do you want to project?
__ Exclusiveness	___ Low Cost	___ High Quality
__ Speedy Service	___ Convenient	___ Innovative

What is the ad headline?

What is the advertising budget for this advertising campaign?

What advertising methods will be used?
__ Radio	___ TV/Cable	__ Yellow Pages
__ Coupons	___ Telemarketing	___ Flyers
__ Direct Mail	___ Magazines	___

Newdispensarypers
__ Press Release	___ Brochures	___ Billboards
__ Other		

When will each advertising method start and what will it cost?

Method	Start Date	Frequency	Cost

Indicate how you will measure the cost-effectiveness of the advertising plan?
Formula: Return on Investment (ROI) = Generated Sales / Ad Costs.

Seminar Outline Worksheet

Objective: To establish your expertise on the subject matter, and produce future possible networking contacts by offering a newsletter sign-up and/or business card exchange.

Warning: Make seminar information rich and not a sales presentation.

1. Start with Attention-Grabbing Headline
    Ex: Hard-hitting Quotation, Thought Provoking Question, Startling Fact
    _____

2. Introduce Yourself and Establish Your Credentials
    _____

3. Present Seminar Overview
    _____

4. Discuss Attendee Participation Guidelines
    _____

5. Solicit a sampling of attendee interests, backgrounds and concerns.
    _____

6. Establish Learning Objectives
    _____

7. Preview the Bulleted Topics To be Covered
    _____
    _____

8. Share a Relevant Success Story (Case Study).
    _____

9. Use analogies and comparisons to create reference points.
    _____

10. Use statistics to support your position.
    _____
    _____

11. Conclusion: - Summarize Benefits for Attendees / Appeal to Action
    _____
    _____
    _____

12. Hold Question and Answer Session

13. Final Thoughts
    - Appreciation for Help Received
    - Indicate after-seminar availability

14. Handout A Remembrance
    - Business Cards   - Glossary of Terms
    - Seminar Outline   - Feedback Survey

Press Release Cover Letter Worksheet
Instructions: Use this form to build a ready-to-use cover letter.

Your Letterhead.

Date

Dear _____,

As a company located in your coverage area, we thought the attached Press Release would be of special concern to your readers/viewers, as it touches upon something that we all have in common, an interest in

_____.

Brief overview purpose of the press release.

_____

I have also enclosed a media kit to give you background information on _____ Company and myself. I hope to follow-up with you shortly.

I also possess expertise in the following related areas:

- _____
- _____
- _____

Should you wish to speak to me or require additional information, I can be reached at _____ or via email at _____.
Additional assistance with company supplied photos can be requested at the same number. This Press Release can also be downloaded from my company website at www. _____.

Thank you for your time and attention,

Contact Name
Company Title
Phone Number
Email Address

New Release Template

News Release

For Immediate Release
(Or Hold For Release Until …(date)….)

Contact:
Contact Person   _____
Contact Title   _____
Company Name   _____
Phone Number   _____
Fax Number   _____
Email Address   _____
Website Address   _____

Date: _____
Attention: _____ (Target Type of Editor)

Headline: Summarize Your Key Message:
                    _____

Sub-Headline: Optional: _____

Location of the Firm and Date.

_____

Lead Paragraph: A summary of the newsworthy content.
                      _____

                      Answers the questions:
                      Who: _____
                      What: _____
                      Where: _____
                      When: _____

Second Paragraph:
Expand upon the first paragraph and elaborate on the purpose of the Press Release.

_____

_____

Third Paragraph:
Further details with additional quotes from staff, industry experts or satisfied patients.

_____

_____

For Additional Information Contact:

_____

About Your Expertise:
Presentation of your expert credentials

_____

_____

About Your Business:
Background company history on the firm and central offerings.

_____

_____

Enclosures: Photographs, charts, brochures, etc.

Special Event Release Format   Notes

1.   Type of Event   _____
2.   Sponsoring Organization   _____
3.   Contact Person Before the Event   _____
4.   Contact Person At the Event   _____
5.   Date and Time of the Event   _____
6.   Location of the Event   _____
7.   Length of Presentation Remarks   _____
8.   Presentation Topic   _____
9.   Question Session (Y/N)   _____
10. Speaker or Panel   _____
11. Event Background   _____
12. Noteworthy Expected Attendees   _____
13. Estimated Number of Attendees   _____
14. Why readers s/b interested in event.   _____
15. Specifics of the Event.   _____
16. Biographies   _____

Track Ad Return on Investment (ROI)

Objective: To invest in those marketing activities that generate the greatest return on invested funds.

Medium	Cost	Calls Received	Cost/Call	No. Act. New Patients	Cost/New Patient
Formula:	A	B	A/B=C	D	A/D=E
Newspaper					
Classified Ads					
Yellow Pages					
Billboards					
Cable TV					
Magazine					
Flyers					
Posters					
Coupons					
Direct Mail					
Brochures					
Business Cards					
Seminars					
Demonstrations					
Sponsored Events					
Sign					
Radio					
Trade Shows					
Specialties					
Cold Calling					
Door Hangers					
T-shirts					
Coupon Books					
Transit Ads					
Press Releases					
Word-of-Mouth					
Totals:					

Internet Article Writing Template

1.   Article Title
Maximum 100 characters (including spaces) - about 12 words.
Write it to catch the attention of readers and publishers. Start with your primary search engine keyword phrase. In printed media titles starting "How to..." or "10 top tips for..." are very popular, but they are not very helpful for search engines. The article title will go into the title of a web page.

2.   Abstract
Maximum 500 characters - about 90 words but 50 or 60 is better.
Make it enticing to hook the publisher and make them want to read the full article. The abstract is primarily targeted at the publisher and will be displayed just below the title on the search pages in the directory, but is secondary to the title in getting attention. Some publishers may also use it.

3.   Description – Meta Tag
Maximum 200 characters but preferably 150 – two lines of text.
This should be a shorter version of the abstract, which must contain your primary keywords. The Mega Tag is needed if you publish on your own website.

4.   Keywords – Meta Tag
Maximum 100 characters - about 12 words comma separated
Start with your primary keyword of phrase then add the other relevant keywords that are used in the article.

5.   Article Text
Length depends on your topic, market and writing style. Research suggests about 500 to 800 words, but some publishers want more of an in-depth analysis. Research your specific market and be flexible, with a prepared mix of lengths, including long and short versions of the same article. Write the basic article with no formatting. If you are using word, disable all the auto-formatting like smart quotes, automatic hypertext links and paragraph dispensarycing because they will all cause problems later.

Include the 'Primary Keyword Phrase' into the first sentence. Include the liberal usage of keywords throughout the article, but don't overdo it. The article still has to be a good read. Remember that even though you are writing for several audiences, content must still be king. Do not promote your own products and services or your article will not be published. Also, do not include self serving links to your web site or affiliate sites in the body of the article, but rather save them for the 'Resource or Byline Box'. If you have links to resources show them as text, as many sites do not allow live html links in the body of the article.
Introduction
1.   Brief outline of what will be covered in the article.
2.   The motivating factor behind why this particular topic was selected and why you

are qualified to address the subject.
3. A brief statement on your credentials, experience and exposure.
4. What you have achieved from your experience to convince readers that you know the subject very well.

Core Subject Matter
1. Define the problem or address the subject areas that will define the gap between the uninformed and the knowledgeable.
2. Provide the benefits the reader will realize from reading the article.
3. Start with simple and general background knowledge, and gradually intensify the technicality of the subject matter.
4. State the expected challenges to be faced in tackling the problem.
5. Discuss the pros and cons of your proposed solution to create the link between the norm and the desired state.

Expand Upon Subject Matter
1. Add technical information to convince readers of the merits of your solution.
2. State a range of requirements needed to implement your solution and their options.
3. Compare players in the market and promote good practice.
4. Place emphasis on desired actions, taking a chronological approach to each stage.
5. Attempt to indirectly answer any questions you think your readers may have.
6. Give supporting points to gain confidence in the approach you recommend.
7. Suggest other options based on price and availability.

Conclusion
1. Summarize problem solution recommendations.
2. Refer readers to other helpful resources.

6. Copyright
Copyright, date, name, country. Few directories ask for this but it makes sense to put it at the bottom of the article or in the field requested.

7. Resource Box
Maximum 500 characters, "including spaces and html code."
This is your opportunity to promote yourself but limit content to 1 or 2 self serving links. Refer to the links in the "Third Person." The directory publisher has to function with this link on their site or ezine so make it acceptable to them. Offer an incentive or reward for people to visit your web site, but make sure that live links show the web address not just keywords. If the publisher doesn't use live links, you still want to present your website address for later referral.

Classified Ad Worksheet

Ad Budget: _____

Ad Objective: ___ Go to Website   ___ Request More Info ___ Mail a Check
                     ___ Introduce a new product/service   ___ Announce a Sale
                     ___ Increase awareness of product
                     ___ Other _____

Target Market: _____

Target Market:
Demographics:
- Age _____
- Gender _____
- Income _____
- Education _____
- Location _____

Reading Interests:
- Daily Newspapers _____
- Weekly Magazines _____
- Magazines _____
- Trade Journals _____

Product. Knowledge Level _____

Purchase Motivators _____

Best Category Heading _____

Select Type of Message
- Strong Offer with Best Value for Money _____
- Point of Difference from Competitors _____
- Listing the Benefits _____

Product Price: $_____

Ad Cost: $_____

Number of Responses: _____
Cost/Response: _____
Number of Sales: _____
Cost/Sales: _____

Made in the USA
Middletown, DE
27 January 2021